A Search in Secret India

The works of Dr Brunton

In chronological order

A SEARCH IN SECRET INDIA

THE SECRET PATH

A SEARCH IN SECRET EGYPT

A MESSAGE FROM ARUNACHALA

A HERMIT IN THE HIMALAYAS

THE QUEST OF THE OVERSELF

DISCOVER YOURSELF

INDIAN PHILOSOPHY AND MODERN CULTURE

THE HIDDEN TEACHING BEYOND YOGA

THE WISDOM OF THE OVERSELF

THE SPIRITUAL CRISIS OF MAN

A SEARCH IN SECRET INDIA

DR. PAUL BRUNTON

SAMUEL WEISER, INC.
York Beach, Maine

First published in England by Rider & Co., London, 1934

First published in America by
E.P. Dutton, New York, 1935

First American paperback published in 1970 by
Samuel Weiser, Inc.
Box 612
York Beach, Maine 03910

Revised edition, 1985

Reprinted, 1989

ISBN 0-87728-602-7
Library of Congress Catalog Card Number: 83-50400

Printed in the United States of America by
McNaughton & Gunn, Inc.

CONTENTS

LIST OF ILLUSTRATIONS

The following illustrations will be found between pages 116 and 117.

A PERSONAL NOTE

Dr. Paul Brunton died July 27, 1981, in Vevey, Switzerland. Born in London in 1898, he authored thirteen books from "A Search in Secret India" published in 1934 to "The Spiritual Crisis of Man" in 1952. Dr. Brunton is generally recognized as having introduced yoga and meditation to the West, and for presenting their philosophical background in non-technical language.

His mode of writing was to jot down paragraphs as inspiration occurred. Often these were penned on the backs of envelopes or along margins of newspapers as he strolled amid the flower gardens bordering Lac Leman. They later were typed and classified by subject. He then would edit and meld these paragraphs into a coherent narrative.

Paul Brunton had lived in Switzerland for twenty years. He liked the mild climate and majestic mountain scenery. Visitors and correspondence came from all over the world. He played an important role in the lives of many.

"P.B.", as he is known to his followers, was a gentle man. An aura of kindliness emanated from him. His scholarly learning was forged in the crucible of life. His spirituality shone forth like a beacon. But he discouraged attempts to form a cult around him: "You must find your own P.B. within yourselves," he used to say.

KTH

FOREWORD TO THE REVISED EDITION

A *Search in Secret India* was an instant success when published in 1934. It continues to be popular after many reprintings, and has been translated into several languages. Written at the age of thirty-five, it was my father's first book. To mark the occasion, he adopted the pen name of *Paul Brunton.*

This is the story of his personal odyssey, his search for holy men to guide him on his quest. To this task he brought all his professional journalistic skills coupled with an extensive background in spiritual research.

My father was a pathfinder. In this book he introduced the terms *yoga* and *meditation* to the Western world. He travelled the length and breadth of the sub-continent interviewing yogis, fakirs, and mystics, exploring a side of India previously unknown to foreigners. His story became a tale of high spiritual adventure.

Fifty years later I retraced my father's steps and journeyed around India giving "in memoriam" lectures in his honor. I learned that his name is still held in highest esteem. Many Indians told me they discovered their country's spiritual dimension from this very book. I made a pilgrimage to the same ashram he discovered and offered my obeisance in the meditation hall where Ramana Maharshi had lived. I saw the small bungalow my father had inhabited, and I gazed up at towering Arunachala.

The highlight of my trip was my encounter with His Holiness Shri Shankara Acharya, the Spiritual Head of South India, whom my father describes in Chapter VIII. I had no prior intention of meeting him, but upon leaving the Ramanashram, decided to seek him out. After driving along country roads for three hours and locating the village where he was staying, history seemed to repeat itself as I was told there was no chance of my being granted an audience with him. However, a friendly disciple agreed to submit my card and returned with the news that His Holiness would received me at the rear of the temple, to avoid the crowds milling in front. His slight figure, clad in a saffron robe, reflected his ninety-one years. I told him I was the son of Paul Brunton. He replied briefly. The interpreter informed me, "He knows!" His Holiness spoke again. "He has been waiting for you! He has been expecting you," said the interpreter. But how did he even know of me? How did he know I was in India, I wondered to myself? I held out a copy of this book and showed him his photograph, taken when he was thirty-eight. "I know!" was his comment.

At this point I had hoped to elicit his views on the world situation as had my father previously. But suddenly all questions melted, as I felt an onrush of peace and love. All I could do was prostrate myself in the time-honored tradition at the feet of His Holiness as he gave me his blessing. He then put around my neck a sacred *mala*, a garland fashioned from fragrant sandalwood. I wear it daily.

Thus the wheel came full circle half a century later.

Kenneth Thurston Hurst
August, 1985

FOREWORD TO THE FIRST EDITION

by

SIR FRANCIS YOUNGHUSBAND, K.C.I.E., K.C.S.I., C.I.E.

"SACRED INDIA" would be as apt a title for this book. For it is a quest for that India which is only secret because it is so sacred. The holiest things in life are not bruited abroad in public. The sure instinct of the human soul is to keep them withdrawn in the inmost recesses accessible to few—perhaps to none. Certainly only to those who care for spiritual things.

And with a country as with an individual. The most sacred things a country keeps secret. It would not be easy for a stranger to discover what England holds most sacred. And it is the same with India. The most sacred part of India is the most secret.

Now secret things require much searching for; but those who seek will find. Those who seek with their whole heart and with the real determination to find will at last discover the secret.

Mr. Brunton had that determination, and he did in the end find. The difficulties were very great though. For in India, as everywhere else, there is much spurious spirituality through which a way must be forced before the true can be found. There is an innumerable crowd of mental acrobats and contortionists through which the seeker after pure spirituality must elbow his way. These men have trained their mental as well as bodily muscles till they are extraordinarily efficient. They have exercised powers of concentration till they have nearly complete control over their mental processes. Many of them have developed what we call occult powers.

These are all interesting enough in their way and are well worth study by scientific men interested in psychic phenomena. But they are not the real thing. They are not the springs whence spirituality comes gushing.

They do not form the secret sacred India that Mr. Brunton was seeking. He saw them. He noted them. He describes them. But he pushed through them. Spirituality at its finest and purest is what he wanted. And this he found at last.

Remote from the haunts of men, deep in the jungles to which—or to the Himalayas—the holiest men in India always return, Mr. Brunton found the very embodiment of all that India holds most sacred. The Maharishee—the Great Sage—was the man who made most appeal to Mr. Brunton. He is not the only one of his kind. Up and down India others—not many, but a very, very few—may be found. They represent the true genius of India, and it is through them that the Mighty Genius of the Universe manifests Himself in peculiar degree.

They, therefore, are among the objects most worth searching for on this earth. And in this book we have the results of one such quest.

FRANCIS YOUNGHUSBAND

PREFACE

Since its original publication in 1934, so much has changed in India that many details of this narrative will seem foreign to today's reader. However, the encounters described in *A Search in Secret India* have lost nothing of their value over the years, and I still fully affirm the fundamental truth of this work.

At the time this book was written, two important groups of mystics existed in India. The well known mystics were snake charmers, hypnotists, soothsayers, and others, who developed special abilities and attained a certain power in their domain. The other group consisted of people who searched for God through various meditation practices. This group of mystics was smaller in number, but they could be found scattered across the whole of India, and they were very important people in Indian culture.

Contacts with Western educational methods and achievements, threats of Japanese and Chinese invasions, as well as the realization of the necessity for a higher standard of living, led the younger Indian people to a more secular and more science-oriented world view. Nehru's policy of modernization and industrialization favored this, while mysticism, metaphysics and yoga promised no great material advantages.

A beneficial result of these changes has enabled women to have more freedom than before. Ananda Mayee leaves her main Ashram in old Benares to wander across the land visiting and teaching her disciples. She is greeted with reverance and admiration, and even met with Nehru on her travels. It is no longer easy for fanatics, charlatans and those obsessed by religious delusions to exploit the local villagers. Progress in the larger cities has caused city dwellers to become more and more motivated by political passions, and their disputes are sometimes violent. When I was there, these people were much more friendly.

Most of the Indian sages whom I portray have parted form the earth, but I shall never forget them. Two of these sages have made the most profound impression on me: one is the Maharishee of Arunachala, who has crossed the threshold of death; the other is Shri Shankara Acharya of Kanchi,* who is the spiritual leader of South India. He is widely respected by all those whom I consider competent to evaluate the spiritual attainment of a man, and he is, of all of India's living holy men, by far the most enlightened.

It is perhaps appropriate to mention another very special person, who for some years has lived as a refugee in the foothills of the Himalayas: the Dalai Lama of Tibet. Although still a young man, he has a profound knowledge of the teachings of Buddhism. To the enemies who so cruelly fight to suppress his homeland, he has demonstrated an attitude that comes close to that of Jesus.

When I first wrote this book, I expressed my regrets that so few people in the West seemed interested in "the Spiritual India." These regrets no longer apply. In the course of the last 20 or 30 years, Westerners have begun to journey to India and the Ashrams of well-known Yoga masters. Many serious books have been published in Western languages in which religious-philosophical Indian writings are presented and explained. What was once the search of a few has now become the longing of hundreds from Europe and the United States.

Paul Brunton
Rome, February 1967

*Not to be confused with three other sages of the same name in North, East, and West India.
(Publisher's Note: Ananda Mayee is no longer living.)

A SEARCH IN SECRET INDIA

CHAPTER I

WHEREIN I BOW TO THE READER

THERE is an obscure passage in the yellowed book of Indian life which I have endeavoured to elucidate for the benefit of Western readers. Early travellers returned home to Europe with weird tales of the Indian faqueers and even modern travellers occasionally bring similar stories.

What is the truth behind those legends which come ever and anon to our ears, concerning a mysterious class of men called Yogis[1] by some and faqueers by others? What is the truth behind the fitful hints which reach us intimating that there exists in India an old wisdom that promises the most extraordinary development of mental powers to those who practise it? I set out on a long journey to find it and the following pages summarize my report.

" Summarize " I say, because the inexorable exigencies of space and time required me to write of one Yogi where I had met more. Therefore I have selected a few who interested me most, and who seemed likely to interest the Western world. One heard much of certain so-called holy men who possessed repute of having acquired deep wisdom and strange powers; so one travelled through scorching days and sleepless nights to find them—only to find well-intentioned fools, scriptural slaves, venerable know-nothings, money-seeking conjurers, jugglers with a few tricks, and pious frauds. To fill my pages with the records of such people would be worthless to the reader and is a distasteful task to me. Therefore I omit the tale of time wasted upon them.

[1] Pronounced *Yogees*.

I feel quite humbly that I have been privileged to see a remote aspect of India seldom seen and less understood by ordinary travellers. Among the English residents in that vast land only an infinitesimal fraction has cared to study this aspect, and of this fraction very few were free enough to examine it more deeply and give their report, for official dignity must needs be respected. Therefore, English writers who have touched on this subject swing over to a hearty scepticism which, by its very nature, renders many sources of native knowledge not readily available to them, and which causes the Indian who really knows something about the less superficial side of the matter to shrink from discussing it with them. The white man will, in most cases, possess but an imperfect acquaintance with the Yogis, if he knows them at all, and certainly not with the best of them. The latter are now but a mere handful in the very country of their origin. They are exceedingly rare, are fond of hiding their true attainment from the public, and prefer to pose as ignoramuses. In India, in Tibet and in China, they get rid of the Western traveller who may happen to blunder in upon their privacy, by maintaining a studied appearance of insignificance and ignorance. Perhaps they would see some sense in Emerson's abrupt phrase: "To be great is to be misunderstood"; I do not know. Anyway, they are mostly recluses who do not care to mingle with mankind. Even when met with they are unlikely to break their reserve except after some period of acquaintance. Hence little has been written in Western continents about the strange life of these Yogis and even that little remains vague.

The reports of Indian writers are indeed available, but they must be read with great care. It is an unfortunate fact that the Hindus lack any critical approach to these matters and will mix hearsay with fact quite indiscriminately. Therefore such reports diminish greatly in truth as documentary records. When I saw the cataract of credulity which covers so many Eastern eyes, I thanked Heaven for such scientific training as the West has given me and for the common sense attitude which journalistic experience had instilled in me. There is a basis of fact underlying much Oriental superstition, but vigilance is needed to discover it. I was compelled to keep a critical but not hostile eye widely open wherever I went. Those who learned that I was interested in the mystical and miraculous, apart from my philosophical concerns, applied liberal paint and plentiful varnish to their few facts; many would think nothing of indulging in breath-taking exaggerations. I might have spent my time trying to teach them that Truth is so strong she can stand upon her own legs without falling to the ground, but I had other things to do. I felt glad, however, that I had preferred to gain my knowledge of Oriental wonders at first hand, just as I prefer Christ's wisdom to his commentators' ignorance. I searched through a welter of crass superstitions, incredible impostures and ancient pretensions for those things which are true, which will stand the acid test of thorough investigation. I flatter myself that I could never have done this did I not contain within my complex nature the two elements of scientific scepticism and spiritual sensitivity, elements which usually range themselves in sharp conflict and flagrant opposition.

I have titled this book *Secret India* because it tells of an India which has been hidden from prying eyes for thousands of years, which has kept itself so exclusive that to-day only its rapidly disappearing remnants are left. The manner in which the Yogis kept their knowledge so esoteric may appear selfish to us in these democratic days, but it helps to account for their gradual disappearance from visible history. Thousands of Englishmen live in India and hundreds visit it each year. Yet few know anything of what may one day prove more worthy to the world than even the prized pearls and valuable stones which ships bring us from India. Fewer still have taken the trouble to go out of their way to find the adepts in Yoga,[1] while not one Englishman in a thousand is prepared to prostrate himself before a brown, half-naked figure in some lonely cave or in a disciple-filled room. Such is the inevitable barrier imposed by this form of caste that even men of generous character and developed intellect, if suddenly taken from their habitations in the British quarters and set down in such a cave, would find a Yogi's company uncongenial and his ideas unintelligible.

Yet the Englishman in India, whether soldier, civil servant, business man or traveller, is not to be blamed because he is too proud to squat on the mat of the Yogi. Quite apart from the business of upholding British prestige, doubtless an important and necessary procedure, the kind of holy man he usually encounters is more likely to repel than attract. It is certainly no loss to avoid such a man. Nevertheless it is a pity that after a sojourn of many years the English resident will often leave

[1] Pronounced *Yohg*. Its spelling is unphonetic.

the country in blameless ignorance of what lies behind the frontal brain of an Indian sage.

I plainly remember my interview with a Cockney under the shadow of Trichinopoly's gigantic rock fort. For over twenty years he had held a responsible post on the Indian railways. It was inevitable that I should ply him with many questions about his life in this sunburnt land. Finally I trotted out my pet interrogation, " Have you met any Yogis ? "

He looked at me somewhat blankly and then replied :

' Yogis ? What are they ? Some kind of animal ? "

Such ignorance would have been perfectly pardonable had he stayed at home within the sound of Bow Bells ; now, after twenty-six years' residence in the country, it was perfectly blissful. I permitted it to remain undisturbed.

Because I put pride underfoot in moving among the varied peoples who inhabit Hindustan ; because I gave them a ready understanding and an intellectual sympathy, a freedom from finicky prejudice and a regard for character irrespective of colour ; and because I had sought Truth all my life and was prepared to accept whatsoever Truth brought in its train, I am able to write this record. I picked my way through a crowd of superstitious fools and self-styled faqueers in order to sit at the feet of true sages, there to learn at first hand the real teachings of Indian Yoga. I squatted on the floor in many a secluded hermitage, surrounded by brown faces and hearing strange dialects. I sought out those reserved and reclusive men, the best Yogis, and listened humbly to their oracular instruction. I talked for hours with the Brahmin pundits of Benares, discussing the age-old questions of philosophy and belief which have tormented the mind and troubled the heart of man since he first began to think. I stopped now and then to divert myself with the magician and wonder-worker, and strange incidents crossed my trails.

I wanted to gather the real facts about the Yogis of to-day by the method of first-hand investigation. I prided myself that experience as a journalist fitted me to draw out, with the least possible delay, much of the information which I sought ; that sitting at the editorial desk and curtly wielding the blue pencil had trained me to become ruthlessly critical in separating wheat from chaff ; and that the contact with men and women in every grade of life which the profession generally gives, with ragged mendicants as well as well-fed millionaires, would help me move just a little more smoothly through the variegated masses of India, among whom I searched for those strange men, the Yogis.

On the other side of the sheet I had lived an inner life totally detached from my outward circumstance. I spent much of my spare time in the study of recondite books and in little-known bypaths of psychological experiment. I delved into subjects which always have been wrapped in Cimmerian mystery. To these items must be added an inborn attraction towards things Oriental. The East, before my first visit, threw out vast tentacles that gripped my soul ; ultimately they drew me to study the sacred books of Asia, the learned commentaries of her pundits and the inscribed thoughts of her sages, so far as English translations could be procured.

This dual experience proved of great value. It taught me never to permit my sympathy with Oriental methods of probing life's mysteries, subvert my scientific desire of critically and impartially finding the facts. Without that sympathy I could never have gone among people and into places where the average Englishman in India may disdain to tread. Without that strict, scientific attitude I might have been led away into the wilderness of superstition, as so many Indians seem to have been led away. It is not easy to conjoin qualities which are usually held to be contradictory, but I sincerely tried to hold them in sane balance.

§

That the West has little to learn from present-day India, I shall not trouble to deny, but that we have much to learn from Indian sages of the past and from the few who live to-day, I unhesitatingly assert. The white tourist who " does " the chief cities and historical sights and then steams away with disgust at the backward civilization of India is doubtless justified in his depreciation of it. Yet a wiser kind of tourist shall one day arise who will seek out, not the crumbling ruins of useless temples, nor the marbled palaces of dissipated kings long dead, but the living sages who can reveal a wisdom untaught by our universities.

Are these Indians mere idlers sprawling in the fierce tropic sun ? Have they done nothing, thought nothing that is of worth to the rest of the world ? The traveller who can see only their material degeneration and mental flabbiness has not seen far. Let him substitute consideration for his contempt and he may open sealed lips and hidden doors.

Grant that India has nodded and snored for centuries ; grant that even to-day there exist millions of peasants in this land who suffer the same illiteracy, share the same outlook blended of puerile superstition and kindergarten religion as did English peasants of the fourteenth century. Grant further that the Brahmin pundits in native centres of learning waste their useless years splitting sacerdotal hairs and drawing metaphysical wire as subtly as our own medieval scholastics ever did. Yet there still remains a small but priceless residue of culture classified under the generic term Yoga, which proffers benefits to mankind as valuable in their own way as any proffered by the Western sciences. It can bring our bodies nearer the healthy condition which Nature intended them to possess; it can bestow one of modern civilization's most urgent needs—a flawless serenity of mind; and it can open the way to enduring treasures of the spirit to those who will labour for them. I admit that this great wisdom hardly belongs to India's present, but to her past; that this guarded knowledge of Yoga flourishes little to-day when once it must have had worthy professors and faithful students. It may be that the secrecy in which it was carefully enshrouded succeeded in killing all spread of this ancient science; I do not know.

It is perhaps not amiss, then, if one asks one's Western fellows to look Eastward, not for a new faith, but for a few pebbles of knowledge to cast upon our present heap. When Orientalists like Burnouf, Colebrooke and Max Müller appeared upon learning's scene and brought us some of the literary treasures of India, the savants of Europe began to understand that the heathens who inhabited that country were not so stupid as our own ignorance had presumed. Those clever people who profess to find Asiatic learning empty of useful thoughts for the West thereby prove their own emptiness. Those practical persons who would fling the epithet "stupid" at its study, succeed only in flinging it at their own narrow-mindedness. If our ideas about life are to be wholly determined by a mere accident of space, by the chance that we were born in Bristol instead of Bombay, then we are not worthy the name of civilized man. Those who close their minds to the entrance of all Eastern ideas, close them also to fine thoughts, deep truths and worth-while psychological knowledge. Whoever will poke about among this musty lore of the Orient in the hope of finding some precious gems of strange fact and stranger wisdom, will find his quest no vain one.

§

I journeyed Eastwards in search of the Yogis and their hermetic knowledge. The thought of finding a spiritual light and diviner life was also entertained, though it was not my primary purpose. I wandered along the banks of India's holy rivers—the quiet, grey-green Ganges, the broad Jumna and the picturesque Godavari—in this quest. I circled the country. India took me to her heart and the vanishing remnant of her sages opened many a door for the unfamiliar Westerner.

Not so long ago I was among those who regard God as a hallucination of human fancy, spiritual truth as a mere nebula and providential justice as a confection for infantile idealists. I, too, was somewhat impatient of those who construct theological paradises and who then confidently show you round with an air of being God's estate agents. I had nothing but contempt for what seemed to be the futile, fanatical efforts of uncritical theorisers.

If, therefore, I have begun to think a little differently about these matters, rest assured that good cause has been given me. Yet I did not arrive at paying allegiance to any Eastern creed; indeed, those which matter I had already studied intellectually much earlier. I did arrive at a new acceptance of the Divine. This may seem quite an insignificant and personal thing to do, but as a child of this modern generation, which relies on hard facts and cold reason, and which lacks enthusiasm for things religious, I regard it as quite an achievement. This faith was restored in the only way a sceptic could have it restored, not by argument, but by the witness of an overwhelming experience. And it was a jungle sage, an unassuming hermit who had formerly lived for six years in a mountain cave, who promoted this vital change in my thinking. It is quite possible that he could not pass a matriculation examination, yet I am not ashamed to record in the closing chapters of this book my deep indebtedness to this man. The production of such sages provides India with sufficient credentials to warrant attention from intelligent Westerners. The secret India's spiritual life still exists, despite the storms of political agitation which now hide it, and I have tried to give authentic record of more than one adept who has attained a strength and serenity for which we lesser mortals wistfully yearn.

I have borne witness in the book to other things also, things marvellous and weird. They seem incredible now, as I sit and type my narrative through the inked ribbon amid the matter-of-fact surroundings of English country-side; indeed, I wonder at my temerity in writing them down for a sceptical world to read. But I do not believe the present materialistic ideas which dominate the world will remain for all time; already one can perceive prophetic indications of a coming change of thought. Yet quite frankly I do not believe in miracles. Neither do most men of my generation. But I do believe that our knowledge of Nature's laws is incomplete, and that when the advance guard of scientists who are pushing forward into unexplored territory have found out a few more of those laws, we shall then be able to do things which are tantamount to miracles.

CHAPTER II

A PRELUDE TO THE QUEST

THE geography master takes a long, tapering pointer and moves over to the large, varnished linen map which hangs before a half-bored class. He indicates a triangular red patch which juts down to the Equator, and then makes a further attempt to stimulate the obviously lagging interest of his pupils. He begins in a thin, drawling voice and with the air of one about to make a hierophantic revelation :

" India has been called the brightest jewel in the British crown. . . ."

At once a boy with moody brow, half wrapt in reverie, gives a sudden start and draws his far-flung imagination back into the stolid, brick-walled building which constitutes his school. The sound of this word INDIA falling on the tympanum of his ears, or the sight of it caught up by the optic nerve of his eyes from a printed page, carries thrilling and mysterious connotations of the unknown. Some inexplicable current of thought brings it repeatedly before him.

When the mathematics master believes that this pupil is laboriously working at an algebraical problem, little does he know that the young rascal uses the school's desk for ulterior purposes. For under the cover of skilfully arrayed books he rapidly sketches turbaned heads, dusky faces and spice-laden ships being loaded from flat junks.

The youthful years pass, but this interest in Hindustan remains undimmed. Nay, it spreads and embraces all Asia within its eager tentacles.

Ever and anon he makes wild projects to go there. He will run away to sea. Surely it would then be a mere matter of enterprise to get some brief glimpse of India ? Even when these projects come to nought, he talks rhetorically to his schoolmates until one of them falls an easy victim to his immature enthusiasm.

Thereafter they conspire in silence and move in secret.

They plan an adventurous tramp across the face of Europe; it is then to continue into Asia Minor and Arabia until the port of Aden is reached. The reader, contemplating the innocent boldness of that long walk, will smile. They believe that a friendly ship's captain could be approached at Aden. He would undoubtedly prove a kindly, sympathetic man. He would take them aboard his steamer and a week later they would begin to explore India.

Preparations for this protracted excursion go on apace. Money is thriftily collected, and what they naively imagine to be an explorer's outfit is secretly brought together. Maps and guide-books are carefully consulted, the coloured pages and attractive photographs raising their wanderlust to fever heat. Finally they are able to fix the date when they intend to snap their fingers at destiny and leave the country. Who knows what lies around the corner?

They might have saved some of their youthful energy and conserved some of their early optimism. For on an unfortunate day the second boy's guardian discovers the preparations, elicits further details of the affair, and comes down with a stern hand. What they suffer as a result is not to be related! The enterprise is reluctantly abandoned.

The desire to view India never leaves the promoter of that unfortunate expedition. The dawn of manhood, however, brings bonds in the form of other interests and holds his feet with enchaining duties. That desire has to be put regretfully in the background.

Time turns page after page of the calendar of years until he meets unexpectedly with a man who gives a temporary but vivid life to the old ambition. For the stranger's face is dusky, his head is turbaned, and he comes from the sun-steeped land of Hindustan.

§

I fling out the fine net of remembrance to sweep the past years for pictures of that day when he steps into my life. The tide of autumn is fast ebbing, for the air is foggy and a bitter cold creeps through my clothing. Clammy fingers of depression strive hard to grip my failing heart.

I wander into a brightly-lit café and seek the borrowed comfort of its warmth. A cup of hot tea—so potent at other times—fails to restore my serenity. I cannot banish the heavy atmosphere which surrounds me. Melancholy has determined to make me serve her dark ends. Black curtains cover the entrance to my heart.

This restlessness is difficult to endure and it ends by driving me from the café into the open street. I walk without aim and follow old tracks until I find myself in front of a small bookshop which I know well. It is an ancient building and harbours equally ancient books. The proprietor[1] is a quaint man, a human relic surviving from an earlier century. This hustling epoch has little use for him, but he has just as little use for this epoch. He deals only in rare tomes and early editions, while specializing in curious and recondite subjects. He possesses a remarkable knowledge—so far as books can give it—of learning's bypaths and out-of-the-way matters. From time to time, I like to wander into the old shop and discuss them with him.

I enter the place and greet him. For a while I finger the yellowed pages of calf-bound volumes or peer closely into faded folios. One ancient book engages my attention ; it seems somewhat interesting and I examine it more carefully. The bespectacled bookseller notes my interest and, as is his wont, commences what he imagines to be an argument anent the book's subject—metempsychosis.

The old man follows habit and keeps the discussion to his own side. He talks at length, appearing to know the pros and cons of that strange doctrine better than my author, while the classic authorities who have written about it are at his finger-tips. In this way I glean much curious information.

Suddenly, I hear a man stirring at the far end of the shop and, turning, I behold a tall figure emerge from the shadows which hide a little inner room where the costlier books are kept.

The stranger is an Indian. He walks toward us with an aristocratic bearing and faces the bookseller.

" My friend," he says quietly, " pardon me for intruding. I could not help overhearing you, while the subject you discussed is of great interest to me. Now you quote the classical authors who first mention this idea of man's continual rebirth upon this earth. The deeper minds among those philosophic Greeks, wise Africans and early Christian Fathers understood this doctrine well, I agree. But where, do you think, did it really originate ? "

He pauses for a moment, but gives no time for a reply.

[1] Now, alas, he has departed from terra firma and his shop has disappeared with him !

"Permit me to tell you," he continues, smiling. "You must look to India for the first acceptance of metempsychosis in the Old World. It was a cardinal tenet among the people of my land, even in remote antiquity."

The speaker's face fascinates me. It is unusual; it would be distinguished-looking among a hundred Indians. Power kept in reserve—this is my reading of his character. Piercing eyes, a strong jaw and a lofty forehead make up the catalogue of his features. His skin is darker than that of the average Hindu. He wears a magnificent turban, the front of which is adorned with a sparkling jewel. For the rest, his clothes are European and finely tailored withal.

His slightly didactic statement does not appeal to the old gentleman behind the counter; in fact, vigorous opposition is offered to it.

"How can that be," comes the sceptical observation, "when the East Mediterranean cities were flourishing centres of culture and civilization in the pre-Christian era? Did not the greatest intellects of antiquity live in the area which embraced Athens and Alexandria? So, surely their ideas were carried Southward and Eastward until India was reached?"

The Indian smiles tolerantly.

"Not at all," is his immediate reply. "What really happened was quite the reverse of your assertion."

"Indeed! You seriously suggest that the progressive West had to receive its philosophy from the laggard East? No, sir!" expostulates the bookseller.

"Why not? Read your Apuleius again, my friend, and learn how Pythagoras came to India, where he was instructed by the Brahmins. Then notice how he began to teach the doctrine of metempsychosis after his return to Europe. This is but a single instance. I can find others. Your reference to the laggard East makes me smile. Thousands of years ago our sages were pondering over the deepest problems while your own countrymen were not even aware that such problems existed."

He stops curtly, looks intently at us, and waits for his words to sink into our minds. I fancy the old bookseller is a little perplexed. Never before have I seen him so struck into silence or so obviously impressed by another man's intellectual authority.

I have listened quietly to the other customer's words and make no attempt to offer a remark. Now there arises a conversational lull which all of us seem to recognize and to respect. Soon the Indian turns abruptly and retires to the inner room, only to emerge a couple of minutes later with a costly folio which he has selected from the shelves. He pays for the book and prepares to leave the shop. He reaches the door, whilst I stare wonderingly at his departing figure.

Suddenly, he turns again and approaches me. He draws a wallet out of his pocket and selects a visiting card.

"Would you care to pursue this conversation with me?" he asks, half smiling. I am taken by surprise, but gladly agree. He offers me the card, adding an invitation to dinner.

§

I set out toward evening to find the stranger's house, a task not without its discomfort, for I am companioned by an unpleasant fog which has descended thickly upon the streets. An artist, I presume, would find a touch of romantic beauty in these fogs which sometimes brood over the town and dim its lights. My mind, however, is so intent upon the forthcoming meeting that I see no beauty and feel no unpleasantness in the surrounding atmosphere.

A terminus is set to my travels by a massive gateway which suddenly looms up. Two large lamps, as in greeting, are held out by iron brackets. My entry into the house is followed by a delightful surprise. For the Indian has given no hint of this unique interior, upon which he has obviously lavished a fine taste and free purse.

Let it suffice that I find myself in a great room, which might be part of some Asiatic palace for aught I know, so exotically is it furnished and so colourful are its gorgeous decorations. With the closing of the outer door I leave behind the grey, bleak Western world. The room has been decorated in a quaint combination of Indian and Chinese styles. Red, black and gold are the predominating colours. Resplendent tapestries, bearing sprawling Chinese dragons, stretch across the walls. Carved green dragon heads glare fiercely from all the corners, where they support brackets which carry costly pieces of handicraft. Two silken mandarin coats adorn both sides of the doorway. Boldly patterned Indian rugs repose on the parquet floor, one's shoes sinking delightfully into their thick pile. A gigantic tiger skin stretches its full length in front of the hearth.

My eyes meet a small lacquered table which stands in one corner. Upon it rests a black ebony shrine with gilded folding doors. I glimpse the figure of some Indian god within the recess. It is probably a Buddha, for the face is calm and inscrutable and the two unwinking eyes gaze down at its nose.

My host greets me cordially. He is impeccably dressed in a black dinner suit. Such a man would look distinguished in any company in the world, I reflect. A few minutes later we both sit down to dinner. Some delightful dishes are brought to the table, and it is here that I receive my initiation into the pleasures of curry, thus acquiring a taste which is never to leave me. The servant who attends on us provides a picturesque note, for he wears a white jacket and trousers, a golden sash and spotless turban.

During the course of the meal our talk is superficial and general, yet whatever my host says, whatever subject he touches, his words invariably carry an air of finality. His statements are so phrased that they leave one with little ground for argument ; his accents are so confident that his talk sounds like the last word upon the matter. I cannot help being impressed by his air of quiet assurance.

Over the coffee cups he tells me a little about himself. I learn that he has travelled widely and that he possesses some means. He regales me with vivid impressions of China—where he has spent a year, of Japan—whose amazing future he tersely predicts, of America, Europe and—strangest of all—of life in a Christian monastery in Syria, where he had once spent a period of retirement.

When we light our cigarettes he touches on the subject which was mentioned at the bookshop. But it is evident that he desires to talk of other things, for he soon leads the way to larger issues, and broaches the subject of India's ancient wisdom.

" Some of the doctrines of our sages have already reached the West," he remarks impressively, " but in most cases the real teachings have been misunderstood ; in a few instances they have somehow been falsified. However, it is not for me to complain. What is India to-day ? She is no longer representative of the lofty culture of her past. The greatness has gone out of her. It is sad, very sad. The masses hold on to a few ideals at the cost of being enmeshed in a fussy tangle of pseudo-religious fetters and unwise customs."

" What is the cause of this degeneration ? " I ask him.

My host is silent. A minute slowly passes. I watch him while his eyes begin to narrow until they are half-closed ; then he quietly breaks the silence.

" Alas, my friend ! Once there were great seers in my land,

men who had penetrated the mysteries of life. Their advice was sought by king and commoner. Under their inspiration Indian civilization reached its zenith. To-day, where are they to be found ? Two or three may remain—unknown, unrecorded and far from the main stream of modern life. When those great sages—Rishees, we call them—began to withdraw from society, then our own decline also began."

His head droops till the chest must support his chin. A sorrowful note has entered his voice with the last sentence. For a while he seems withdrawn from me, his soul wrapped in melancholy meditation.

His personality impresses me again as being provocatively interesting and decidedly attractive. Eyes, dark and flashing, reveal a keen mentality ; voice, soft and sympathetic, reflects a kindly heart. I feel anew that I like him.

The servant noiselessly enters the room and approaches the lacquered table. He lights a joss stick and a blue haze rises to the ceiling. The strange perfume of some Eastern incense spreads around the room. It is not unpleasant.

Suddenly my host raises his head and looks at me.

" Did I tell you that two or three still remain ? " he asks queerly. " Ah, yes ! I said that. Once I knew a great sage. It was a privilege about which I rarely speak to others now. He was my father, guide, master and friend. He possessed the wisdom of a god. I loved him as if I were really his own son. Whenever I stayed with him at fortunate intervals, I knew then that life at its heart is good. Such was the effect of his wonderful atmosphere. I, who have made art my hobby and beauty my ideal, learnt from him to see the divine beauty in men who were leprous, destitute or deformed ; men from whom I formerly shrank in horror. He lived in a forest hermitage far from the towns. I stumbled upon his retreat seemingly by accident. From that day I paid him several visits, staying with him as long as I could. He taught me much. Yes—such a man could give greatness to any country."

" Then why did he not enter public life and serve India ? " I question frankly.

The Indian shakes his head.

" It is difficult enough for us to understand the motives of such an unusual man. It would be doubly difficult for you, a Westerner, to understand him. His answer might probably be that service can be rendered in secret through the telepathic power of the mind ; that influence can be exerted from a distance in an unseen yet no less potent manner. He might also say that a degenerate society must suffer its destiny until the fated hour of relief strikes."

I confess to being puzzled by this answer.

" Quite so, my friend, I expected that," observes the other.

§

After that memorable evening I visit the Indian's home many times, drawn by the lure of his unusual knowledge as much as by the attractiveness of his exotic personality. He touches some coiled spring among my ambitions and releases into urgency the desire to fathom life's meaning. He stimulates me, less to satisfy intellectual curiosity than to win a worth-while happiness.

One evening our conversation takes a turn which is destined to have important results for me. He describes on occasions the queer customs and peculiar traditions of his countrymen ; sometimes he portrays in words a few of the types who people his amazing land. He drops a remark this evening anent a strange type, the Yogi. I possess but a vague and incoherent idea of what the term really means. It has come to my notice a few times during the course of my reading, but on each occasion the terms of reference differ so much from the others that confusion is the natural result. So, when I hear my friend use the word I stop him short and beg for further information.

" That I shall do with pleasure," he answers, " but I can hardly tell you, in a single definition, what constitutes a Yogi. No doubt, a dozen of my countrymen will define the word in a dozen different ways. For instance, there are thousands of wandering beggars who pass by this name. They swarm through the villages and attend the periodic religious fairs in droves. Many are only lazy tramps and others vicious ones, while most are totally illiterate men, unaware of the history and doctrines of the science of Yoga, under whose shelter they masquerade."

He pauses to flick the ash off his cigarette.

" Go, however, to some place like Rishikesh, over which the mighty Himalayas keep eternal guard. There you will find a totally different class of men. They live in humble huts or caves, eat little food and constantly pray to God. Religion is their breath ; it occupies their minds day and night. They are mostly good men studying our sacred books and chanting prayers. Yet they, too, are called Yogis. But what have they in common with the beggars who prey on the ignorant masses? You see how elastic the term is! Between these two classes there are others who partake of the nature of both."

"And yet there seems to be much made of the mysterious powers possessed by Yogis," I remark.

"Ah! now you must listen to a further definition," he laughs back at me. "There are strange individuals in solitary retreats far from the big cities, in the seclusion of lonely jungles or mountain caves, men who devote their entire existence to practices which they believe will bring marvellous powers. Some of these men will eschew all mention of religion and scorn it; others, however, are highly religious; but all of them unite in the struggle to wrest from Nature a mastery over forces invisible and intangible. You see, India has never been without her traditions of the mysterious, the occult, and many are the stories told of those adepts who could perform miraculous feats. Now these men, too, are called Yogis."

"Have you met such men? Do you believe these traditions?" I ask innocently.

The other man is silent. He seems to be ruminating over the form in which to couch his reply.

My eyes turn to the shrine which stands upon the lacquered table. I fancy, in the soft light which fills our room, that the Buddha is smiling benignantly at me from its lotus throne of gilt wood. For half a minute I am ready to believe that there is something uncanny in its atmosphere; and then the Indian's clear voice breaks into my thoughts and arrests my wandering fancies.

"Look!" he says quietly, holding something out for my inspection. He has loosed it from under his collar. "I am a Brahmin. This is my sacred thread. Thousands of years of strict segregation have made certain qualities of character instinctive in my caste. Western education and Western travelling can never remove them. Faith in a higher power, belief in the existence of supernatural forces, recognition of a spiritual evolution among men—these things were born in me as a Brahmin. I could not destroy them if I would, while reason is overpowered by them whenever the issue comes to battle. So, although I am quite in sympathy with the principles and methods of your modern sciences, what other answer can I give you, except this—I believe!"

He looks intently at me for a few moments. Then he proceeds:

"Yes, I have met such men. Once, twice, three times.

They are difficult to come across. Once they were easier to find, I believe, but to-day they have almost disappeared."

"But they still exist, I presume?"

"Most likely, my friend. To find them is another matter. It would require a protracted search."

"Your master—was he one of them?"

"No, he belonged to a higher order. Did I not tell you that he was a Rishee?"

The term needs some elucidation before my mind can digest it. I tell him so.

"Higher than the Yogis stand the Rishees," he answers. "Transfer the Darwinian theory to the realm of human character; accept the Brahmin teaching that there is a spiritual evolution running parallel with the physical one; look upon the Rishees as men who have attained the crest of this upward climb; then you may form some rough conception of their greatness."

"Does a Rishee also perform those wonders of which we hear?"

"Yes, he certainly does, but he will not value them for their own sake, whereas many of the Yogi wonder-workers do. Such powers arise in him naturally by reason of his great development of will and mental concentration. They are not his chief concern; he may even disdain them and use them little. You see, his first purpose is to become inwardly something akin to those divine beings of whom Buddha in the East and Christ in the West are the most illustrious examples."

"But Christ worked miracles!"

"He did. But do you think he performed them for any vain self-glory? Not so; he desired to help the souls of ordinary people by thus catching their faith."

"Surely, if such men as Rishees existed in India, multitudes would flock after them?" I conjecture.

"Undoubtedly—but they would first have to appear in public and announce themselves for what they are. Only in the most exceptional cases have Rishees ever been known to do that. They prefer to live apart from the world. Those who wish to perform a public work may emerge for a limited time and then disappear again."

I object that such men could hardly be of much service to their fellows if they hide themselves in inaccessible places.

The Indian smiles tolerantly.

"That is a matter which comes within the province of your Western saying: 'Appearances are sometimes deceptive.'

Without intimate knowledge of these persons, the world is not in a position to judge them accurately, if you will pardon my saying so. I have mentioned that the Rishees did sometimes live for a while in towns and move in society. In olden times, when that was a little more frequent, their wisdom, power and attainment became obvious to the public; their influence was then openly acknowledged. Even Maharajahs did not disdain to pay reverent homage to those great sages and to consult them for guidance in their policies. But as a matter of fact, it is certain that the Rishees prefer to exert their influence in a silent and unknown manner."

"Well, I would like to meet such men," I mutter, half to myself. "And I should certainly like to encounter some real Yogis."

"You shall do so one day, without a doubt," he assures me.

"How do you know that?" I ask, somewhat startled.

"I knew it that day we first met," is the astonishing answer. "It came to me as an intuition—does it matter what you call it?—as a message deeply felt but inexplicable by outward evidences. My master taught me how to train this feeling, to develop it. Now, I have learnt to trust it implicitly."

"A modern Socrates guided by his daemon!" I remark half-jocosely. "But tell me, when do you think your prophecy will come true?"

He shrugs his shoulders.

"I am not a prophet. So I regret that I cannot date the event for you."

I do not press him, though I suspect he could say more if he would. I meditate upon the matter and then offer a suggestion.

"I suppose you will return to your own country eventually. If I am ready at the time, could we not travel together? Would you not help me locate some of these men we have been discussing?"

"No, my friend. Go alone. It will be better that you do your own finding."

"It will be so difficult for a stranger," I complain.

"Yes—very difficult. But go alone; one day you will see that I am right."

§

From that time I feel strongly that a momentous day will dawn which will find me at anchor in the sunny East. I reflect that if India has harboured such great men as the Rishees in the past, and if, as my friend believes, there may be a few of them still in existence, then the trouble of locating them might be balanced by the reward of learning something of their wisdom. Peradventure, I might then gain an understanding and content which life has so far denied me. Even if I fail in such a quest, the journey will not be a vain one. For those queer men, the Yogis, with their magic, their mysterious practices and their strange mode of living, excite my curiosity and arouse my interest. The journalistic grindstone has sharpened to an abnormal keenness my concern with the unusual. I am fascinated by the prospect of exploring such little-known trails. I decide to carry out my fancy to its full proportions and, when opportunity allows, take the first boat to India.

My dark-skinned friend, who has thus clinched and rendered final this determination to trek towards the rising sun, continues to receive me at his house for several months. He assists me to take my bearings upon the swirling ocean of life, though he always refuses to act as a pilot across the uncharted waters which stretch ahead of me. To discover one's position, to be made aware of latent possibilities, and to get one's vague ideas clarified, is nevertheless of indubitable value to a young man. It is not amiss, then, if I pay my meed of gratitude to that early benefactor of mine. For a dark day comes when fate spins its wheel once again, and we part. Within a few years I hear, seemingly by accident, of his death.

Time and circumstance are not ready for my journey. Ambition and desire lure a man into responsibilities from which it is not easy to extricate himself. I can do little more than resign myself to the life which hems me in, and watch and wait.

I never lose my faith in the Indian's prophecy. One day it is strengthened by an unexpected confirmation.

Professional work throws me for several months into frequent contact with a man for whom I entertain a high respect and friendly regard. He is exceedingly astute and knows human nature through every letter of its alphabet. Many years earlier he held the post of Professor of Psychology at one of our universities, but an academic life was not to his taste. He deserted it for pastures where he could put his amazing range of knowledge to more practical use. For a time he acted as adviser to magnates of the business world. How often has he boasted of drawing several retaining fees from the chiefs of large firms!

He is born with the remarkable gift of inspiring others to

their best endeavours. Every person he meets—from office boy to millionaire magnate—finds practical help and new enthusiasm from the contact; sometimes they receive golden advice. I make it a practice to take careful note of any counsel he gives me, for his foresight and insight usually receive startling verification in both business and personal matters. I enjoy his company because he has succeeded in fusing the elements of introspection and extrospection in his own nature, with the result that he can talk profound philosophy one minute and deal with a commercial report the next. Withal he is never dull, always witty and radiating good-humour.

He admits me into the circle of intimate friendship and, sometimes, we spend several hours at a time in mingled work and pleasure. I never tire of listening to his talk, for its latitude of subject enthrals me. I wonder often that one small head can carry all he knows !

One night we go out to dine together in a little Bohemian restaurant where pleasantly shaded lights and nicely cooked food accompany each other. After the meal we find a full moon resplendent in the heavens, and tempted by the witchery of its poetic light, decide to walk homewards.

The conversation has been somewhat light and frivolous for most of the evening, but as we walk on through the city's quieter streets, it drifts into philosophical depths. The close of our nocturnal peregrination finds us discussing subjects so abstruse that some of my companion's clients would take fright at the mere sound of the names. Outside his door, he turns and proffers a hand in farewell. As he grips mine, he suddenly addresses me in grave tones and says slowly :

" You ought never to have entered this profession. You are really a philosopher caught up in the ink-slinging business of writing. Why did you not become a university don and spend your life in secluded research ? For you like to put on those carpet slippers of yours and walk around inside your brain. You are trying to reach the very source of the mind. One day you will go out to the Yogis of India, to the Lamas of Tibet and the Zen monks of Japan. Then you will write some strange records. Good night ! "

" What do you think of these Yogis ? "

The other man bends his head towards mine and half-whispers in my ear :

" My friend, they know, *they know !* "

I walk away greatly puzzled. This Eastern journey is not likely to happen for a long time ahead. I am sinking deeper and deeper into a maze of activities from which escape becomes proportionately more difficult. For a while pessimism seizes me. Am I not doomed by destiny to remain imprisoned in this maze of private bonds and personal ambitions ?

Yet my guess at the unseen writ is wrong. Fate issues its orders every day, and though we are not literate enough to be able to read them, nevertheless we unconsciously move about to obey ! Before twelve months pass I find myself disembarking at Alexandra Dock, Bombay ; mingling with the motley life of that Eastern city, and listening to the weird medley of Asiatic tongues which contribute to its cacophony !

CHAPTER III

A MAGICIAN OUT OF EGYPT

IT is a singular fact—and perhaps a significant one—that before I can begin to try my luck in this strange quest, fortune herself comes in quest of me. I have not even taken the tourist's privilege of exploring the show places of Bombay. All I know of the city can be comfortably written down on a postcard. My trunks, save one, remain in a sedate, unpacked condition. My sole activity consists in an attempt to familiarize myself with my surroundings in the Hotel Majestic, which a shipboard acquaintance had described as one of the most comfortable hotels in the city. It is through this activity, then, that I make a startling discovery. For, staying as a fellow guest of the hotel, I find a member of the magician's fraternity, a weaver of strange spells, in short, a wonder-worker in the flesh !

Not that he is one of those juggling fellows, mind you, who make their own and theatres' fortunes by bewildering jaded audiences. He is not some clever individual attempting to emulate the feats of Maskelyne and Devant in a less prosaic environment than that of Regent Street. No ! This man belongs to the line of medieval sorcerers. He engages daily in commerce with mysterious beings, invisible to normal human eyes, but plain enough to his own ! Such, at least, is the peculiar reputation which he has created. The hotel staff regard him with fearful looks and speak of him with bated breath. Whenever he passes by, the other guests instinctively break off conversation and a puzzled, questioning look comes into their eyes. He makes no overtures to them and usually insists on dining alone.

What makes him more intriguing in our eyes is that he bears neither European nor Indian nationality ; he is a traveller from the country of the Nile ; in very sooth, a magician out of Egypt !

It is not easy for me to reconcile the appearance of Mahmoud

Bey with the sinister powers with which he has been credited. Instead of the stern visage and lean body which I look for, I observe a good-looking smiling face, a well-built figure with massive shoulders and the quick walk of a man of action. Instead of the white robe or voluminous cloak, he is sprucely dressed in well-fitting, modern clothes. He looks like a handsome Frenchman, such as one might see any evening in the better restaurants of Paris.

I ruminate upon the matter for the rest of the day. Next morning, I wake up with a clear-cut decision. Mahmoud Bey must be forthwith interviewed. I shall "get his story," as my fellow scribes of the Press might say.

I write a few lines, expressive of my desire, on the back of a visiting card and then, in the right-hand corner, I draw in tiny characters a certain symbol which will indicate that I am not unfamiliar with the traditional side of his mysterious art and which, I hope, may help me to obtain an interview. I slip the card into the hand of a soft-footed servant, add a silver rupee, and send him up to the magician's room.

Five minutes later the response arrives: "Mahmoud Bey will see you at once, sir. He is just about to take breakfast and invites you to join him."

This first success encourages me. The servant leads the way upstairs and I find Mahmoud Bey seated at a table whereon there is tea and toast and jam. The Egyptian does not rise to greet me. Instead, he points to a chair opposite him and says, in a firm, resonant voice:

"Please be seated. Excuse me, but I never shake hands."

He wears a loose grey dressing-gown. There is a leonine mane of brown hair on his head. A curling lock strays over his forehead. His teeth flash white in a charming smile as he asks:

"You will share my breakfast, eh?"

I thank him. Over the cups I inform him of the awe-inspired reputation which belongs to him in the hotel, and of the prolonged meditation in which I have indulged before having the temerity to approach him. He laughs heartily and half raises a hand into the air, as a gesture of helplessness, but says nothing.

After a pause, he asks: "Are you representing any paper?"

"No. I have come to India on a private mission—to study some out-of-the-way things, and possibly make a few notes for literary work."

"Will you stay here long?"

" That depends on circumstances. I have fixed no period," I answer, with a queer feeling that the affair is becoming a case of the interviewer interviewed. But his next words reassure me :

" I, too, am here on an extended visit. Possibly one year, possibly two years. After that, I am off for the Far East. I would like to see the world and then return home to Egypt, if Allah permits."

The servant enters and clears the table after we have finished. I feel that it is time to plunge into deeper water.

" Is it true that you possess these magical powers ? " I question him, pointedly.

Calmly and confidently, he says : " Yes ! Allah, the All-Powerful, has granted me such powers."

I hesitate. His dark grey eyes gaze fixedly at me.

" You would like me to demonstrate them, I believe ? " he asks, suddenly.

He has correctly gauged my desire. I nod assent.

" Very well. Have you a pencil and some paper ? "

I hastily feel in a pocket for my notebook, tear out a page, and then produce a pencil.

" Good," he remarks. " Now please write some question on the paper." With that he withdraws and sits at a small table in the window recess. He half turns his back upon me and looks down into the street below. Several feet of space now separate us.

" What kind of question ? " I query.

" Anything you wish," he replies promptly.

My brain plays with a few thoughts. Finally, I write down a brief question. It is : " Where did I live four years ago ? "

" Now fold the paper repeatedly until it forms a tiny square," he instructs me. " Let it be the smallest possible fold."

I obey him. Thereupon he draws his chair back to my table and faces me once again.

" Please clench the piece of paper, together with the pencil, in the palm of your right hand."

I hold the articles tightly clutched. The Egyptian closes his eyes. He appears to fall into a profound concentration. Then the heavy lids open once more, the grey eyes look steadily at me, and he quietly says :

" The question which you asked—was it not, ' Where did I live four years ago ? ' "

" You are correct," I reply, astonished. This is a case of mind reading extraordinary !

"Now, please unfold the piece of paper in your hand," his voice breaks in.

I place the tiny scrap upon the surface of the table and slowly open out its many folds until the paper lies flat, extended to its original size.

"Examine it!" commands the other man. I do so and make a surprising discovery. For some unseen hand has written in pencil the name of the town where I lived four years ago. The answer has been placed immediately beneath the written question.

Mahmoud Bey smiles triumphantly.

"There is the answer. Is it correct?" he demands.

I give a wondering assent, for I am baffled. The feat hardly seems credible. As a test, I ask him to repeat it. He readily agrees and moves away to the window while I write down a further question. Thus he avoids any possible accusation of being close enough to read my writing. Besides, I watch him carefully and note that his eyes are set upon the colourful scene in the street below.

Once again I fold the paper and clutch it tightly against the pencil which is in my hand. He returns to the table and plunges again into close concentration, his eyes fast shut. Then come the words:

"Your second question—'What journal did I edit two years ago?'"

He has given my query quite accurately. Thought-reading again, I presume.

Once more he requests me to unfold the tiny scrap in my right hand. I place it flat on the table and it reveals to my astounded gaze the name of the journal in question, clumsily written in pencil!

Conjuring? I dismiss the suggestion as absurd. The paper and pencil were supplied from my own pockets, the questions were unpremeditated, while Mahmoud Bey has scrupulously put several feet between us at each writing. Moreover, the entire feat has been performed in the morning daylight.

Hypnotism? I have studied the subject and know well when any attempt at undue influence is being made. I know equally how to guard against it. And the mysteriously added words still remain on the paper.[1]

[1] The scrap of paper remained in my possession for several months, and the writing did not disappear during the whole of that time. I showed it to two or three persons who readily identified the added answers. It is therefore evident that the experience had not been a hallucination.

I am baffled again. For a third time I request the Egyptian to repeat the experiment, and he agrees to a final test. From this, too, he emerges completely successful.

The facts cannot be gainsaid. He has read my mind (as I believe); he has somehow, by some inexplicable magic, caused certain words to be written by an invisible hand upon a piece of paper which I clutch tightly in my hand; and, finally, those words form correct replies to my question.

What is the strange process he uses?

As I ponder over the matter, I feel the presence of uncanny forces. To the normal mind, the thing is incredible. It is something alien and apart from sane existence. My heart almost stands still with a sense of eeriness.

"Have you men in England who can do this?" he asks, half boastfully.

I am compelled to admit that I know of none who can perform the feat under similar test conditions, though several professional conjurers can doubtless perform it if allowed to use their own paraphernalia.

"Would you care to explain your methods?" I inquire weakly, fearing that in asking him to reveal his secrets I am asking for the moon.

He shrugs his broad shoulders.

"I have been offered large sums of money to give my secrets away, but I do not intend to do so yet."

"You are aware that I am not entirely ignorant of the psychic side of things?" I venture.

"Assuredly. If I ever come to Europe—which is quite possible—you may be able to render certain services to me. In that case, I promise to train you in my methods so that you could do the same things, if you wish."

"How long does the training last?"

"That would differ with different persons. If you worked hard and gave the whole of your time to it, three months would be enough to get an understanding of the methods, but after that years of practice may be required."

"Can you not explain the broad basis of your feats, the theoretical side alone, without explaining your secrets?" I persist.

Mahmoud Bey muses over my query for a while.

"Yes, I am willing to do that for you," he answers softly.

I feel for my shorthand book, draw it out of a pocket, and poise the pencil in readiness to take notes.

" No, please. Not this morning," he protests, smiling. " I am busy ; you must excuse me now. Come here to-morrow at one hour before noon, and we shall continue our talk."

§

Precisely at the appointed time I sit again in Mahmoud Bey's room. He pushes a box of Egyptian cigarettes over the table towards me. I pick one out and, as he proffers the light, he remarks :

" These come from my native country. They are good."

We lean back in our chairs, puffing a few preliminary whiffs. The smoke is fragrant, aromatic ; certainly these cigarettes are excellent indeed.

" So I must now describe my theories, as your English friends would call them ; to me they are certainties." Mahmoud Bey laughs good-naturedly. " Perhaps you will be surprised to hear that I am a man expert in scientific agriculture and that I hold diplomas in the subject ? " he adds irrelevantly.

I begin to scribble a note.

" That does not seem to fit in with my—shall we say, interest in magic, I know," he continues. I look up at him and notice a smile hovering around his lips. He gazes back at me. There is a good " story " in this man, I reflect.

" But you are a journalist ; probably you would like to know how I became a magician, eh ? " he queries.

I express an eager assent.

" Good ! I was born in an interior province, but brought up in Cairo. Let me tell you that I was just a normal boy, with the usual interests which schoolboys possess. I was very keen on making agriculture my profession, so I attended the Government Agricultural College for that purpose. I worked hard at my studies and went on with them most enthusiastically.

" One day an old man took an apartment in the house where I lived. He was a Jew, with bushy eyebrows and a long grey beard, and his face was always grave and serious. He seemed to be living in the past century, for he wore very old-fashioned clothes. His manner was so reserved that the other inhabitants of the house were kept at a distance. Strangely enough, instead of having the same effect upon me, this mysterious reserve piqued my interest. Being young, self-assertive and utterly without a trace of shyness, I persistently strove to make his acquaintance. At first he rebuffed me, but that only added fuel to the fire of my curiosity. Eventually, he gave way to my constant attempts to engage him in conversation. He opened his doors to me and permitted me to enter his life. Thus I came to learn that he spent much of his time in strange studies and weird practices. In short, he confessed to me that he was making researches into the supernatural side of things.

" Imagine it ! Hitherto my life had run along the even channel of youthful study and healthy sport. Now, I was forced abruptly face to face with a totally different kind of existence. And it appealed to me. The thought of the supernatural did not frighten me, as no doubt it would have done other boys. Really, it thrilled me because I saw the possibilities of great adventures opening up through it. I begged the old Jew to teach me something about the subject, and he yielded to my desire. In this way I was brought into a new circle of interests and friends. The Jew took me with him to a society in Cairo which conducted practical investigations into magic, spiritualism, theosophy and the occult. He often delivered lectures to them. The group was composed of society people, learned savants, Government officials and other persons of good standing.

" Although I had only just reached manhood, I was permitted to accompany the old man to every meeting of the society. On each occasion I listened eagerly ; my ears drank in every word of the talk around me ; my eyes watched with keen fascination the strange experiments which were so often made. Of course, it was inevitable that my technical studies in agriculture were neglected, so that more time could be given to the researches into supernatural matters. However, I had a natural genius for the former studies and scraped through my diploma examinations without difficulty.

" I studied the musty old books which the Jew lent me, and practised the magical rituals and other exercises which he taught me. I made such quick progress that I began to discover things which he himself did not know. At length, I became acknowledged as an expert in these arts. I delivered lectures and gave demonstrations to the Cairo Society, until its members appointed me as its President. For twelve years I remained its leader. Then I resigned, because I wanted to leave Egypt and travel to certain countries—and, incidentally, to acquire a fortune ! "

Mahmoud Bey stops speaking; his carefully manicured fingers, which I have not failed to observe, flick the ash from his cigarette.

"A difficult task!"

He smiles. "For me it will be easy. I need only a few clients among the super-rich who wish to make use of my magical powers. Already I am known to certain wealthy Parsees and rich Hindus. They come here to consult me about their problems or troubles, or they wish to discover certain things which elude them, or they want information which is only to be procured by occult means. I charge them high fees, naturally. One hundred rupees is my minimum. Frankly, I want to make a lot of money and then throw the whole thing up and retire to some quiet interior province in Egypt. I will buy a large orange-grove plantation and take up my agricultural work once again."

"Did you come here direct from Egypt?"

"No—I spent some time in Syria and Palestine, after leaving Cairo. The Syrian police officers heard of my powers and occasionally asked me to help them. Whenever they were puzzled by some crime, they used my services as a last resource. Almost always I succeeded in finding the criminal for them."

"How were you able to do that?"

"The inner secrets of the crimes were revealed to me by my attendant spirits, who created a vision of the scenes before my eyes."

Mahmoud Bey relapses for a minute into reminiscent thought. I wait patiently for his next words.

"Yes, I suppose you could call me a practising Spiritualist of a sort, since I do invoke the aid of spirits," he goes on. "But I am also what you call a magician in the real sense—not a conjurer—as well as a thought reader. I do not claim to be anything more than this."

His claim is sufficiently startling to require no further additions!

"Please tell me something about your invisible employees," I ask him.

"The spirits? Well, it took me three years of difficult practice to get my present control of them. You see, in the other world which exists outside our material senses, there are bad as well as good spirits. I try to use good spirits only. Some of them are human beings who have passed through what the world calls death, but most of my attendants are *jinns* —that is, native inhabitants of the spirit world who have never possessed a human body. Some of them are just like animals, others are as shrewd as men. There are also evil *jinns*—we call them *jinns* in Egypt and I do not know any suitable English word for them—who are used by low sorcerers, especially by the African witch doctors. I refuse to have anything to do with them. They are dangerous servants and will sometimes turn treacherously on the man who is using them and kill him."

"Who are these human spirits you employ?"

"I can tell you that one of them is my own brother. He 'died' some years ago. But remember—I am not a Spiritualist medium, for no spirit ever enters my body or is allowed to control me in any way. My brother communicates with me by impressing upon my mind whatever thought he wishes, or by bringing a picture-vision before my mind's eye. That is how I knew the questions you wrote down yesterday."

"And the *jinns?*"

"I have as many as thirty at my command. Even after obtaining mastery over them, I had to train them how to do my bidding, just as you train children to dance. I have to know the name of each one, because you cannot bring or use them without knowing their names. Some of these names I learned from the musty old books which the Jew lent me."

Mahmoud Bey pushes the cigarette-box towards me again, and then continues:

"I have given each spirit a particular duty; each one is trained to do a separate work. Thus, the *jinns* who produced the pencil-written words on your piece of paper yesterday would be quite unable to help me discover the nature of your questions."

"How do you get into contact with these spirits?" is my next query.

"I can call them to me very quickly merely by concentrating in thought upon them, but in practice I usually write down in Arabic the name of the spirit required; that is sufficient to bring it to me almost at once."

The Egyptian looks at his watch. He rises and says:

"And now, my friend, I regret to say that I cannot give you any further explanation of my methods. Perhaps you will now understand why I must keep them secret. We may meet again one day, if Allah wills. Good-bye."

He flashes his teeth in a smile as he bows. The interview is at an end.

§

Night in Bombay. I go to bed late, but not to sleep. The heavy air suffocates me; it seems to contain no oxygen; and its heat is intolerable. The whirring blades of an electric fan which hangs from the ceiling bring little relief, certainly not sufficient to induce my weary eyes to close. I find that the simple act of breathing is a distinct labour. The air is hot enough to hurt my inexperienced lungs with every dilation. My wretched body becomes flaccid and drips a continuous stream of perspiration which my pyjamas soak up. Worse, my oppressed brain finds no rest. The devil of insomnia enters my life this night and is destined to haunt me until the day when my shoes tread Indian soil for the last time. I have begun to pay the inevitable price of acclimatization to the tropical world.

A mosquito net hangs around my bed like a white shroud. Through a tall window which opens on the veranda balcony the moonlight comes streaming and casts eerie shadows on the pale ceiling.

Musing over the morning's talk with Mahmoud Bey and the astounding phenomena of the previous day, I seek for some explanation other than that he has given me, but can find none. If those thirty or more mysterious servitors of his really exist, then one is back in the medieval period when—assuming legend does not always lie—magicians flourished in every city of Europe, though often hindered in their dark work by Church and State.

The more I seek for an explanation, the more I retreat baffled.

Why had Mahmoud Bey instructed me to hold the pencil simultaneously with the piece of paper? Did his alleged spirits draw some constituent atoms from the lead to enable them to write the answers?

I cast about in memory for instances of similar feats. Does not the famous Venetian voyager, Marco Polo, relate somewhere in his book of travel how he came across certain magicians in China, Tartary and Tibet and how they were able to perform pencil writing without contact? And did not those wizards inform him that this weird art was known and practised among their people since centuries before?

I remember, too, that Helena Petrovna Blavatsky, the enigmatic Russian lady who founded the Theosophical Society, produced somewhat parallel phenomena fifty years ago. Certain favoured members of her society received somewhat lengthy messages through her agency. They propounded philosophical questions and the replies were scrawled—precipitated, she called it—upon the actual letter paper bearing the questions! It is curious that Mme Blavatsky claimed intimate acquaintance with both Tartary and Tibet, the very lands where Marco Polo met with the same phenomena. Yet Mme Blavatsky did not claim to control any mysterious spirits, as Mahmoud Bey had done. Her assertion was that the mysterious writings emanated from her Tibetan masters, who lived in the flesh and lurked unseen as the inspirers of her society. Apparently they were better hands at the feat than the Egyptian, for they produced such writings hundreds of miles away from Tibet. There had been much dispute at the time whether the Russian lady's phenomena were really genuine, and whether her Tibetan teachers really existed. But that is not my concern, for that brilliant woman has long since gone to the other world in which she seemed so much at home while yet here. I know my own experience and what I have witnessed with my own eyes. I must accept the genuineness of the performance, even if I reserve its explanation.

Yes, Mahmoud Bey is a magician, a twentieth-century wizard. My discovery of him so soon after landing on Indian earth seems to be a herald, apt and prophetic, of even stranger discoveries yet. Metaphorically, I have cut the first notch in my stick of Indian experience. Actually, I have put down the first note on the virgin white sheets of my note-book.

CHAPTER IV

I MEET A MESSIAH

"I AM pleased to see you" is the somewhat conventional greeting with which I am received by Meher Baba. He is destined, had I but known it, to flash like a meteorite across the Western sky and to rouse the curiosity of millions of people in Europe and America. Moreover, like a meteorite, he will fall ingloriously to earth. I am the first Western journalist to interview him, for I track him down to his Indian abode when he is almost unknown to more than local fame.

I have become acquainted with one of his chief disciples, and, after some correspondence, wonder what manner of man has joined the ranks of self-appointed deliverers of mankind. Two Parsee disciples come to Bombay to escort me. Before we leave the city, they inform me that it is necessary to make a present of choice flowers and fruits to their master. So we proceed to the bazaar and they collect a large hamper of these commodities on my behalf.

Our train arrives at Ahmednagar next morning, after travelling through the night. I remember it as the historical place where the cruel Emperor Aurungzeeb, Preserver of the Faith and Ornament of the Moghul Throne, stroked his heavy beard for the last time, for Death caught him here in his tent.

A rackety old war-time Ford car, which does duty for the transport needs of Meher Baba's retreat, waits for us at the station. The seven-mile run which follows takes us through flat country. An avenue of neem trees lines part of the road. We pass a village whose huddled brown roofs rise against the elaborate little spire of the local temple. Then I sight a stream, whose banks are lined with pink and yellow flowers, and in whose muddy water buffaloes are blissfully resting.

We arrive at Meher Baba's curious colony, which is spread out in scattered erections. Three odd-looking stone structures, which I learn later are the remnants of a dismantled army camp site, stand in a field. Three plain wooden bungalows stand in an adjacent one. A quarter of a mile away is a little village whose name is given as Arangaon. The whole place presents a bare appearance and seems half deserted. My Parsee escorts are at pains to inform me that this is only the country headquarters of their master, and that his principal centre is near the town of Nasik, where the majority of his intimate disciples reside and where visitors are usually received.

A few men emerge from one of the bungalows as we pass. They lounge on the veranda, smile, gesticulate, and seem pleased at the arrival of a European in their midst. We cross a field and reach a queer-looking structure, which is nothing less than an artificial cave. It is built of stones and rubble cemented together and is about eight feet deep. It faces due south and receives the bright morning sunlight full into its interior. I look around and see the rolling expanse of fields, the ring of hills which bounds the horizon on the east, and the tree-shaded village down in a hollow. This Parsee holy man is doubtless a great lover of Nature, for he has set his retreat in a scene of aloof, untroubled peace. I am, indeed, glad to find such a quiet backwater after the whirl of Bombay life.

Two men stand on guard like sentries outside the cave's entrance. They move at our approach and go inside to consult their master. "Put out your cigarette," whispers one of my escorts, "Baba does not like smoking." I throw the offending cigarette away. A minute later I am conducted into the august presence of the so-called "new messiah."

He squats at the far end of the cave, the entire floor of which is covered with a beautifully patterned Persian rug. He proves to be somewhat different from the person I have imagined. His eyes do not penetrate me, his facial expression lacks strength, and although I am aware of something ascetic, unworldly and gentle in his atmosphere, I wonder why I feel no responsive thrill, such as one may reasonably expect to feel in the presence of one who proposes to win the allegiance of millions of people.

He is clothed in a long, spotless white robe, which looks ludicrously like an old-fashioned English nightshirt! His amiable and kindly face is framed in chestnut-coloured hair, which falls in long curly waves to his neck. I am struck by the soft, silky texture of the hair, which is remarkably like the hair of a woman. His nose rises into arched prominence and then descends into aquiline depth. The eyes are dark, medium sized and clear, but I find them unimpressive. A heavy brown moustache stretches across his upper lip. The light-tinted olive skin betrays his Persian origin, for his father hails from the land of the Shahs. Withal he is young, apparently somewhere in the thirties. A final feature which remains in memory is his forehead. It is so low as to appear less than average height, and it is so receding as to make me wonder. Do brain areas carry qualitative significance ? Does a man's forehead indicate his powers of thought ? But possibly a messiah is above such physical limitations !

" I am pleased to see you," he remarks, but not, mind you, in the usual manner of human speech. For he holds a small alphabet board upon his lap and points rapidly with his index finger to one letter after another. As the words are spelt out in this dumb pantomime manner, his secretary interprets them aloud for my benefit.

Since the tenth of July, 1925, the holy man has not uttered a single word. His younger brother tells me that when the new messiah breaks into speech, his message will startle the world ! Meanwhile, he adopts a pose of strict silence.

Still fingering the board, Meher Baba makes some kindly inquiries into my personal well-being, asks questions about my life, and expresses his gratification at my interest in India. He possesses an excellent knowledge of English, so there is no necessity to translate my speech. He postpones till the late afternoon the lengthy interview which I request. " Food and rest are your immediate needs," he says, or rather, communicates.

I adjourn to one of the stone structures. It possesses a bare gloomy interior, but contains an old bedstead without bedding, a ramshackle table and a chair which might have rendered good service during the Indian Mutiny. Here I am to make my home for nearly a week. I peer through the glassless window and am rewarded by a view of sparse, untilled fields stretching away into scrub bush dotted with cactus.

Four hours creep lethargically around my watch. Once again I sit upon the Persian rug, face to face with Meher Baba, whose colossal claim that he is destined to give spiritual light and practical leading to the whole of mankind, I have yet to investigate.

He puts this claim into the first sentence which he flicks out on the alphabet board.

" I shall change the history of the whole world ! "

My note-taking disturbs him, however.

" Can you not make your notes after you leave me ? "

I agree, and henceforth inscribe his words upon the pages of memory.

" As Jesus came to impart spirituality to a materialistic age, so have I come to impart a spiritual push to present-day mankind. There is always a fixed time for such divine workings, and when the hour is ripe I shall reveal my true nature to the entire world. The great teachers of religion—Jesus, Buddha, Muhammed and Zoroaster—do not differ in their essential doctrines. All these prophets came from God. The chief commandments run through all their teachings like a golden thread. These divine ones came out into public when their help was most needed, when spirituality was at its lowest ebb and materialism was apparently everywhere victorious. Such a time we are fast approaching at present. The whole world is now enmeshed in sensual desires, in racial selfishness and money worship. God is forsaken. True religion is abused ; man seeks life and the priests usually give him a stone. God, therefore, must send his true prophet among men once again to establish true worship and to awaken people out of their materialistic stupor. I but follow in the line of those earlier prophets ; this is my mission. God has given me a mandate."

I listen quietly while the secretary voices these amazing assertions. I keep my mind open, uncritical, and offer no mental resistance. This is not to say that I accept them, however, but that I am aware one must know how to listen among these Orientals. Otherwise a Westerner will get little for his pains, even where there might be something worthy of acceptance. Truth can stand a ruthless investigation, but the methods of the Occident must be modified to suit the mental atmosphere of the Orient.

Meher Baba smiles genially at me, and then proceeds:

" The prophets lay down certain rules and regulations to help the masses lead better lives and to incline them towards God. Gradually these rules become the tenets of an organized religion, but the idealistic spirit and motive force which prevail during the founder's lifetime, disappear gradually after his death. That is why organizations cannot bring spiritual truth nearer and why true religion is always a personal concern. Religious organizations become like archæological departments trying to resuscitate the past. Therefore I shall not attempt to establish any new religion, cult or organization. But I shall rejuvenate the religious thought of all peoples, instil a higher understanding of life into them. Dogmas invented centuries after the founder's death, frequently differ startlingly, but the fundamentals of all religions are really the same, because all issue from the same source—God. Therefore, when I appear publicly I shall run down no existing religion, but then I shall not uphold any special one. I want to turn men's minds away from sectarian differences, so that they will agree on essential truths. Remember though, that every prophet considers the times, the circumstances and the prevailing mentality of the people before his public manifestation. He therefore preaches doctrines best understood and best suited to such conditions."

Meher Baba pauses for a while to let these exalted ideas soak into my head, and then his words take a new turn.

"Have you not noticed how all the nations have been brought into quick communication with each other during this modern epoch? Do you not see how railways, steamships, telephones, cables, wireless and newspapers have caused the whole world to become a closely-woven unit? An important event which happens in one country is made known within a day to the people of a country ten thousand miles away. Therefore a man who wishes to deliver an important message can find almost the whole of mankind as a ready audience. For all that there is a sound reason. The time is soon coming to give mankind a universal spiritual belief which shall serve all races of people and all countries. In other words, the way is being prepared to enable me to deliver a world-wide message!"

This breath-taking announcement indicates sufficiently that Meher Baba possesses an unlimited faith in his own future, and indeed, his whole manner confirms it. In his own estimation, his stock will one day stand at infinitely more than par!

"But when shall you tell the world about your mission?" I ask.

"I shall break my silence and deliver my message only when there is chaos and confusion everywhere, for then I shall be most needed; when the world is rocking in upheavals—earthquakes, floods and volcanic eruptions; when both East and West are aflame with war. Truly the whole world must suffer, for the whole world must be redeemed."

"Do you know the date of this war?"

"Yes. It is not far off. But I do not wish to reveal the date."[1]

[1] See also Chapter XIV.

" That is a terrible prophecy ! " I exclaim.

Meher Baba spreads out his thin tapering fingers apologetically.

" It is. The war will be terrible in its nature because scientific ingenuity will make it more intense than the last war. However, it will last only a short time—a few months—and at its worst I shall make myself publicly known and declare my mission to the entire world. By my material efforts and spiritual powers, I shall speedily bring the conflict to an abrupt end, thus restoring peace to all the nations. Yet great natural changes must take place on this planet simultaneously. Life and property in different parts of the globe will suffer. If I play the role of a messiah it will be because world conditions require it. Be assured that I shall not leave my spiritual work undone."

His secretary, a short dusky-faced man who wears the round black cap of the Mahratta people, looks at me impressively after he finishes speaking the last word. The expression on his face seems to say : " There ! how do you like that ! You see what important things we know here ! "

His master's fingers begin to move over the board once more, and he hastens to tell me their new import.

" After the war will come a long era of unique peace, a time of world tranquillity. Disarmament will then no longer be a matter of mere talk, but an actual fact. Racial and communal strife will cease ; sectarian hatred between religious organizations will come to an end. I shall travel widely throughout the world and the nations will be eager to see me. My spiritual message will reach every land, every town, every village even. Universal brotherhood ; peace among men ; sympathy for the poor and downtrodden ; love of God—I shall promote these things."

" What of India—your own country ? "

" In India I shall not rest till the pernicious caste system is uprooted and destroyed. India became depressed in the scale of nations with the establishment of caste. When the outcastes and lower castes are elevated, India will find herself to be one of the influential countries of the world."

" And what of her future ? "

" Despite its faults, India is still the most spiritual country in the world. The future will find it the moral leader of all the nations. All the great founders of religions were born in the East, and it is to the East that the peoples must continue to look for spiritual light."

I try to visualize the great Western nations sitting at the feet of the meek little brown men, but fail. Perhaps the white-robed figure squatting in front of me grasps my difficulty, for he adds :

" The so-called subjection of India is not real subjection. It is of the body, and therefore temporary. The soul of the country is deathless and great, even if outwardly the nation has lost its power."

This subtle explanation somewhat eludes my understanding. I return to our earlier theme.

" We in the West have heard most of the things in your message from other sources. You have nothing new to tell us, then ? "

" My words can only echo the old spiritual truths, but it is my mystic power that will bring a new element into the world's life."

Upon this point I seek to rest my brain. For a while there is silence ; I ask no more questions. I turn my head and gaze out of the cave. Far across the quiet fields, a line of hills rises in the distance. In the sky, a pitiless sun scorches man, beast and earth alike. The minutes pass. In this secluded cave, in this unending heat, surrounded by absorbent minds, it is easy to weave grandiose schemes of world reformation, to possess oneself of extravagant religious ideas. But out in the world of reality, amid the hard life of materialistic cities, these things would soon dissipate like mists before the dawning sun.

" Europe is hard, sceptical," I remark, turning and looking at the new messiah. " How are you going to convince us that you speak with real divine authority ? How can you convert unfamiliar peoples to your brand of spiritual belief ? The average Westerner will tell you that it is impossible, and very likely he will laugh at you for your pains."

" Ah, you do not realize how changed the times will be."

Meher Baba strokes his pale slender hands. And then he adds some astounding claims, which sound fantastic to Western ears, yet his manner is quite matter-of-fact.

" Once I publicly announce myself as a messiah, nothing will be able to withstand my power. I shall openly work miracles in proof of my mission at the same time. Restoring sight to the blind, healing the sick, maimed and crippled, yes, even raising the dead—these things will be child's play to me ! I shall work these miracles because through them people will everywhere be forced to believe in me, and then believe in my message. These wonders will not be done to satisfy idle curiosity, but to convince the sceptically minded."

I hold my breath. The interview has reached the boundary of common sense. My mind begins to falter. We are entering the region of Oriental fantasy.

" Make no mistake, however," continues the Parsee messiah. " I tell my disciples that these miracles are to be done only for the masses, not for them. I should not care to perform a single wonder, but I know that this will turn the minds of common people to my words. If I shall astonish the peoples of the world with these feats, it will be only because I wish to spiritualize them."

" Baba has already done marvellous things," breaks in the secretary.

I am instantly alert.

" Such as—— ? " I demand quickly.

The master smiles self-deprecatingly.

" Tell him another time, Vishnu," he communicates. " I can perform any miracle when necessary. It is easy to one who has reached my divine state."

I make a mental note to buttonhole the secretary on the morrow and get some details of these reputed marvels. They will form an interesting part of my investigation. I come as a circumspect inquirer and every kind of fact will make grist for my mill.

There is another interlude of silence. I request the holy man to give me certain information about his career.

" Tell him that also, Vishnu," he answers, directing me again to his secretary. " You will have plenty of opportunity to talk to my disciples, since you are staying here for a little while. They can tell you about the past."

The talk drifts into the domain of general matters. Soon after, our meeting disperses. The first thing I do on getting back to my quarters is to light a cigarette, thus atoning for the one forbidden me, and then watch its fragrant smoke rise erratically upward.

§

I witness a curious spectacle in the early evening. The stars have just begun to twinkle faintly, the day is not quite dead, and in this queer half light a few oil lanterns glow palely. Meher sits inside his cave while a motley crowd, composed of disciples, visitors and people from the nearby village of Arangaon, gather in horseshoe fashion around the entrance.

A ceremony which is repeated every evening wherever

Meher may be at the time is about to take place. A devotee holds aloft a shallow metal bowl which serves as a lamp, its wick being dipped in oil which is strongly perfumed with sandalwood. He waves it seven times around the saintly head of his master. The assembled audience thereupon break into a vigorous chorus of chants and prayers. Through the intonations of their Mahratti dialect, I catch the name of Baba several times. It is obvious that the chants are hyperboles of adulation for their master. Everyone looks at him with adoring eyes. Meher's younger brother sits at a small portable harmonium, and makes a wailing kind of music to accompany the singers.

During the course of the ceremony, each devotee files up to the cave in turn, prostrates himself before Meher and kisses his uncovered feet. Some are so overwrought with pious emotion that they prolong the act of osculation to a full minute! I am told that this act is deemed extremely beneficial spiritually, since it brings Meher's blessing upon the devotee and automatically washes away some of his sins.

I walk back to my quarters, wondering what the next day will bring forth. Somewhere across the fields and out in the jungle a jackal bays and breaks the night's silence.

The next day I gather the secretary and some of the English-speaking disciples outside one of their wooden bungalows. We sit in a half circle. Those who do not understand English stand a little distance away and watch us with smiling faces and interested eyes. I proceed to extract from all these collective minds and memories such facts about their amazing master's career as I do not already know.

His personal name is Meher, but he calls himself Sadguru Meher Baba. Sadguru means "perfect master," while Baba is simply a term of affection in common use among some of the Indian peoples, and it is by this name alone that his disciples usually address him.

Meher Baba's father is a Persian[1] who is an adherent of the Zoroastrian creed, and who emigrated to India as a poor youth. Meher was his first son and was born in 1894 at Poona City. The boy was put to school at five, proved good at his studies, and passed the matriculation examination at seventeen. He then entered Deccan College in Poona and received a good modern education for two years.

Now began the tortuous and incomprehensible phase of his career. He was cycling back from school one evening and was

[1] Hence the appellation *Parsee*.

about to pass the dwelling-place of a well-known Muhammedan woman faqueer. Her name was Hazrat Babajan, and she was reputed to be over a century old. She was reclining on a long couch which stood upon a railed veranda outside her humble wooden one-roomed house. When the cycle drew abreast of her, the old woman rose and beckoned to the boy. He dismounted and approached her. She clasped his hands and embraced him and then kissed his forehead.

What happened afterwards is not very clear. I gathered that the youth reached his home in a dazed mental state, and that during the following eight months his mental faculties progressively weakened until he became unable to study properly. In the end he had to bid a final farewell to his college, because he could no longer follow his lessons.

Thereafter young Meher fell into a semi-idiotic condition and was hardly able to look after himself. His eyes became dull and lifeless, and he lacked the intelligence to perform the most elementary duties of a human being, such as taking food, washing oneself, attending to the calls of nature, and so on. When his father said, " Eat ! " he took his food in a mechanical manner ; otherwise he did not understand why the food was put before him. In short he became a human automaton.

A young man of twenty, whose parents have to care for him like a child of three, seems a case of mental regression, and the distracted father concluded that he had overworked his mind while cramming for an examination. Meher was taken to various doctors, who diagnosed mental breakdown and gave him injections. In nine months' time improvement in his lamentable condition set in and gradually increased, until he was able to understand his environment intelligently and to act more normally.

After his recovery it was discovered that his character had changed. His scholastic ambitions were gone, his ambitions for a worldly career had disappeared, while his interest in games and sports had collapsed. All these things were replaced by a deep thirst for the religious life and by a continuous aspiration to spiritualize himself.

Because he believed that these changes took their root in the kiss which the Mudammedan woman faqueer had bestowed on him, Meher approached the old lady for advice about his future. She directed him to find a spiritual teacher. He inquired where this boon was to be obtained. She waved her hand vaguely into space for reply.

He visited several holy men of repute in the locality. Then

he went farther afield to the villages within a hundred miles of his native Poona. One day he walked into a little stone-built temple near Sakori. It was a poor humble shrine but it was the abode of a very holy man, or so the villagers said. And so, when Meher came face to face with Upasani Maharaj, he felt that he had found his master.

The young aspirant for holiness made periodic excursions from home to Sakori. He usually spent a few days at a time with his teacher, but once he remained for four months. Meher asserts that during this period he was being perfected, made ready for his mission. One evening he collected thirty of his old schoolmates and boyhood friends, gave them mysterious hints of an important meeting, and brought them to the little temple in Sakori. The doors were locked and Upasani Maharaj, the stern-looking holy man who lived there, rose and addressed the gathering. He spoke to them about religion, told them to seek virtue, informed them that he had made Meher the spiritual inheritor of his own mystic powers and knowledge, and finally announced to the surprised young men that Meher had attained divine perfection! He strongly advised them to become followers of their Parsee friend, for then they would receive great spiritual benefit, both in this life and in that to come.

Some of his listeners took his advice and others remained sceptical. About a year later, when Meher had reached the age of twenty-seven, the young Parsee announced to his small flock that he had become conscious of a divine mission which he was to carry out, and that God had given him a work of colossal importance to mankind. He did not straightway reveal the precise nature of that mission, but within a few years he let the secret emerge. He was destined to become a messiah!

In 1924 Meher left India for the first time. He embarked on a journey to Persia with a company of half a dozen disciples, telling them that he would tour the country of his ancestors. When the ship touched port at Bushire, he suddenly changed his mind and left the place by the next homeward boat. Three months later rebel forces captured Teheran, the Persian capital and deposed the old regime. A new Shah came to the throne.

Meher Baba then turned to his followers and said:

"Now you see the result of my mystic workings during my visit to Persia!"

His disciples told me that Persia was a happier land under the new ruler, and that Muhammedans, Zoroastrians, Jews and Christians were living amicably together, whereas there had been constant strife and cruel outrages among them under the old regime.

Some years after this mysterious excursion, Meher Baba began a curious educational institution. At his suggestion a disciple purchased the colony's present site near the village of Arangaon. Several rough bungalows were constructed, together with many thatch-and-pole huts. A free boarding school was then declared open, the teachers being recruited from the Parsee's educated disciples and the pupils from the families of devotees or their friends. No fees were charged for tuition, while even board and lodging were free. In addition to the usual secular subjects, there was special instruction in undenominational religion by Meher himself.

On such attractive terms it was an easy matter to collect nearly one hundred boys. A dozen of them arrived from distant Persia. The boys were taught the moral ideals which are more or less common to most religions, and the life stories of the great prophets were unfolded to them. The class on religion gradually became the central feature of the curriculum and Meher Baba led the older boys into a devotional mysticism which appears to have been of a somewhat watery nature. They were taught to regard him as a sacred personage, even to worship him. A few boys began to manifest signs of religious hysteria in the sequence. Strange scenes occurred among them every few days.

A noticeable feature of this unusual school was that the pupils belonged to varying castes, races and creeds. Hindus Muhammedans, Indian Christians and Zoroastrians mingled freely, but Meher Baba wanted a still wider enrolment. He sent his chief disciple on a mission to England to find a few white pupils. The emissary, however, encountered much difficulty because the white parents were unwilling to entrust their children to a stranger, who wanted to haul the latter off to a school in distant Asia. Moreover, the idea of a school combining all religions did not mean much to them. There are plenty of schools in England where pupils of different creeds foregather in a natural spontaneous manner without the fuss that is made of it in a creed-ridden country like India.

One day the emissary from India met an Englishman who straightaway became converted to acceptance of the Parsee messiah after a conversation or two. The man was possessed of an enthusiastic temperament and having rapidly travelled through all the cults which honeycomb London, he was ready for what seemed to be the loftier message of Meher Baba. So he assisted in the quest for white pupils and found three children, whose poverty-stricken parents were willing to ease their own burdens at the price of parting with them. At this stage the India Office bestirred itself into activity, investigated the matter, shook its official head and put a ban on the project. The children did not sail. The representative of the Parsee messiah returned to India, accompanied by the Englishman and the latter's wife and sister-in-law. Five or six months after their arrival, Meher Baba sent them back to England at the expense of his chief disciple.

I learnt from Meher that his object in founding this school was twofold. First, he wanted to break down the racial and religious barriers among the pupils ; secondly, he sought to train a selected number of them as future ambassadors for his spiritual cause. When the years had sufficiently ripened them and the time came for public announcement of his own mission, he would send them out to all the five continents to act as apostles and helpers in his destined work of spiritualising mankind.

Another activity developed into being alongside the school. A primitive hospital was opened and ardent disciples were sent out to collect the blind, the ailing and the crippled from the locality. The latter were given free medical treatment, food and accommodation, while the Parsee holy man provided them with spiritual consolation. Five lepers were cured by his mere touch, says an enthusiastic devotee. Alas, I am a trifle sceptical, for no one knows who they are, where they are or how to find them now. 'Tis a piece of Oriental exaggeration, I fear. Surely one of the lepers would have attached himself to Meher Baba's train of disciples in sheer gratitude. Surely the news would have spread like a prairie fire across leprosy-ridden India, and all the stricken souls of the country would have eagerly flocked to the hospital near Arangaon.

There grew up a large camp-following of devotees, visitors and hangers-on from nearby villages. The population of this unusual colony reached into hundreds ; intense religious fervour pervaded the whole place ; and Meher Baba was, of course, the centre of the whole picture.

Eighteen months after the colony was founded, it was suddenly closed down and all these activities were abandoned. The boys were sent back to their parents and the patients to their homes. Meher Baba vouchsafed no reason for this move on his part. I learnt that sudden inexplicable impulses of this kind were a regular feature of his conduct.

In the spring of 1929 he sent out his first missionary disciple, a man named Sadhu Leik, who was bidden to go on tour round India. The latter was told as a parting injunction :

" You have the advantage of a messiah to work for. Be cosmopolitan and do not run down any religion. Be sure that I will know all about you. Do not be disheartened by the remarks of others. I will lead you, and follow none but me."

From the information which I picked up it was obvious that the poor fellow was physically unfitted for a wandering life. He was able to create a small following in Madras, but soon sickened on the way and then returned to die.

Such is a rapid outline of the Parsee holy man's career.

§

I have had several fugitive talks of a chatty nature with Meher Baba, but I want to hear something more definite about his self-appointed mission to the world. So I seek and obtain my final interview with him.

He wears a soft blue scarf to-day and the alphabet board rests upon his knees in readiness for our conversation. The disciples present form an admiring audience and provide the requisite background. Everyone smiles at everyone else until I shoot a sudden question through the silence.

" How do you know that you are a messiah ? "

The disciples look aghast at my temerity. The master moves his bushy eyebrows. But he is not disconcerted, for he smiles at the enquiring Westerner and quickly answers :

" I know ! I know it so well. You know that you are a human being, and so I know that I am a messiah ! It is my whole life. My bliss never stops. You never mistake yourself for some other person ; so I cannot mistake who I am. I have a divine work to do and I will do it."

" What really happened when the Muhammedan woman faqueer kissed you. Can you remember ? "

" Yes. Until then I was as worldly as other youths. Hazrat Babajan unlocked the door for me. Her kiss was the turning point. I felt as though the universe was receding into space ; and I was left entirely alone. Yes—I was alone with God. For months I could not sleep. And yet I grew no weaker but remained as strong as before. My father did not understand ; he thought I was going mad. He called in one doctor and then another. They gave me medicines and tried injections, but they were all wrong. I was with God and there was nothing to cure. Only, I had lost hold of normal existence and it took me a long time to get back. Do you understand ? "

" Quite. Now that you have got back, when will you let the public know ? "

" My manifestation will happen in the near future, but I cannot give you the exact date."

" And then—? "

" My task on this earth will last for thirty-three years. Afterwards I shall undergo a tragic death. My own people, the Parsees, will be responsible for my violent end. But others will continue my work."

" Your disciples, I presume ? "

" My circle of twelve selected disciples, of whom one will become a master at the appointed time. It is for their sake that I fast often and observe silence, for this wipes their sins away and will enable them to become perfect spiritually. They have all been with me in past births, and I am bound to help them. There will also be an outer circle with forty-four members. They will be men and women of lower spiritual grade ; their duty will be to assist the twelve chief disciples, after the latter have attained perfection."

" There are other claimants to messiahship ? "

Meher laughs in deprecation of those absurd persons.

" Yes. There is Krishnamurti—Mrs. Besant's protégé. The Theosophists deceive themselves. Their chief wire-pullers are supposed to be somewhere on the Himalayas in Tibet. You will find nothing but dust and stones in their supposed abodes. Besides, no real spiritual teacher ever required someone else's body to be prepared and trained for his use. That is ridiculous."

Other strange statements emerge from this final conversation ; a curious jumble of assertions, which come through slim fingers flickering from letter to letter. . . . " America has a great future ; she will become a spiritually-minded nation. . . . I am aware of everyone who puts his faith in me, and he is always helped. . . . Do not try to read my actions, you will never fathom them. . . . Once I visit a place and stay there, however short a time, its spiritual atmosphere becomes greatly elevated. . . . The general spiritual push that I shall give the world will soon put right all material problems—economic, political, sexual, sociological—for selfishness will be destroyed and brotherhood will replace it. . . .

Shivaji, the chieftain who built up the Mahratta empire in the seventeenth century, is also here (he points to himself; the meaning is that Meher is a reincarnation of Shivaji). . . . Some of the planets are inhabited; they resemble this globe in culture and material advancement, but spiritually our earth is most advanced. . . ."

One observes that Meher suffers from no modesty when discussing his claims. I am a little startled, however, when he communicates a command to me at the finish of the interview.

"Go to the West as my representative! Spread my name as that of the coming divine messenger. Work for me and my influence, and you will then be working for the good of mankind."

"The world will probably scout me as a madman," I reply uneasily, for such a task staggers my imagination.

Meher disagrees.

I answer that nothing short of working a series of miracles will convince the West that anyone is a spiritual superman, let alone a messiah, and that since I cannot perform miracles I cannot undertake the job of being his herald.

"Then you shall perform them!" is his comforting assurance.

I remain silent. Meher misconstrues my silence.

"Stay with me and I shall confer great powers on you," he urges. "You are very fortunate. I will help you to obtain advanced powers, so that you will render service in the West."

§

It is unnecessary to describe the remainder of this incredible interview. Some men are born great, some achieve greatness, and others appoint a press agent. Meher seems to favour the latter course.

Next day I prepare to leave. I have imbibed sufficient pious wisdom and prophetic forebodings to suffice me for the time. I have not wandered to distant parts of the world merely to hear religious assertions or declarations of grandeur. I want facts, even if they are to be facts of a strange, uncommon kind. And I want reliable evidence; better still, something personal, something to which I can testify for my own satisfaction.

My kit is packed, I am about to leave. I go to Meher and bid him a polite farewell. He informs me that within a few months he will be in residence at his central headquarters, which are situated near the town of Nasik. He suggests that I should visit him there and stay for a month.

" Do this. Come when you can. I will give you wonderful spiritual experiences and enable you to know the real truth about me. You will be shown my inner spiritual powers. After that, you will have no more doubts. You will be able to prove by your own personal experiences what I claim. Then you can go to the West and win many people for me."

I decide to return at my leisure and spend a month with him. Despite the theatrical character of the Parsee holy man and the fantastic nature of his mission, I decide to investigate the whole thing with an open mind.

§

A brief return to the stir of city life in Bombay, and then I entrain for Poona. My wanderings around this ancient land are about to begin.

The old Muhammedan holy woman, whose sudden intervention started Meher Baba off on his queer tangent, engages my interest. I deem a short visit to her will not come amiss. I have already made a few preliminary enquiries about her in Bombay, where I learn from former Judge Khandalawalla, who has known her for fifty years, that her age is really about ninety-five. I remember that Meher's followers informed me that it is one hundred and thirty, but I generously ascribe this exaggeration to the heat of their enthusiasm.

The Judge briefly tells me her story. She is a native of Baluchistan, that vague territory situate between Afghanistan and India, and she ran away from home quite early. After long and adventurous wanderings afoot, she arrived at Poona about the beginning of this century and has never moved from the city since. At first, she made her home under a neem tree, where she insisted on remaining in all seasons. Her reputation for sanctity and strange powers spread throughout the Muhammedan people in the vicinity, until even the Hindus came to treat her with due reverence. Some Muhammedans eventually built a wooden shelter under the tree for her, since she refused to live in a proper house. This gives her the semblance of a home and provides some protection against the inclemencies of the monsoon season.

I ask the Judge for his personal opinion. He replies that he does not doubt but that Hazrat Babajan is a genuine faqueer The Judge happens to be a Parsee, so I make some judicious enquiries about Meher Baba, who is well known to him. What I learn is unlikely to make me more favourable to the Parsee messiah. I ask him finally about Upasani Maharaj, who is now the inspirer of Meher. My informant, a shrewd, discerning old man of vast experience in these and worldly matters, enters into a lengthy account of his own unfortunate contact with him. I give two instances :

" Upasani has made ghastly mistakes. He once induced me to go to Benares, where he was staying at the time. After a while, I got a premonition of death and wanted to return to Poona, where my family was living. Upasani prevented me from going by repeatedly prophesying that everything would be all right. Nevertheless, two days later I received a telegram saying that my son's wife had given birth to a child, and that it died within a few minutes. In the other case, Upasani told my son-in-law, who was thinking of going on the Bombay Stock Exchange, that such a move would prove extremely fortunate for him. Acting on this advice, he embarked on the Exchange and was almost ruined ! "

Judge Khandalawalla impresses me with the independence of his outlook. He debunks Upasani Maharaj, whom Meher Baba has described to me as " one of the greatest spiritual personalities of this age," yet he does not hesitate to admit that Meher himself is honest and really believes in his spiritual attainment, although this attainment remains unproven.

I reach Poona, put up at a hotel in the cantonment, and then drive straight to the abode of Hazrat Babajan. A guide, who knows her personally and who will eke out my little Hindustani as an interpreter, accompanies me.

We find her in a narrow street, whose lighting is a quaint mixture of gaudy little oil lamps and electric globes. She lies, in full view of passers-by, upon a low divan. A fenced veranda rail separates it from the street. Above the wooden shelter rises the shapely outline of a neem tree, whose white blossoms make the air slightly fragrant.

" You must take off your shoes," my guide warns me. " It is considered disrespectful to wear them when you enter." I obey him and a minute later we stand by her bedside.

She lies flat on her back, this ancient dame. Her head is propped by pillows. The lustrous whiteness of her silky hair offers a sad contrast to the heavily wrinkled face and seamed brow.

Out of my slender store of newly-learnt Hindustani I address a phrase of self-introduction to the old lady. She turns her aged head, stretches out a skinny, bony forearm, and then takes one of my hands in her own. She holds it tightly, staring up at me with unworldly eyes.

Those eyes puzzle me. They seem to be quite uncomprehending, entirely vacant. She silently grips my hand for three or four minutes and continues to look blankly into my own eyes. I receive the feeling that her gaze penetrates me. It is a weird sensation. I do not know what to do. . . .

At last she withdraws her hand and brushes her forehead several times. Then she turns to my guide and says something to him, but it is in the vernacular and I cannot grasp its meaning.

He whispers the translation :

" He has been called to India and soon he will understand."

A pause, and then she croaks forth another sentence, but its meaning were better kept in my memory than in print.

Her voice is extremely feeble ; her words emerge slowly and with much difficulty. Is it possible that this aged and decrepit fleshly frame, this haggard and huddled figure, contains the soul of a genuine faqueer with wondrous powers ? Who can say ? It is not always easy to read the pages of the soul by the letters of the body.

But the woman is nearing her century. I have been warned that continued conversation with her is not permissible, owing to her enfeebled condition. I prepare to withdraw quietly, strongly impressed by one thought. I think that the vacancy of her eyes is a signal that she is near the gate of death. The mind is parting from the worn-out body, but drags itself back now and again to pay a feeble attention to this world through strange eyes.[1]

In the hotel, I sum up my feelings. That some deep psychological attainment really resides in the depths of her being, I am certain. Respect rises unbidden within me. I find that the contact has diverted my normal thought currents and raised up an inexplicable sense of that element of mystery which surrounds our earthly lives, despite all the discoveries and speculations of the scientists. I see with unexpected clarity that those scientific writers who profess to reveal the fundamental secrets of the great world puzzle, profess what is nothing more than surface scratching. But I cannot under-

[1] I visited her again some months later. The impression of her near decease was confirmed. She died soon after.

stand why a brief contact with the woman faqueer should so sap at the very base of my confident mental certainties.

The cryptic prophecy she made recurs to my mind. I am unable to grasp its meaning. No one has called me to India ; have I not gone freely of my own whim ? . . . Only now, as I write these lines, long after the event, do I believe that I begin dimly to understand. 'Tis a strange world, my masters !

CHAPTER V

THE ANCHORITE OF THE ADYAR RIVER

THE hands race around my watch, the weeks move across the face of my calendar, while I work my way southwards across the Deccan plateau. I visit several remarkable places, but find few remarkable men. Some inscrutable, impelling force—which I cannot understand, but which I blindly obey—hurries my pace so that sometimes I rush onwards as though I am a tourist.

At last I am on the train to Madras, where I intend to halt and establish myself for a while. During the long night journey, when sleep is difficult to procure, I take count of the invisible gains which I have reaped during these travels in Western India.

I force myself to confess that so far I have not tracked down any Yogi, about whose discovery I can feel unduly elated ; as for the thought of finding a Rishee, that now lies in the remote depths of my mind. On the other hand, I have seen enough of the gross superstitions and suffocating customs of sleepy India, to make me realize that the scepticism and warnings of some chance Bombay acquaintances are well justified. I realize, too, that my self-imposed task will be difficult of fulfilment. Pious men are here in all their fifty-seven varieties, but they do not provide sufficient attraction. One wanders by temples whose mysterious interior seems to promise much. I cross the sacred precincts and stand at the threshold. I peep inside and behold the fantastic worshippers, who toll a bell as they pray, that their prayers may not escape the ears of their chosen deity !

I am glad to reach Madras, whose straggling and colourful appearance appeals to me, and I settle in a charming suburb about two miles outside the city so as to get easier contact with the Indian, rather than the European, element. My house is in the Street of the Brahmins. The road is choked with a thick layer of sand, into which my shoes readily sink ;

the sidewalk is made of beaten earth : everything is free from the improving touch of the twentieth century. The white-washed houses have pillared porches and open verandas. In the interior of mine, there is a tiled courtyard, around which runs a covered gallery. Our water is hauled up by a bucket from an old well.

The luxuriant tropical scenery which unfolds as soon as one gets away from the two or three streets which compose this suburb affords me perpetual delight. Soon I discover that the Adyar River is less than half an hour's walk away. There are several shady palm groves near this wide stream, and they take my fancy. I spend my spare time loitering among them or walk for a few miles beside the languid water.

The Adyar River flows down to Madras, of which city it forms the southern boundary, and then joins the ocean amid the ceaseless rise and fall of the Coromandel surf. Alongside this beautiful stream I slowly amble one morning, accompanied by a Brahmin acquaintance who learns where my interests lie. After some time he suddenly seizes my arm.

" Look ! " he exclaims. " Do you see that young man who is approaching us ? He is known to be a Yogi. He would interest you, but, alas ! he never talks to us."

" Why not ? "

" I know where he lives, but he is the most reserved man in the whole district."

By this time the stranger has almost reached us. He possesses an athletic figure, and I judge him to be about thirty-five. He is slightly above medium height. What strikes me most, however, is the negroid character of his face. The skin has darkened to a shade of black, and the broad flat nose, the thick lips and muscular frame, all betoken non-Aryan blood. His long neatly-plaited hair is gathered around the crown of his head in a sort of top-knot. He wears a peculiar kind of large ear-ring. A white shawl is wrapped around his body and then flung across the left shoulder. The legs are bare and the feet uncovered.

He completely ignores us and paces onwards with slow steps. His eyes are downcast, as though intent on searching the ground. One gathers the impression that the mind behind those eyes is pondering over some matter. What, I wonder, is the subject of this walking meditation ?

He piques and arouses my interest still further. An intense desire to break down the barriers which separate us grips me suddenly.

" I want to talk to him. Let us turn back," I suggest.

The Brahmin protests firmly.

" It is useless."

" At least I can try," I answer.

The Brahmin again endeavours to dissuade me.

" That man is so inaccessible that we know hardly anything of him. He keeps himself quite aloof from his neighbours. We must not interfere with him."

But I am already moving in the reputed Yogi's direction and my companion has perforce to follow me.

We are soon behind the other man, who gives no sign of his awareness of our presence, but continues to pace slowly onward. We follow with parallel steps.

" Please ask if I may converse with him," I tell my companion. The latter hesitates, and then shakes his head.

" No—I dare not," he declares weakly.

The unpleasant possibility that I might be missing a valuable contact stirs me to further effort. There is no alternative but to address the Yogi myself. I throw all conventions—Hindu and European—to the wind, stand directly in his path and face him. I try a brief sentence out of my slight stock of Hindustani. He looks up ; there is a half-smile around his mouth, but he makes a negative gesture of the head.

At this time I know only a single word of Tamil, which is the vernacular of Madras, and doubtless the Yogi knows even less of English. Few people know Hindustani in the South, but of this fact I am not yet aware. Fortunately, the Brahmin begins to feel that he cannot leave me so helpless, and advances to the rescue.

In a hesitant, apologetic voice, he says something in Tamil.

The Yogi does not reply. His face hardens, the eyes become cold and unfriendly.

The Brahmin looks at me embarrassed. A prolonged pause follows. Neither of us knows what to do. I realize ruefully what a difficult task it is to help hermits to find their tongues. They dislike being interviewed, and they do not wish to talk to strangers about their intimate experiences. They dislike, especially, being asked to break their chronic silence for the sake of a sun-helmeted white man, who is tacitly assumed to possess neither sympathy with nor understanding of the subtleties of Yoga.

This feeling is succeeded by another. I become strangely aware of a penetrating inspection on the Yogi's part. Somehow, I sense that he is mentally probing my innermost thoughts. Yet outwardly he remains aloof, indifferent. Am I mistaken ?

But I cannot shake off this weird feeling that I have become a kind of human microscopical specimen.

The Brahmin becomes very nervous and nudges me as a hint to be off. Another minute and I shall yield to his silent importunity and go away defeated.

The Yogi makes a sudden gesture of his hand, leads us towards a tall palm tree close by, and silently bids us sit down at its foot. He then drops to the ground himself.

He addresses some Tamil words to the Brahmin. I notice that his voice possesses a peculiar resonance and a quality which is almost musical.

"The Yogi says that he is willing to converse with you," my companion interprets, and then volunteers the statement that the other man has peregrinated an unfrequented part of the river for some years.

The first thing I ask is the man's name, whereupon I hear such a lengthy string of appellations that I immediately christen him anew. It appears that his first name is "Brama-suganandah," that he possesses four other names all equally long or longer, and that the only useful thing to do seems to be to call him Brama. If I am to give all five of the names, the words would stretch right across this page, so many letters are there in each name ! I am both awed and appalled at the length of the young man's patronymic.[1] It is, therefore, better to maintain a discreet silence about them, and make matters easier for unacclimatized readers by referring to him henceforth as Brama, the shorter name which I bestow on him in conversation.

"Please tell him that I am interested in Yoga and wish to know something about it," I say.

The Yogi nods his head on hearing the translated statement.

"Yes, I can see that," he replies with a smile. "Let the sahib ask questions."

"What kind of Yoga practice do you follow ?"

"Mine is the system of Body Control. It is the most difficult of all the Yogas. Body and breath must be fought as though they were obstinate mules, and they must be conquered. Thereafter the nerves and mind are more easily controlled."

[1] Tamil, the vernacular of South-eastern India, is similar to German in the ease with which it forms lengthy compound words. With the result that a train will carry you past a railway station called Kulasekharapatnam, and—but I had better stop my pen in time !

" What benefit do you get from it ? "

Brama gazes across the river.

" Health of the body, strength of the will, length of years these are a few benefits," he says. " The Yogi who has become a master in the training which I follow, brings the flesh to iron-hard endurance. Pains do not move him. I know one who submitted to an operation at the hands of a surgeon, when no sleep-giving drug could be used. He endured it without a murmur. Such a one can also experience in his unprotected body the most intense cold, yet receive no hurt."

I whip out my note-book, for I perceive that our conversation is likely to prove more interesting than I anticipated. Brama smiles again at my stenography, but does not object.

" Tell me more about your Yoga system," I beg him.

" My master has lived on the open mountains of the Himalayas, surrounded by snow and ice and wearing a cinnamon-coloured robe for his only comfort. He can sit down for several hours at a stretch in a place where it is so cold that water instantly freezes. Yet he will feel no distress. Such is the power of our Yoga."

" You are a disciple, then ? "

" Yes. There are still many hills to climb. I have given twelve years of unstopping effort to practise our exercises every day."

" And you have attained some unusual powers——? "

Brama nods his head, but maintains a stolid silence.

I am intrigued more and more by this strange young man.

" Is it permissible to ask how you became a Yogi ? " I query, somewhat uncertainly.

At first there is no answer. We three continue to squat under the fronded palm. I hear the hoarse cries of errant crows among a group of coconut trees on the opposite bank of the river. Mingling with this noise comes the fitful chatter of a few monkeys, who explore the tree-tops. From the shore rises the quiet plash of the water.

" Most willingly ! " comes Brama's sudden reply. I think he realizes that my questions are prompted by something deeper than mere academic curiosity. He hides his hand beneath his shawl, fixes his gaze upon some object on the other side of the river, and begins to speak :

" I was a quiet and lonely child ; there was no pleasure for me in the usual habits of children. I did not care to play with the others, but liked to wander alone in gardens or in the fields. Few people understand a brooding boy, and I cannot say that I was happy with life. About the age of twelve I happened, by mere chance, to overhear the conversation of some older persons, and it was through their talk that I first discovered the existence of Yoga. This event aroused in me a desire to learn more of the matter. I began to enquire into it among several people and in this way was able to get a few books in Tamil, which revealed many interesting things about the Yogis. As a horse riding through a desert thirsts for water, so did my mind thirst for still further knowledge about them. But I came to a point where it seemed impossible to get to know more. One day I re-read, as if by chance, a sentence in one of my books. It was: 'To succeed on the path of Yoga, one must have a personal teacher.' These words now made a tremendous impression on me. I felt that only by leaving home and travelling about could I find a suitable teacher. To this course, my parents would not give permission. Not knowing what else to do, I began to practise in secret some breathing exercises, about which I had collected some scraps of information. These practices did not help me; instead, they injured me. I did not then realize that without the guidance of an expert teacher, it is not safe for anyone to do them. But my eagerness was such that I could not wait till I met a teacher. Within a few years the effect of these breathing exercises showed itself. A small rupture made its appearance on the top of my head; it seemed that the skull was broken in its weakest spot. Anyway, blood streamed from the wound and my body became cold and numb. I thought I was dying. Two hours later a strange vision crossed my mind's eye. I seemed to see the figure of a venerable Yogi, who addressed me, saying: 'You now see what a dangerous condition you have brought yourself into by these forbidden practices. Let this be a severe lesson to you.' The vision disappeared and, peculiarly enough, from that moment my state grew better and I completely recovered. But the scar remains still."

Brama bends his head so as to show the crown to our eyes. A tiny rounded scar is plainly visible on his poll.

"After this unfortunate experience I gave up breathing exercises and waited for some years until home ties were looser," he goes on. "When my opportunity for freedom came, I left home and went out in search of a teacher. I knew that the best way to test a teacher is to live with him for a few months. I found several teachers and divided my time between staying with them for a while and returning home disappointed. Some were the heads of monasteries; others were the chiefs of institutions of spiritual learning, but somehow none of them satisfied me. They gave me plenty of philosophy, but little from their own experience. Most of them could only repeat what the books said; they could offer no really practical guidance. I did not want book theories so much as practical experience of Yoga. Thus, I visited no less than ten teachers, but they did not seem to be the real Yoga masters. I did not despair, though. My youthful eagerness burnt more strongly, for rebuffs only increase my determination to succeed.

"I was now at the gate of manhood. I resolved to leave the home of my fathers for ever, to renounce the worldly life and to search till death for a true master. I then set out from home on my eleventh wandering or pilgrimage. I moved about until I came to a large village in the district of Tanjore. I went down to the river-side for my morning bath and afterwards walked along the bank. Soon I came to a small shrine built of red stone, or rather, it was a miniature temple. I peered inside out of curiosity and was surprised to see a number of men gathered in a circle around a man who was almost nude; in fact, he was wearing only a cod-piece.[1] The men were looking at him with expressions of the utmost respect. There was something venerable, dignified and mysterious in the face of the central figure. I remained at the entrance, awed and fascinated. I soon gathered that the little meeting was receiving some kind of instruction and I had a strong feeling that the man in the centre was a real Yogi, a genuine master and not merely a book-filled scholar. I cannot explain why I felt that.

"Suddenly, the teacher turned his face towards the door and our eyes met. I then obeyed my inner urge and walked into the temple. The teacher greeted me warmly, bade me sit down, and said: 'Six months ago I was directed to take you as a pupil. Now you have come.' I remembered with a pleasant shock that it was exactly six months since I left home to begin my eleventh journey. However, it was thus that I met my master. Thereafter, I accompanied him wherever he travelled. Sometimes he would go into the towns; sometimes he would withdraw into secluded forests or lonely jungles. With his help I began to make good progress upon the path of Yoga, and I was satisfied at last. My teacher was a Yogi of great experience, though the path he followed was that of Body Control. There are several systems of Yoga; they are

[1] A semi-loincloth.

very different in their methods and exercises; and the system I was taught is the only one which begins with the body instead of the mind. I was also taught how to obtain breath control. On one occasion I had to fast for forty days, to prepare myself to receive one of the Yogic powers.

"You may imagine how surprised I was one day when my teacher sent for me and said: 'The life of total withdrawal from the world is not yet for you. Go back to your people and live a normal life. You will marry and have one child. At the age of thirty-nine certain signs will be given you, and after that you will find yourself free to retire from the world again. You will then go to the forests and practise solitary meditation until you reach the goal which every Yogi seeks. I shall be waiting for you and you can return to me.'

"I obeyed his commands and returned to my native place. In due course I married a faithful and devoted woman, who bore me one child, exactly as my teacher had predicted. But not long after, my wife died. My parents were no longer living, so I left my native town and came here to stay in the house of an old widow who also comes from there and who knew me as a child. She looks after my domestic needs and yet, because the years have made her discreet, she permits me to live the reserved existence which the rules of our school enjoin."

Brama ceases talking and I am so impressed by his narrative that my questioning tongue is likewise stilled. There are two or three minutes of complete silence and then the Yogi rises, turns his face homewards, and begins to walk slowly. The Brahmin and myself follow him.

Our path leads through lovely palm groves and through pretty clumps of casuarina. The river shines in the bright sunlight and an hour or so is passed pleasantly as we stroll along its banks. Anon, we begin to enter the haunts of men. Fisher folk wade into the water to carry on their work in the ancient way. For they fish neither from boats nor from the shore, but stand waist high in the stream and hold their nets and baskets.

The beauty of the scene is enhanced by the brightly-plumed birds which flutter down to the river. The air is slightly scented by a gentle breeze, which blows pleasantly in our faces from the direction of the sea. We reach a road where I leave the river regretfully. A herd of squeaking pigs passes us. They are under the care of a grey-haired, low caste woman, who hits unfortunate stragglers with a bamboo stick.

Brama turns eventually to bid us farewell. I express the hope that I may be allowed to see him again. He assents. I then venture to ask whether I may have the honour of a visit from him. To the great surprise of my Brahmin companion, the Yogi readily agrees to call in the evening.

§

With the fall of dusk I await Brama's arrival somewhat eagerly. Several questions tumble over each other in my mind. His brief autobiography has intrigued me, while his strange character has puzzled me.

When the servant announces him, I descend the few steps which lead from the veranda and hold up my hands, with palms touching, as a token of welcome. The symbolism of this common Hindu greeting, which I have soon learnt, will appear quaint to the Western mind. For the gesture indicates, " My soul and yours are one ! " The Hindus delight to receive it from a European, which reveals the rarity of that event, though it is nothing more than the Indian substitute for shaking hands. I want to be accepted as one with friendly intent, and therefore I try to respect the Indian customs and conventions, so far as I am aware of them. This does not mean that I am going to " turn native "—I have no such purpose—but that I believe in treating others as I would have them treat me.

Brama accompanies me into the large room and immediately squats cross-legged on the floor.

" Will you not sit on the divan ? " I ask him, through the interpreter. " It is well cushioned and extremely comfortable." But no—he prefers the hard floor ! And Indian floors are laid with tiles, not boards.

I express my gratitude for his visit and offer him some food, which he accepts and eats in silence.

After the meal I feel that I must tell him something about myself, something that will explain my sudden intrusion into his existence. And so I enter into a brief account of the forces which drew me to India. At its close, Brama emerges from the bulwark of aloofness behind which he has so far hidden, and puts his hand on my shoulder in a friendly way.

" That such men should exist in the West it is pleasant to hear. You have not wasted your journey, for you shall learn much. It is a happy day for me that destiny brought our feet to the same spot. Whatever you wish to know, ask, and, so far as my oaths permit me, I shall gladly tell you."

This sounds like good luck, indeed! I ask him about the nature of his Yoga system, its history and its aims.

" Who dare say how old is the system of Body Control which I have studied? Our secret texts declare that it was revealed by the god Shiva to the sage Gheranda. From his lips it was learnt by the sage Marteyanda, who then taught it to others, and thus it came down in a continuous line through thousands of years; but how many thousands we neither know nor care, though we believe that it is the last of the Yoga sciences that were born in antiquity. Such was the decline of man even in those days, that the gods had to give him a way of spiritual salvation which led purely through the body. The Yoga of Body Control is little understood except by the adepts who have mastered it, and the common people possess the most false notions of our ancient science. And since such adepts are, alas! so infrequently to be found to-day, the most foolish and distorted practices pass as our system without hindrance among the multitude. Go to Benares and you will see a man who sits all day and sleeps all night on a bed of sharp spikes; and in another place you will see a man who holds one arm aloft in the air until it is half withered from disuse and until the nails are several inches long. You will be told that they are men who practise our system of Yoga, but it is not so. Such men bring shame on it, rather. Our aim is not to torture the body in foolish ways for the sake of public wonder; these self-torturing ascetics are ignorant men who have picked up by hearsay, or from some friendly person, a few exercises in the forced contortion of the body. But since they know not what are our objects, they distort these practices and prolong them unnaturally. Yet the common people venerate such fools and bestow food and money upon them."

" But are they to blame? If the real Yogis make themselves so scarce and keep their methods so secret, then misunderstandings will surely arise," I object.

Brama draws up his shoulders and a scornful expression passes across his mouth.

" Does a Rajah keep his jewels on the highway for public display?" he asks. " No, he hides them in the treasure chambers deep down in the vaults of his palace. The knowledge of our science is one of the greatest treasures a man can have. Is he to offer it in the bazaar for all and sundry? Whoever desires to grasp this treasure—let him search for it. That is the only way, but it is the right way. Our texts enjoin secrecy again and again, while our masters will reveal the important teachings only to tested disciples who have been faithful to them for some years at least. Ours is the most secret of all the Yogas ; it is full of grave dangers, not only to the disciple himself, but to others. Think you that I am allowed to reveal any but its most elementary doctrines to you, or even those without extreme discretion ? "

" I see."

" But there is a branch of our science about which I may talk to you more freely. It is that wherein we strengthen the will and improve the body of beginners, for only so can they be fit to attempt the difficult practices of real Yoga."

" Ah, that would interest the West ! "

" We have nearly a score of body exercises which strengthen the different parts and organs, and remove or prevent certain diseases. Some of them are postures which press upon special nerve centres ; these in turn affect certain organs which are not working properly, and help to put them right."

" Do you use medicines ? "

" Certain herbs, plucked under a waxing moon, are used if necessary. We have four kinds of exercises or methods to accomplish this early work of putting the body's health in good order. First, we learn the art of repose so that the nerves may be soothed. For that, there are four suitable exercises. Then we learn the ' stretches,' which are exercises copied from the natural stretching of healthy animals. Third, we clean the body thoroughly by a variety of methods which may seem very curious to you, but which are indeed excellent in their effect. Lastly, we study the art of breathing and its control."

I express a desire to receive a demonstration of some exercises.

" There is no dark secret in those which I shall show you now," Brama smiles. " Let us begin with the art of repose. We can learn something of this matter from the cat. Our master places a cat in the circle of his pupils and gets them to notice how graceful the animal becomes when in repose. He instructs them to observe it carefully when the midday heat sends it to sleep. He tells them to watch it closely when it crouches in front of a mouse hole. He makes it clear to them that the cat sets a perfect example of true rest, and that it knows how to store and keep every bit of strength. You imagine that you know how to rest, but really you do not. You sit in that chair for a while, then move from side to side, then fidget, and then sprawl out your legs. Though you do not rise from the chair and outwardly seem to be at ease, one thought after another races through your brain. Can you call that repose? Is it not a way of still being active?"

"That is a point of view which has never occurred to me," I say.

"Animals know how to rest themselves, but not many men have this knowledge. This is because animals are guided by instinct, which is the voice of Nature, while men are guided by their thoughts. And since men largely lack control over their brains, their nerves and bodies are affected as a result; there is little real repose for them."

"What must we do, then?"

"The first thing you must learn is nothing more than the Oriental form of sitting! Chairs may indeed be useful in the cold rooms of your Northern countries, but you must learn to do without them during the times of exercise which shall prepare you for Yoga. Our way of sitting is really most restful. After working or walking, it gives peace to the entire body. The easiest way for you to learn it is to place a small rug or mat before the wall of your room; sit upon this as comfortably as you can and use the wall to support your back. Or you can place the mat in the centre of the room, and then use a couch or chair to lean against. After that, bend the legs inwards at the knees and cross the feet. There need be no feeling of strain and you must not tighten the muscles. So your first exercise will be to sit like that and keep your body quite still, except for the effort of gentle breathing. And having got into that position, you must promise yourself that you will withdraw your thoughts from all worldly burdens and affairs; just rest your mind on a beautiful object, a picture or a flower."

I leave my easy chair and drop on the floor, facing Brama, assuming the attitude he has just described. It is the position of an old-time tailor sitting cross-legged at his work.

"Yes, you do it easily," observes Brama, "but other Europeans may not find it comfortable, because they are not accustomed to it. You have one fault—keep your backbone straight, not bent. Let me show you another of our exercises."

Brama proceeds to raise his knees toward his chin, though still keeping his feet crossed. This position draws his feet away somewhat from the trunk. He clasps his hands around the front of his knees.

"This position is very restful after you have been standing on your legs for a long time. Be careful to throw most of the body's weight upon the seat. You may practise this for a few minutes, whenever you feel very tired. It will soothe important nerve centres."

"It is extremely simple, anyway."

"We need nothing complicated to learn the art of repose; in fact, our easiest exercise gives excellent results. Lie flat on your back, legs stretched out side by side. Turn the toes outward. Let your hands be extended and rest them alongside the body. Relax every muscle. Close the eyes. Give your whole weight to the floor. You cannot do this exercise properly in a bed, as it is important to keep the backbone perfectly flat. Use a rug laid upon the floor. In this attitude, Nature's healing forces will rest you. We call this the corpse position. By practice, you may learn to rest in any of these attitudes for an hour, if you wish. They take away tension of muscle and soothe nerves. Repose of muscle comes before repose of mind."

"Really, your exercises seem to consist of nothing more than sitting still in some way or other!"

"Is that nothing? You Westerners thirst to be active, but is repose to be despised? Do calm nerves possess no meaning? Repose is the beginning of all Yoga, but it is not our need alone; it is also the need of your world."

Brama's words are not without justification.

"Those exercises are enough for this evening," he adds. "I must go."

I thank him for what he has told me, and beg for further instruction.

"To-morrow morning you may find me along the river," he replies.

Gathering his white shawl around his shoulders, he touches his palms in farewell and is gone. I am left to ruminate upon the interesting conversation which has so abruptly ended.

§

I meet the Yogi again on many occasions. At his desire, I intercept him on his morning walks, but when I can cajole him indoors, he spends his evenings with me. Those evenings prove extremely fruitful for me and my quest, because he unfolds a more arcane knowledge when the moon displays herself than he is willing to unfold under a high sun.

A little enquiry enables me to solve a point which has puzzled me for a while. I have been under the impression that the

Hindus are a brown race. Why, then, is Brama's skin dark to the point of negroid blackness ?

The answer is that he belongs to an indigenous population which appears to be India's first inhabitant. When the Aryans—India's earliest invaders—broke through the mountains in the north-west thousands of years ago and descended into the plains, they found this native race of Dravidians and drove them into the South. These Dravidians remain a separate people to this day, except that they have absorbed the religion of their conquerors. The fiery tropic sun has pigmented their skins almost black, which, together with other evidences, makes certain ethnologists think that they primally arose out of some African stock. As in those early days of their undisputed sway over the entire country, the Dravidians still wear their hair long and tied in a knot behind their heads, and they still speak their primal, half-chanted tongues, of which the most important is Tamil.

Brama makes the confident assertion that the brown invaders took their knowledge of Yoga from his own race, just as they took certain other things in addition. But scholarly Hindus to whom I mention this claim deny it as absurd ; I, therefore, leave the less important question of origin to settle itself !

Because I am not writing a thesis around the subject of Yogic physical culture, I do not purpose to describe more than two or three exercises in the art of adopting and maintaining fixed bodily attitudes, which appears to be so prominent a feature of the Yoga of Body Control. The twenty or more postural methods which Brama demonstrates, either in a palm fringed grove or in my more prosaic quarters, involve strangely contorted attitudes, and, to Western eyes at least, must appear either ludicrous or impossible, or both. Some of them require balancing on both knees with feet upturned, or balancing the entire weight of the body upon the tips of one's fingers ; others take the arms behind the back and somehow bring the hands to the front again on opposite sides ; others again tie up all the limbs in a complicated knot ; still others put the legs round the neck or over the shoulders, in acrobatic manner ; while a fifth group twist and turn the trunk in the queerest imaginable style. It is while watching Brama perform some of these feats that I begin to perceive how difficult will this art of Yoga be.

" How many of these exercises comprise your system ? '
I enquire.

" There are eighty-four postures in the Yoga of Body Control," replies Brama, " though I do not know more than sixty-four at present." Even as he speaks he practises one of these postures and sits in it as comfortably as I sit in a chair. Indeed, he tells me that this is his favourite posture. It is not a difficult one, this, but it does seem uncomfortable. His left foot is tucked into the groin and the heel of the other foot is placed under the base of the body, the right leg being doubled back so as to carry most of the weight.

" What is the use of such a posture ? " I ask again.

" If a Yogi enters into it and then practises a certain breathing exercise, he will become more youthful."

" And that breathing exercise——? "

" I am not permitted to reveal it to you."

" What is the object of all these postures, then ? "

" The mere fact of sitting or standing for regular periods in certain fixed postures may seem of small importance in your eyes. But the concentration of attention and will power upon the chosen posture is so intense—if success is to be gained—that sleeping forces awaken within the Yogi. Those forces belong to the secret realms of Nature ; therefore they are seldom fully aroused until our breathing exercises are also practised, for the breath possesses deep powers. Though the awakening of such forces is our real aim, no less than a score of our exercises are capable of being used for benefiting one's health or to remove certain diseases ; while others will drive impurities out of the body. Is this not of great use ? Still other postures are intended to assist our efforts to get control over the mind and soul, for it is a truth that the body influences thought no less than thought influences the body. In the advanced stages of Yoga, when we may be plunged for hours in meditation, the proper posture of the body not only enables the mind to remain undistracted in its efforts, but actually assists its purpose. Add to all these things the tremendous gain in will power which comes to the man who perseveres in these difficult exercises, and you may see what virtues there are in our methods."

" But why all this twisting and turning ? " I object.

" Because there are many nerve-centres scattered throughout the body, and each posture affects a different centre. Through the nerves we can influence either the organs of the body or the thoughts in the brain. Those twists enable us to reach nerve centres which otherwise might remain untouched."

" I see." The basis of this Yogic physical culture begins to shape itself a little more clearly in my mind. It is interesting to ascertain how it compares with the basic principles of our

European and American systems. I tell Brama about the existence of the latter.

"I do not know your Western systems, but I have seen white soldiers being drilled at the great camp near Madras. By watching them I have understood what their instructors wished to do. Strengthening the muscles seems to have been their first object, because you Westerners find your highest virtues in being bodily active. Therefore, you make much use of the limbs in a most energetic manner, repeating those movements again and again. You spend energy vigorously, so that you may build up the muscles and receive greater strength in return. That is a good thing to do in the cold countries of the North, doubtless."

"What is the chief difference between the methods, as you see it?"

"Our Yoga exercises are really poses and require no further movements after the pose has been taken up. Instead of seeking more energy with which to be active, we seek to increase the power of endurance. You see, we believe that though the development of the muscles may be useful, it is the power which is behind them that is of greater value. Thus, if I tell you that standing on your shoulders in a particular way will wash the brain with blood, soothe the nerves and remove certain weaknesses, you as a Westerner would probably do the exercise for a moment and repeat it several times with a rush. You may strengthen the muscles which are called into action by this exercise, but you would get little of the benefits which a Yogi gets by doing it in his own way."

"And what may that be?"

"He will do it slowly, with deliberation, and then maintain the position as steadily as he can for some minutes. Let me show you this All-Body posture, as we call it."

Brama lies flat upon his back, hands at sides and legs together. He raises his legs into the air, keeping the knees quite straight, until they have attained about two-thirds of a right angle with the floor. He supports his back with his hands, resting the elbows on the floor. The body is then tilted completely upward, his trunk and hips becoming vertical. The chest is brought forward to touch the chin. The hands form a bracket which supports the trunk. The weight of the body is supported by the shoulders and the back of the neck and head.

After maintaining this upside down position for about five minutes, the Yogi gets up and explains its value.

"This posture brings blood flowing down to the brain by its

own weight for a few minutes. In the ordinary position the blood has to be forced upwards by the pumping action of the heart. The difference between the two ways is shown by the soothing effect of the posture upon the brain and nerves. For men who work with their minds, thinkers and students, the quiet practice of this all-body posture brings quick relief when their brains are tired. This is not its only virtue. It strengthens the sex organs. But these benefits come only if the exercise is done in our way and not in your hasty Western manner."

"If I am not mistaken, you mean that the Yoga attitudes keep the body fixed in a state of poised stillness, whereas our Western exercises violently agitate it?"

"Even so," agrees Brama.

A further exercise which I select from Brama's repertory as being more within the compass of Western limbs, is one which should quickly yield to patience and practice. In this posture, the Yogi sits with extended legs, raises both arms over his head and crooks the first fingers. He bends his trunk forward, exhaling the breath while doing so, and grasps the big toes of his feet inside the hooked fingers. The right toe is caught by the right index finger, and so on. Then he slowly bends his head forward until it falls between his outstretched arms and the forehead lies flat against his thighs. He keeps this curious position for a little while and then gradually returns to a normal attitude.

"Do not try to do this all at once," he warns me. "Try to bring the head a little closer to the knees little by little only; even if it takes a few weeks to succeed in this posture, once you have mastered it, it will be yours for years."

I learn that this exercise strengthens the spine, as indeed one might expect it to do; that it removes nervous troubles caused through spinal weakness; and that it will work wonders with the blood circulation.

In the next posture, Brama sits on the floor and then doubles his legs up underneath him; thus the soles of his feet come under the base of his body. He drops the trunk backward until his shoulders touch the floor. He crosses his arms underneath the back of the head, which is then cushioned upon them. Each hand now grasps the opposite shoulder joint. He remains in this not unshapely pose for some minutes. On emerging from it, he explains that nerve centres situate in the neck and shoulders, as well as in the legs, are favourably affected by the exercise; and that even the chest is benefited.

The average Englishman is so apt to regard the average

Indian as a weakling, as an enervated product of tropic sun and under-feeding, that it surprises one to learn that such a carefully thought out native system of physical culture has existed in India since antiquity. If our Western systems possess such a usefulness that no one would dream of disputing their value at this day, this is not to say that they are consequently complete and that they have pronounced the last word on bodily development, health preservation and the eradication of disease. Perhaps if the West, with its thorough methods of scientifically directed research, would pick some dust-covered practices out of the traditional teaching of Yoga, we might arrive at a completer knowledge of our bodies and a fuller regime for the healthy life.

Yet I know that perhaps not more than a round dozen of the Yoga postures are easy enough to be worth our time and trouble. The seventy odd postures which compose the remainder of the system are hardly likely to yield to any except the most enthusiastic, and that only if they are young enough to have flexible limbs and supple bodies.

Brama himself admits :

" I have practised hard each day for twelve years ; only in this way could I master the sixty-four postures which I know. And then I was fortunate enough to begin while young, for a man of mature years could not even attempt these postures without feeling much pain. Bone, muscle and flesh settle down into stiffened positions in a grown man and can be disturbed only with difficulty and with pain. Yet even then it is remarkable how the postures can be conquered by continued efforts."

I do not doubt Brama's assertion that anyone may master these exercises by persistent practice, only the slow breaking-in of limbs, joints and muscles to the novel positions into which they are introduced must necessarily be such a dilatory process as to embrace the years. He has the advantage of beginning these postures when hardly out of his 'teens, and the value of this early beginning cannot be over-estimated. Just as successful acrobats are usually those who have been trained in childhood, so is it obvious that successful Yogis of the school of Body Control must start their training before the growing period ends, say before twenty-five. I certainly do not know how it is possible for any adult European to adventure with the scores of intricate postures which comprise most of their system without breaking a bone or two in the undertaking. When I argue this with Brama, he grants only a partial agreement and stubbornly maintains that continued efforts may succeed in many cases, though not in all. But he agrees that Europeans may have a harder task.

"We Orientals have the advantage of having learnt to sit with folded legs from childhood. Can a European bend his legs and sit steadily for two hours without pain? Yet the crossing of the legs with intertwined ankles forms but the beginning of several of our postures. We look upon it as one of the best. Shall I show it?"

Thereupon Brama assumes that position which has been made familiar to the Western world by the numerous pictures and images of the Buddha. Sitting perfectly erect, he folds the right leg so as to tuck the foot into the left groin. Then he folds the other leg and brings his left foot across to the right thigh, where its heel touches the lower corner of the abdomen. The soles of his feet are turned up. It is an artistic and balanced pose; the thought occurs to me that such an attractive posture may be worth trying.

I try to imitate him and am rewarded for my labours with excruciating pains in the ankles. I complain that I cannot achieve this position even for a single moment. How picturesquely exotic has this Buddha seat seemed to me in the past, when I have seen it exemplified in some attractive bronze figure which is placed in the window of a curio shop! But how unnatural does this twisting of the lower limbs now seem to me in India, when I attempt to exemplify it in my own person! Brama's smiling encouragement fails to reassure me. I tell him that I must postpone my efforts.

"Your joints are stiff," he observes. "Rub a little oil into the ankles and knees before you practise it again. You are so accustomed to sitting in chairs that the posture will put some strain on your limbs. A little practice every day will slowly remove the difficulty."

"I doubt whether I could ever do it."

"Say not that it is impossible. It will take you a long time, but you shall surely master it. Success will take you by surprise one day; it comes suddenly."[1]

"It is so painful that it feels like a new torture!"[2]

"But the pain will lessen, and though it may take a much

[1] I state the fact for what it is worth that, lured by the attractiveness of the Buddha position, I succeeded, after sporadic and painful efforts, in achieving it eight months later. Thereafter the difficulty disappeared.

[2] It is necessary to warn amateur dabblers in these Yoga posturings against the grave risks they incur. A surgeon to whom I described them, said that a strained ankle or a broken tendon are likely injuries.

longer time than it will to reach success, you will reach a point where the posture brings no pain with it."

" But is it worth while for me to attempt it ? "

" Assuredly. The Lotus posture—for that is what we name it—is so important that none of our novices are permitted to miss it, however much he is allowed to avoid other postures. It is the chief attitude in which advanced Yogis perform their meditations. One reason is that it gives a solid base to the body, which is unlikely to topple over should the Yogi pass into a deep trance—an event which sometimes occurs unexpectedly, though the adepts can pass into trance at will. You see, the Lotus posture locks the feet together and holds the body quiet and steady. A restless and irritated body will disturb the mind, but in the Lotus posture one feels poised and self-controlled. In this attitude it becomes easier to win the power of mind concentration, which is so greatly prized among us. Lastly, we practise our breathing exercises mostly when sitting in this posture, for the combination arouses the spirit-fire which sleeps in the body. When this unseeable fire awakens, all the blood in the body is redistributed afresh, while the nerve force is sent with great keenness to certain important points."

With this explanation I remain content and bring our talk of postures to a close. For Brama has earlier thrown himself into a large number of fearful contortions and convulsive posturings for my edification, just to show me something of his mastery over flesh and bone. What Westerner has the patience to go through all these complicated exercises and master them ? What Westerner has even the time to do so ?

CHAPTER VI

THE YOGA WHICH CONQUERS DEATH

BRAMA expresses a wish that I shall visit his dwelling. He tells me that he does not actually stay in the house, but has erected a roomy hut in the garden at the rear so as to keep his freedom and preserve his independence.

Accordingly—and I must confess, with some eagerness—I call at the house one afternoon. The building stands in a dusty street, which bears a desolate and neglected air. I stand for a moment outside the ancient whitewashed structure and survey its wooden upper storey, whose projecting window is so reminiscent of our medieval European houses. I push open the heavy old door which confronts me, an act which sends a rattling echo through the rooms and passages.

An old woman, whose motherly smile stretches broadly across her face, appears almost at once and bows repeatedly before me. She leads me through a long darkened passage until we emerge through a kitchen into the back garden.

The first thing I notice is a spreading peepul tree and then, under the protective shade of its branches, an old fashioned well. The woman guides me to a hut on the other side of the well and close enough to it to receive some of the tree's shade. It is lightly built of bamboo posts, thin wooden cross beams and a thatched grass roof.

The dame, whose face is as black as Brama's, becomes visibly excited and bursts out into a series of trembling Tamil sentences, apparently addressed to the hut. A musical voice answers from within, the door slowly opens, the Yogi appears and then affectionately draws me into his simple hermitage. He omits to close the door. The widow remains in the entrance for the next few minutes, her eyes glued upon me, her face exuding indescribable happiness.

I find myself in a plain room. A low cushionless divan stands along the farther wall and a rudely made wooden bench, which is littered with papers, fills a corner. A heavily chased brass water-pot hangs by a cord from one of the roof beams. The floor is covered with a large piece of matting.

"Seat yourself!" says Brama, waving a hand towards the floor. "We have no chair to offer you; I am sorry."

We all squat around the mat—Brama, myself, and a young student-teacher who has attached himself to me and is now acting as interpreter. Within a few minutes the old widow departs, only to return later with a pot of tea, which is served upon the mat in lieu of a table. She departs again and reappears with biscuits, oranges and plantain fruits, which are heaped upon brass dishes.

Before we begin to take these pleasant refreshments, Brama produces a garland of yellow marigolds and hangs it around my neck. I am astonished and protest strongly, for I know that this Indian custom is usually reserved for distinguished persons and I have never classed myself in that sublime category.

"But, brother—," he pleads smilingly. "You are the first European to visit my abode and the first to become my friend. I must express my delight, and the delight of this lady here, by honouring you in this way."

My further protests prove of no avail. I have perforce to sit on the floor with a wreath of marigolds draped ceremoniously over my jacket. I am indeed glad that Europe is sufficiently far away for none of my friends to notice this odd sight and laugh at me!

We drink our tea, eat the fruit and chat pleasantly for a while. Brama informs me that he built the hut and made the rude furniture with his own hands. The sight of the papers on the corner bench arouse my curiosity, and I beg him to tell me their *raison d'être*. For I observe that the papers are all of a pink colour and that they have been written on in green ink. Brama picks up a handful, which I perceive are written in quaint characters easily recognizable as Tamil. The student-teacher examines the documents but finds them hard to read and harder to understand. He informs me that they are written in an obsolete form of Tamil which was the literary form of early centuries, but is nowadays understood only by few persons. He adds that the great classics of Tamil philosophy and literature are unfortunately written in this archaic form of language, which is called high Tamil, and which presents more difficulties for those only familiar with the modern living vernacular than medieval English presents to the average present-day English-knowing person.

"These papers are written by me mostly at night," Brama explains. "Some of them are accounts of my Yoga experiences written in verse, and some are lengthy poems where I let my heart speak its religion. There are a few young men who call themselves my pupils, who often come here to read these writings aloud."

Brama picks up an artistic-looking document, which consists of a few pages of pink paper written on in red and green inks and tied with a green ribbon, and smilingly presents it to me.

"I have written this especially for you," he declares.

The young interpreter finds it to be a poem of eighty-four lines. It opens and closes with a mention of my name, but beyond this the young man can hardly travel. He deciphers occasional words and tells me that the poem evidently contains some kind of personal message, but it is written in such high Tamil that he is not competent to render a proper translation of it. However, I am extremely pleased to receive this unexpected gift, especially as it is an expression of the Yogi's good will.

After the celebrations of my visit are finally over, the old lady departs and we settle down to serious talk. I plunge anew into that matter of breathing which seems to play so important a part in Yoga, and which is wrapped in such secrecy. Brama regrets that he can show me no further exercises for the present, but he is willing to tell me a little more of his theories.

"Nature has measured out 21,600 breath-rhythms to every man, which he must use up daily and nightly from one sunrise till the next. Quick, noisy and tumultuous breathing exceeds this measure and therefore shortens one's life. Slow, deep and quiet breathing economizes this allowance, and so lengthens life. Every breath which is saved goes to build up a great reserve, and out of this reserve a man can draw extra years for living. Yogis do not take so many breaths as other men; nor do they need to for—but, alas! how can I explain further without transgressing my oaths?"

This reserve of the Yogi tantalizes me. Is it possible that a knowledge which is hidden away with so much pains cannot have something of real worth in it? If that is really the case, then one can understand why these strange men cover up their tracks and conceal the treasure of their teachings in order to ward off the superficially curious, the mentally unready and perhaps the spiritually unworthy. Is it likely that I, too, may come within one of these latter classifications and eventually leave the country with little more than my trouble for reward ?

But Brama is speaking again :

" Have not our masters the keys to the powers of breath ? They know how close is the connection between the blood and the breath ; they understand how the mind, too, follows the path of the breath ; and they have the secret of how it is possible to awaken awareness of the soul through workings of the breath and thought. Shall I not say that breath is but the expression in this world of a subtler force, which is the real sustainer of the body ? It is this force which hides in the vital organs, though it is unseeable. When it leaves the body the breathing stops in obedience and death is the result. But through the control of breath it is possible to get some control over this unseeable current. But though we bring our body under extreme control—even to the point of controlling the beats of the heart—do you think that our ancient sages had only the body and its powers in view when they first taught our system ? "

Whatever I think about the ancient sages and their purpose, disappears in the intense curiosity which is suddenly aroused in my mind.

" You can control the working of your heart ? " I exclaim in surprise.

" My self-acting organs, the heart, the stomach and the kidney, have been brought to some degree of obedience," he answers quietly, without a trace of boastfulness.

" How do you do that ? "

" One gains the power by practising certain combinations of posture, breathing and will-power exercises. Of course, they belong to the advanced degrees of Yoga. They are so difficult that few persons can ever do them. Through these practices I have conquered somewhat the muscles which work the heart ; and through the heart muscles, I have been able to go on and conquer the other organs."

" This is indeed extraordinary ! "

" You think so ? Place your hand upon my chest, just over the heart, and keep it there." With that, Brama changes his position, takes up a curious posture, and closes his eyes.

I obey his command and then wait patiently to see what is going to happen. For some minutes he remains as steady as a rock, and almost as motionless. Then the beating of his heart begins to diminish gradually. I am startled to feel it become slower and slower. A thrill of eerieness spreads over my nerves as I distinctly feel his heart completely stop its rhythmic functioning. The pause lasts for about seven anxious seconds.

I try to pretend that I am hallucinated, but my nervousness is such that I know the attempt is useless. As the organ returns to life from its seeming death, relief seizes me. The beats begin to quicken and normality is safely reached at length.

The Yogi does not emerge from his motionless self-absorption till some minutes later. He slowly opens his eyes and asks :

" Did you feel the heart stop ? "

" Yes. Most distinctly." I am certain that there was no hallucination about the feat. What other strange Yogi tricks can Brama play with his internal mechanism, I wonder ?

As if in answer to my unspoken thought, Brama says :

" It is nothing compared with what my master can achieve. Sever one of his arteries, and he is able to control the flow of blood ; yes, even to stop it ! I, too, have brought my blood under some measure of control, but I cannot do that."

" Can you show me that control ? "

He requests me to take his wrist and grip it where I can feel the flow of blood through his artery. I do so.

Within two or three minutes I become aware that the curious rhythm which beats under my thumb is lessening. Soon it comes to a definite halt. Brama has brought his pulse to a stop !

I anxiously await the resumption of circulation in his artery. A minute passes but nothing occurs. A second minute, during which I am acutely conscious of each second, likewise ticks itself away in my watch. The third minute is equally fruitless. Not until half-way through the fourth minute do I become conscious of a faint return to activity within the artery. The tension is relieved. Before long, the pulse beats at its normal rate.

" How strange ! " I exclaim involuntarily.

" It is nothing," he modestly replies.

" This seems to be a day of strange feats, so will you not show me another ? "

Brama hesitates.

" Only one more," he says at length, " and then you must be satisfied."

He looks thoughtfully at the floor and then announces :

" I shall stop the breath ! "

" But then you will surely die ! " I exclaim nervously.

He laughs but ignores the remark.

" Now hold your hand flat under my nostrils."

I obey him hesitantly. The warm caress of exhaled air touches and retouches the skin of my hand. Brama closes his eyes; his body becomes statuesque in its steadiness. He appears to fall into a kind of trance. I wait, continuing to hold the back of my hand immediately under his nose. He remains as still and as unresponsive as a graven idol. Very slowly, very evenly, the caress of his breath begins to diminish. Ultimately it completely ceases.

I watch his nostrils and lips; I examine his shoulders and chest; but in no single case can I discover any external evidence of respiration. I know that these tests are not final and wish to make a more exhaustive test, but how? My brain works rapidly.

There is no hand-mirror in the room, but I find an excellent substitute in a small polished brass dish. I hold the dish under his nostrils for a while, and again in front of his lips. Its shining surface remains unmarred by any dullness or moisture.

It seems impossible to believe that in this quiet conventional house near a quiet conventional city, I have established contact with something significant, something that Western science may one day be forced to recognize against its will. But the evidence is there, and it is indubitable. Yoga is really more than a worthless myth.

When Brama ultimately emerges from his trance-like condition, he seems a little tired.

"Are you satisfied?" he asks, with a fatigued smile.

"I am more than satisfied! But I am at a loss to understand in what way you can do it."

"It is forbidden me to explain. The restraint of breath is a practice which is part of advanced Yoga. To a white man it may seem a foolish thing to strive for, yet to us it is of much importance."

"But we have always been taught that man cannot live without breathing. Surely that is not a foolish idea?"

"It is not foolish; nevertheless it is not true. I can hold my breath for two hours, if I wish. Many times I have done that, but I am not yet dead, you see!" Brama smiles.

"I am puzzled. If you are not permitted to explain, perhaps you can throw a little light upon the theory behind your practices?"

"Very well. There is a lesson we can draw from watching certain animals, which is a favoured method of instruction with my master. An elephant breathes much more slowly than a monkey, yet it lives much longer. Some of the large serpents breathe far more slowly than a dog, yet they live far longer. Thus, creatures exist which show that slowness of breathing may possibly prolong age. If you can follow me so far, the next step will be easier for you to grasp. Now, in the Himalayas, there are bats which go into winter sleep. They hang suspended in the mountain caverns for weeks, yet they do not draw a single breath until they again awaken. The Himalayan bears, too, will sometimes sink into trance throughout the winter, their bodies apparently without life. In deep burrows of the Himalayas, when food cannot be found during the winter, there are hedgehogs which pass into sleep for some months, a sleep in which breathing is suspended. If these animals cease to breathe for a time, and yet live, why should not human beings be able to do the same ? "

His statement of curious facts is interesting, but it is not so convincing as his demonstration. The common notion that breathing is an essential function in every condition of life is not to be thrown aside at a few minutes' notice.

" We Westerners will always find it difficult to understand how life can continue in a body unless breathing continues also."

" Life always continues," he answers cryptically. " Death is but a habit of the body."

" But surely you cannot mean that it may be possible to conquer death ? " I enquire incredulously.

Brama looks at me in a strange manner.

" Why not ? " There is a tense pause. His eyes search me, but they do it in a kindly way.

" Because there are possibilities in you, I shall tell you one of our old secrets. But I must first demand your agreement to one condition."

" And that—— ? "

" You shall not attempt to practise any breathing exercise as an experiment, except those which I may teach you later."

" I agree."

" Keep your word, then. Now you have hitherto believed that the complete stoppage of breathing brings death ? "

" Yes."

" Is it not reasonable to believe, also, that the complete holding of the breath within one's body keeps life within us for so long as the breath is held, at least ? "

" Well—— ? "

" We claim no more than that. We say that an adept in breath control, who can completely retain his breath at will, thereby retains his life current. Do you grasp that ? "

" I think so."

" Imagine, now, an adept in Yoga who can keep the locked breath, not merely for a few minutes as a curiosity, but for weeks, for months and even for years. Since you admit that where there is breath there must be life, do you not see how the prospect of prolonged life opens up for man ? "

I am dumb. How can I dismiss this assertion as preposterous ? Yet how can I accept it ? Does it not recall to memory the idle dreams of our European alchemists of medieval times, dreamers who sought an elixir of life, but who succumbed to the sickle of death one by one ? But if Brama is not self-deceived, why should he seek to deceive me. He has not sought my company and he makes no effort to acquire disciples.

A strange fear touches my brain. What if he is merely mad ? No—he seems so sensible and rational in other matters. Would it not be better to regard him as mistaken ? Yet something in me doubts even that conclusion. I am bewildered.

" Can I not convince you ? " He speaks again. " Have you not heard the story of the faqueer who was buried by Ranjeet Singh in a vault at Lahore ? The burial of the faqueer took place in the presence of English army officers, while the last of the Sikh kings watched it himself. The living tomb was guarded by soldiers for six weeks, but the faqueer emerged healthy and alive. Enquire into this story, for I have been told that it is written somewhere in the records of your Government. This faqueer had brought his breathing under great mastery and could stop it at will without danger of dying. Yet he was not even an adept in Yoga, for I have heard from an old man who knew him when he was alive that his character was not good. His name was Haridas and he lived in the North. If this man could live in an airless space for such a long time without breathing, how much more can be done by the true masters of Yoga, who practise in secret and will not perform these marvels for gold ? "[1]

A pregnant silence follows our conversation.

" There exist other strange powers which can be acquired

[1] I have since verified this reference and find that the actual episode occurred in 1837 at Lahore. The faqueer was buried in the presence of King Ranjit Singh, Sir Claude Wade, Dr. Honigberger, and others. A guard of Sikh soldiers watched the grave day and night to prevent fraud. The faqueer was dug up alive forty days later. Fuller particulars can be found in the archives at Calcutta.

by the way of our Yoga, but who, in these degenerate days, will pay the heavy price to obtain them ? "

There is another pause.

" We who live and work in the everyday world have sufficient to do without seeking such powers," I venture, in defence of my epoch.

" Yes," agrees Brama, " this path of Body Control is only for the few. Therefore the teachers of our science have kept it a silent secret through the centuries. It is not often that they seek after pupils ; pupils must seek after them."

§

The next time we meet, Brama visits my quarters. It is evening and we soon adjourn for dinner. After the meal and a short rest, we go out on the moonlit veranda where I plant myself in a deck chair, while the Yogi finds a mat on the floor more comfortable.

For several minutes we silently enjoy the bright radiance of the full moon.

As I have not forgotten the astonishing events of our last meeting, it is not long before I broach anew this incredible matter of men who snap their fingers at death.

" Why not ? " Brama asks his favourite question. " There is an adept in our Yoga of Body Control who is hidden among the Neilgherry Hills, here in the South. He never stirs from his retreat. In the North, there lives another whose home is a cave upon the snowy Himalayas. These men you cannot meet, for they disdain this world, yet their existence is a tradition among us and we are told that they have extended their lives to hundreds of years."

" You really believe this ? " I exclaim in deferential doubt.

" Without a doubt ! Have I not the visible example of my own master ? "

A question which has been on my mind for many days, presses itself to the fore again. Hitherto I have hesitated in voicing it, but now that our friendship has come so close I decide to give the query a bold outlet. I look earnestly at the Yogi and ask him :

" Brama, who is your master ? "

For a while he returns my gaze, but yields no answer. He looks at me hesitatingly.

When he speaks, his voice is slow and grave :

" He is known to his Southern disciples as Yerumbu Swami, meaning The Ant Teacher."

" What a curious name ! " I exclaim involuntarily.

" My master always carries a bag of rice powder from which he feeds the ants wherever he may be. But in the North and among the Himalayan villages where he sometimes stays, he bears another name."

" Is he, then, perfect in your Yoga of Body Control ? "

" Even so."

" And you believe that he has lived——? "

" I believe that he is over four hundred years old ! " Brama quietly finishes the sentence for me.

There is a tense pause.

I stare at him in bewilderment.

" Many a time he has described to me what happened during the reigns of the Moghul Emperors," supplements the Yogi. " And he has told me stories of the days when your English India Company first came to Madras."

Sceptical Western ears are unable to accept these statements.

" But any child who has read a history book could tell you such things," I counter.

Brama ignores my remark. He goes on :

" My master remembers clearly the first battle of Panipat[1] and he has not forgotten the days of the battle of Plassey.[2] I recollect how he once referred to a brother disciple, one Beshudananda, as a mere child of eighty years ! "

In the clear moonlight I notice that Brama's swarthy, broad-nosed countenance remains peculiarly unmoved while he utters these strange words. How can my brain, nurtured in the strict methods of inquiry which modern science has called forth, entertain such assertions ? After all, Brama is a Hindu and must possess some of the legend-swallowing ability of his people. It is useless to contend with him ; I shall remain silent.

The Yogi continues :

" For more than eleven years my master was spiritual adviser to one of the old Maharajahs of Nepal, the State which lies between India and Tibet. There he is known and loved by some of the village people, who dwell among the Himalayan

[1] In 1526, the invading army of Baber, a descendant of the ruthless Tamerlane, and the forces of the King of Agra met in conflict at Panipat.

[2] This famous battle, which opened the British path to power in India, occurred in 1757.

mountains. They revere him as a god when he visits them, yet he talks to them in a kindly way, in the manner of a father talking to his children. He gives no heed to caste rules, and he eats neither fish nor meat "

" How is it possible for a man to live so long ? " My thoughts involuntarily voice themselves again.

Brama looks away, seems to forget my presence.

" There are three ways in which this is possible. The first is to practise all the postures, all the breathing exercises and all the secret exercises which comprise our system of Body Control. This practice must take place until one is perfect, which can be done only under a proper master who can show you in his own body what he teaches. The second way is to partake regularly of some rare herbs which are known only to the adepts who have studied this matter. These adepts carry the herbs secretly, or hide them in their robes when travelling. When the time arrives for the final disappearance of such an adept, he selects a worthy disciple, makes the secret known to him, and presents him with the herbs. To none else are they given. The third way is not easy to explain." Brama stops abruptly.

" Will you not try ? " I urge.

" It is possible that you will laugh at my words."

I assure him that, on the contrary, I shall treat his explanation with due respect.

" Very well. There exists a tiny hole inside the brain of man.[1] Within this hole dwells the soul. There is also a kind of valve which protects this hole. At the bottom of the spine there comes into being the unseeable life-current which I have mentioned to you more than once. The constant loss of this current causes the body to grow old, but its control fills the flesh with new life and perpetuates it. When a man has conquered himself, he can begin to get this control by certain practices which are known only to advanced Yogis of our school. And when he can withdraw this life-current up his spine, he may then try to concentrate it into the hole in the brain. But, unless he finds a master who will assist him to open the protecting valve, he cannot succeed. If he finds a master who is willing to do this, then the unseeable current will enter the hole and turn into the Nectar of Longevity, as we name it. It is no easy task, for ruin waits in ambush for the man who attempts it alone. But the man who succeeds can

[1] It is possible that Brama refers to the cavity caused by the four inter-communicating ventricles of the brain, but I am not sure.

induce a condition similar to death whenever he pleases, and so obtains the victor's power when real death seeks him out. In fact, he can choose the exact moment of his death at any time, and to the severest examination he will appear to have died naturally. One who has all these three methods at his command can live for many hundred years. So have I been taught. Even when he dies, the worms will refrain from attacking his body. A century later his flesh will still be free from decay."

I thank Brama for his explanation, but I wonder. I am profoundly interested, but I am not convinced. Anatomy does not know this current of which he talks, and it has certainly never known his Nectar. Are these stories of physiological marvels mere superstitious misunderstandings? With them one returns to the age of fable, the ancient days of long-lived wizards and magicians who hold the elixir of life. Yet the demonstrations of breath and blood control which Brama has given me provide some assurance that Yogic powers are not mere chimeras, that these powers can undoubtedly be responsible for the performance of feats which must appear fabulous to the uninitiated. Beyond this point I find it difficult to walk with him.[1]

I remain respectfully silent, careful not to allow my intellectual struggles betray themselves on my face.

"Such powers as these would be much desired by men who are nearing the grave," Brama resumes, "but forget not that the way to them is full of danger. Can you wonder that our masters say of these exercises: 'Keep them as secret as you would keep a box of diamonds.'"

"So you are unlikely to reveal them to me?"

"Those who wish to become adepts should first learn to walk before they try to run?" he replies, with a faint smile.

"A last question, Brama."

The Yogi nods.

"Where is your master now living?"

"He has entered a temple retreat in the mountains of Nepal, on the yonder side of the Terai jungle."

[1] The entire conversation, with its amazing statements and cool assertions, now seems like a fantastic dream. My attempt to transfer it to paper is a task which, more than once, makes me contemplate omitting it completely from this book as I have perforce to omit many other conversations. I do not doubt but that it will cause many superior European lips to curl in contempt of Asiatic superstition. If I finally let it pass into publication, it is at the bidding of other judgments than mine.

" Is he likely to return to the plains again ? "

" Who can foretell his movements ? He may remain in Nepal for many years, or he may begin his travels again. He likes Nepal best because our school of Yoga flourishes better there than in India. You see, even the teaching of Body Control differs with different schools. And ours is the Tantra school, which is better understood in the atmosphere of Nepal than among the Hindus."

Brama reverts to silence. I guess that he is dwelling in devoted thought upon this enigmatic figure of his master. Ah ! if these things I have heard to-night are more real than legendary, then, indeed, one may catch a glimpse of what is around the corner—Man, Ageless and Immortal !

§

If I do not hurry my pen, this chapter will never be brought to a close. Therefore I shall endeavour to transfix the last memorable scene of my association with the Yogi of the five names.

The Indian night comes quickly on the heels of evening; there are no lingering sunsets as in Europe. And as the swift dusk begins to descend on his garden hut, Brama lights an oil lantern and suspends it by a cord from the roof. We settle down anew.

The old widow discreetly slips away and leaves me alone with the Yogi and the student-teacher who translates our words. The odour of burning incense touches the room with a mystical atmosphere.

This evening sad thoughts of parting steal over me. I try to brush them off, but fail. I cannot clearly tell this man, through the irritating barrier of speaking through a third person, what is in my heart. How far the novel facts and strange theories he has put forward are correct, I am little able to say, but I have appreciated his readiness to let me enter his solitary existence ; I have felt at times that our hearts have drawn sympathetically near to each other ; and I know now what it has meant to him to break his habitual reserve.

To-night I have made a last attempt, under the shadow of impending departure, to induce him to reveal his deeper secrets.

" Are you ready to abandon the life of cities and to retire into a solitary place in the hills or the jungle for some years ? " he asks me, searchingly.

" I must first think this out, Brama."

" Are you ready to give up all other activities, all your work, renounce your pleasures and put your whole time into the exercises of our system—and that not merely for a few months, but for several years ? "

" I do not think so. No—I am not ready. One day, perhaps——"

" Then I can take you no farther. This Yoga of Body Control is too serious to become the mere sport of a man's leisure hours."

I see my chances of becoming a Yogi fade swiftly into nothing. I regretfully realize that the full system, with its many years of difficult training, its rigorous and austere discipline, is not for me. But there is something else which is closer to my heart than strange powers of the flesh. I confide in the anchorite.

" Brama, these powers—they are wonderfully fascinating. One day I would really like to go more deeply into your training, yet, after all, how much lasting happiness do they bring ? Is there not something finer still in Yoga ? Perhaps I do not make myself clear ? "

Brama nods his head and says :

" I understand."

We both smile.

" Our texts say that the wise man will follow up his practice of the Yoga of Body Control with the Yoga of Mind Control," he remarks, slowly. " It can be said that the first prepares the way for the second. When our ancient masters received the principles of our system from the god Shiva, they were told that the final goal was not to be purely material. They understood that the conquest of the body was to be looked upon as a step towards the conquest of the mind, and this again as a way to becoming spiritually perfect. So you see that our system deals with things close at hand, indeed, with the body, but only as an indirect means of penetrating to the spirit. Therefore, my own master has taught me : ' First run your course in Body Control ; then you can take to the kingly science, the Mind Control.' Remember that a body which is mastered ceases to distract the mind ; only a few can plunge straight into the path of holding the thoughts. Yet if a man feels strongly drawn to the way of Mind Control we do not interfere ; for that, then, is his path."

" And that is a purely mental Yoga ? "

" Even so. It is a training to make the mind like a steady

light, and then that light is turned on to the abode of the spirit."

"How can one start such training ?"

"For that again, it is necessary to find a master."

"Where ?"

Brama shrugs his shoulders.

"Brother, people who are hungry look eagerly for food; those who are starving, however, will search like madmen. When you want a master as much as a starving man wants to eat, you will surely find one. Those who search sincerely will most assuredly be led towards him at the appointed hour."

"You believe that there is a destiny about the matter ?"

"You speak truly."

"I have seen some books——"

The Yogi shakes his head.

"Without a master, your books are mere pieces of paper. Our word for him, *guru*, means : 'One who dispels darkness.' The man whose efforts and destiny favour him sufficiently to find a real teacher, steps quickly into a state of light, for the master uses his own higher gifts to benefit the disciple."

Brama moves away to his bench of littered papers and presently returns with a large document, which he hands to me. It is covered with an orderly arrangement of cabbalistic signs, peculiar symbols and Tamil characters drawn in red, green and black inks. The top of the sheet is adorned with a large hieroglyphic symbol patterned like a scroll, in which I recognize representations of the sun, moon and the human eyes. All the sketches and writings fall around a central blank space.

"Last night, I spent some hours preparing this," says Brama. "When you get back, paste one of my photographs in the centre."

He informs me that if I will concentrate my mind upon this queer but not inartistic document for five minutes before going to sleep at night, I shall dream clearly and vividly of him.

"Even if five thousand miles separate our bodies, place your thoughts upon this paper and our spirits shall meet at night," he asserts confidently. And he explains that these dream meetings will be as actual and as real as our physical meetings have been so far.

This brings me to mention that my trunks are all but packed, and that I shall soon be off; I am doubtful when and where I may see him again.

He replies that he does not doubt that whatever destiny has been allotted us, must be fulfilled. And then he confides in me :

" I leave this place in the spring, when I shall go to the Tanjore district, where two students await me. As for what will happen thereafter, who can say, for, as you know, I hope one day to receive the call from my master."

There is a long silence, which Brama eventually breaks by addressing me in a voice which is lowered to a hushed whisper. I turn to the student-teacher, preparing myself to receive some new revelation.

" Last night my master appeared to me. He spoke to me about yourself. He said : ' Your friend, the sahib, is eager for knowledge. In his last birth he was among us. He followed Yoga practices, but they were not of our school. To-day he has come again to Hindustan, but in a white skin. What he knew then, has now been forgotten ; yet he can forget for a while only. Until a master bestows his grace upon him he cannot become aware of this former knowledge. The master's touch is needed to help him recover that knowledge in this body. Tell him that soon he shall meet a master. Thereafter, light will come to him of its own accord. This is certain. Bid him cease his anxiety. Our land shall not be left by him until this happens. It is the writing of fate that he may not leave us with empty hands.' "

I draw back, astounded.

The lamp throws its beams of light upon the little assembly. My young interpreter's face seems stricken with awe in that yellowish glare.

" Did you not tell me that your teacher was in distant Nepal ? " I demand reproachfully.

" Indeed, he remains there still ! "

" Then how on earth can he travel twelve hundred miles in a single night ? "

Brama smiles cryptically.

" My master is ever present to me, though India's span lies between our bodies. I receive his message without letter or bearer. His thought speeds through the air. It reaches me and I understand."

" Telepathy ? "

" If you wish ! "

I rise, for it is time to go. We wander out on our last moonlight walk together, and pass the ancient walls of the temple which stands not far from Brama's house. The moon filigrees through the many-branched trees as we halt at a lovely group of palms which borders the road.

Whilst he is bidding me farewell, Brama murmurs :

" You know that I have but few possessions. This is the thing I value most. Take it."

He grasps the fourth finger of his left hand, and pulls at it. He holds forward the palm of his right hand. I see a golden ring glistening in the centre under the rays of the moon. Eight slender claws grip a round green stone, whose face is veined with reddish-brown markings. Brama puts it in my hand as we clasp in farewell. I attempt to return the unexpected gift, but he meets my refusal by pressing it more determinedly upon me.

" One who enjoys great wisdom in Yoga gave this to me. In those days I was travelling far and wide for knowledge. Now—I beg you to wear it."

I thank him and enquire, half jokingly :

" Will it bring me good fortune ? "

" No, it cannot do that. But there is a powerful charm within the stone, which will help you penetrate to the company of secret sages, and which will help you awaken your own mystic powers. This you will realize by experience. Wear it when you need these things."

There is a final and friendly parting, and we go our ways.

I walk slowly away, my head filled with a strange medley of thoughts. I muse over the extraordinary message from Brama's far-off master. It is too extraordinary for me to dispute. I remain silent before it while belief and scepticism fight a fantastic conflict in my heart.

I glance at the golden ring and ask myself, " How can a mere ring possess any real efficacy in these matters ? " I do not understand how or why it can influence me or others in any mental or spiritual manner. The belief savours of superstition. Yet Brama seems so confident of the reality of its fanciful properties. Is it possible ? I feel almost impelled to answer : In this strange land all things may be possible ! But intellect rushes to the rescue and puts up a barricade of question marks.

I fall into a fit of musing abstraction, so that I move away, startled, when I stumble against something and knock my forehead. Looking up, I behold the poetic silhouette of a palm tree and the fireflies making a myriad dancing points of light between the branches.

The night sky is deep blue. Venus—a point of intense brightness—seems quite close to our planet. Infinite peace broods over the road as I walk. A mysterious stillness enthrals me. Even the large bats which occasionally appear and sweep over my head, move their wings silently. The scene charms me. I stop for a moment. The moon diffuses a light which turns a man, who is approaching me, into a flitting ghost.

When I reach my quarters, I find that wakefulness lingers late this night. Close to dawn sleep comes at last, drowning my whirl of thoughts in forgetfulness.

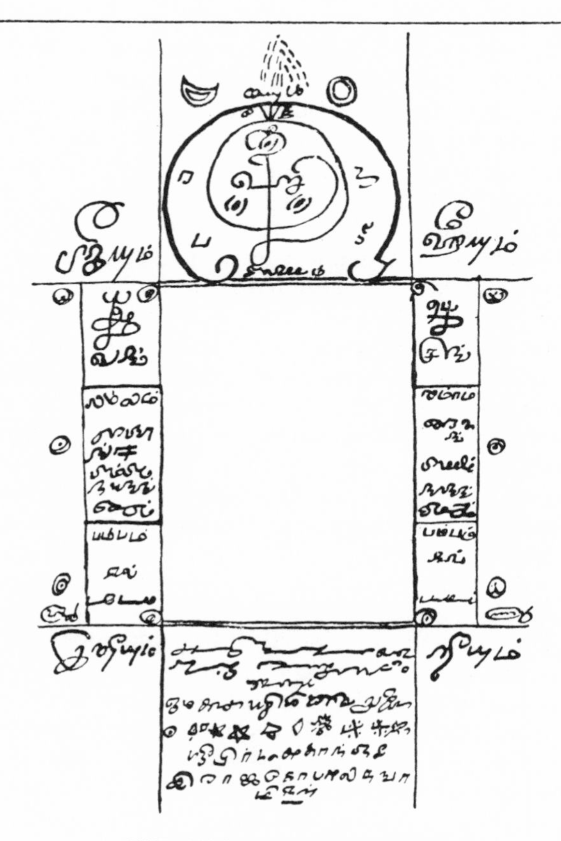

THE YOGI'S MAGIC CHART

"Paste one of my photographs in the centre. Even if five thousand miles separate our bodies, place your thoughts upon this paper and our spirits shall meet at night."

CHAPTER VII

THE SAGE WHO NEVER SPEAKS

I MUST break the chronological character of this record, and wander backwards in time for a week or so, if I am to catch the record of a not uninteresting encounter.

During my stay in the suburb outside Madras, I have not neglected to pursue diligent enquiries within Indian circles in the city itself, with reference to the existence of outstanding figures of the kind in whom I am interested at the time. I talk to judges, lawyers, teachers, business people and even one or two pious notables. I interview the interviewers and spend a few pleasant hours with men of my own profession. I discover an assistant editor who tells me privately that he was a keen student of Yoga in his younger days. He sat then at the feet of one whom he still regards as being indubitably an adept in the science of Mind Control, but this master died ten years ago.

The erstwhile pupil is a charming and highly intelligent Hindu, but alas ! he does not know where high-grade Yogis can now be found.

Aside from this, I meet with little more than vague tales, foolish legends and positive rebuffs. It is true that I meet with one holy man whose Christlike face and robes would have created a sensation in prosaic Piccadilly, but he, too, tells me that he is wandering the land in search of a higher life. He has renounced an estate of good farming land to become a gypsy, a holy beggar. He offers me this estate, provided that I shall settle down and serve benighted, suffering Indians. Alas, I too am a benighted, suffering mortal. His munificent offer is passed on elsewhere.

Word is brought me one day concerning a reputed Yogi. He lives about half a mile outside Madras, yet, because he discourages acquaintance, appears to be known to few persons. My curiosity is quickly excited and I determine to have an audience with him.

The house is hidden behind tall bamboo poles which fence a square compound, and which stands completely isolated in the centre of a field.

My companion points to the compound.

" I am told that the Yogi is immersed in trance most of the day. It is unlikely that he will hear us even if we rattle the gate or shout his name; even if we did those things, it would be thought rude."

A rough gate gives entrance to the enclosure, but as it is strongly padlocked I begin to wonder how we are to get into the house. Complete silence pervades the scene. We wander around the field, turn away from a piece of adjoining waste land, and eventually meet a boy who knows where to find the residence of the Yogi's attendant. A circuitous walk brings us to the place.

The man proves to be a hired servant. His wife and many children come outside to see us and trail behind his heels. We tell him our desire, but he refuses to help us. He firmly declares that the Sage Who Never Speaks is not on view to stray visitors, but lives in strict seclusion. The Sage's days are spent in deep trances and he would be highly offended if all and sundry were allowed to break in on his privacy.

I beg the attendant to make an exception in my favour, but he is adamant. It becomes necessary for my friend to threaten Government interference, if we are not admitted forthwith—a totally unjustifiable procedure, of course, but one which I illegally reinforce, though our eyes wink towards each other. There ensues an animated discussion. I supplement our threats by the lure of liberal baksheesh and it is not long before the attendant reluctantly yields and brings out his keys. My companion informs me that it is clear the man is no more than a paid servant, because if he were a personal disciple of the Sage, neither threats nor money could have moved him.

We march back to the gate of the compound and unlock a massive iron padlock. The servant informs us that the Sage's belongings are so few that they do not include a key. He is locked in the compound from the outside and has no means of egress until the attendant's visits, which take place twice daily. We learn further that the Sage is occupied with his trances throughout the day, but in the evening he partakes of some fruit, sweetmeats, and a cupful of milk. There have been many evenings, however, when the food has remained untouched. The fall of darkness sometimes brings the recluse out of his cottage, though a walk around the fields is the only exercise he takes.

We cross the compound and arrive at a modern cottage. It is solidly built of stone slabs and painted timber posts. The attendant produces another key and unlocks a heavy door. I express surprise at all these precautions, for did not the servant tell us that the Sage's belongings are very few ? Thereupon the man tells us a brief explanatory story.

Some years earlier the silent Sage lived in the cottage without the protection of any locks or fastenings upon the entrances. But one unfortunate day there came a man who was drunk with toddy liquor, and who took advantage of the defenceless state of the Sage to attack him. The drunkard pulled his beard, belaboured him with a stick and shouted disgusting epithets.

Chance intervened to draw some young men into the field, intent upon playing a ball game. The noise of the assault drew their attention. They entered the cottage and rescued the Sage from his assailant, while one of them ran off to the nearest houses to inform all and sundry. Before long a group of excited people gathered together, Indian fashion, and began to mishandle the drunken ruffian who had dared attack a revered holy man. There was a likelihood that the man who was so dastardly would be lynched.

Throughout this episode the Sage had maintained his usual stoic calmness and endurance. Now he intervened and wrote down the following message.

" If you beat this man, it is the same as beating me. Let him go, for I have forgiven him."

Since the Sage's word was unwritten law, his request was unwillingly obeyed and the miscreant set free.

§

The attendant peers into the room and then warns us to be perfectly quiet, because the Sage is sunk in trance. I unlace my shoes and leave them behind on the veranda, in obedience to the inexorable dictates of Hindu custom. As I bend my head I notice a small flat stone in the wall. Its face is inscribed with Tamil characters. " The Abode of the Sage Who Never Speaks," translates my companion.

We enter the one-roomed cottage. It is lofty, well-roofed

and scrupulously clean. A raised marble dais, which is about one foot high, is built into the floor's centre. Its surface is covered with a richly patterned Persian rug. Upon this rug sits the entranced figure of the silent Sage.

Imagine a handsome man, whose skin shines with a tawny blackish colour, whose body is finely erect, and who sits in a peculiar attitude which I immediately identify as one of the Yoga postures which Brama has shown me. The left leg is doubled back so that the foot is under the base of the body, and the right leg is swung across the left thigh. The Sage's back, neck and head form a perfectly straight line. His hair falls in long black strands almost to his shoulders, and hangs thickly around his head. There is a sweeping black beard upon his chin. His hands are clasped over his knees. I notice that the trunk is remarkably well developed ; it is very muscular and he is clearly in a healthy condition. The only covering he wears is a loin cloth.

His face photographs itself immediately in my memory as the face of a man who smiles in triumph over life, a man who has conquered the frailties which we, feebler mortals that we are, harbour willingly or unwillingly. The mouth is slightly stretched—as though about to break into a smile. The nose is short and straight, almost Grecian in type. The eyes are wide open ; they stare straight ahead in a fixed and unblinking gaze. The man sits like a carved rock and never moves.

My informant has earlier told me that the silent Sage is without doubt deeply immersed in an entranced communion wherein the human part of his nature is presumed to be sunk into temporary abeyance, and that he is quite unaware of his physical surroundings. I watch the Sage steadily but can find no room for doubt that he is in a cataleptic trance. The minutes add up into hours but he remains motionless.

What impresses me most is that throughout that time he never blinks his eyes. I have never before met any human being who could sit down and look steadily ahead for two hours without the flicker of an eyelid. Little by little, I am compelled to conclude that if the recluse's eyes are still open, they are nevertheless quite unseeing. If his mind is awake, it is not to this sublunary world. The bodily faculties seem to have gone to sleep. Occasionally, a tear drop falls from his eyes. It is clear that the fixation of the eyelids prevents them carrying out their usual office on behalf of the tear ducts.

A green lizard descends from the roof, creeps across the

carpet, crawls over one of the Sage's legs, and then passes behind the marble dais. Yet, had it crawled over a stone wall, it would not have found a steadier surface than that leg. From time to time flies settle upon his face and journey over his swarthy skin, but no muscular response can be observed. Had they alighted upon the face of a bronze statue, precisely the same effect might be observed.

I study the figure's breathing. It is extremely gentle, almost imperceptible, quite inaudible but quite regular. It is the only sign he provides that life has not parted from the body.

While we are waiting I decide to use the time to take a photograph or two of this impressive figure. I slip my folding camera out of its leather case and focus the lens upon him from my seat on the floor. The lighting of the room is not good ; therefore I give a couple of time exposures.

I look at my watch. Two hours have passed. The Yogi still shows no signs of emerging from his long trance. The sculptural rigidity of his form is remarkable.

I am prepared to stay all day in order to achieve my object, in order to interview this strange man. But the attendant now comes up to us and whispers that it is useless to wait any longer. Nothing will be gained by doing so. If we will come again in a day or two, better fortune might be ours ; nevertheless, he cannot promise anything definitely.

We leave the place, temporarily defeated as we are, and turn our steps toward the city. My interest has not waned ; on the contrary, it has heightened.

During the next two days I endeavour to collect some information relative to the Sage Who Never Speaks. This endeavour involves a scattered and discursive investigation, which varies from a lengthy cross-examination of his attendant to a brief interview with a police inspector. In this way I succeed in piecing together a fragment of the Sage's story.

Eight years ago he arrived in Madras district. No one knew who he was, what he was or whence he came. He took up his residence on the piece of waste land which now adjoins the field containing his cottage. Inquisitive inquirers who addressed him received no reply for their pains. He spoke to none, heeded no sounds and no persons, and could not be drawn even into the most casual conversation. He begged a little food occasionally by holding out his coconut-shell bowl.

Day after day he persisted in squatting amid these unattractive surroundings, despite his exposure to the relentless rays of a burning sun, to the heavy downpours of the monsoon season, and to dust and unpleasant insects. Never at any time did he make any effort to seek shelter, but always remained serenely oblivious of external circumstances. There was no protection for his head and no covering for his body, except for a narrow loin cloth.

He never changed the Yoga posture in which he sat for any other. Now, the outskirts of a large city like Madras were hardly suitable for a hermit who wished to seat himself in the open air and in full public gaze in order to plunge his mind into abstracted meditations for lengthy periods. Such conduct would have won great respect in ancient India, but the modern Yogi can find favourable conditions for his mystic practices only in sparse jungle spaces, forest retreats, mountain caves or in the seclusion of his room.

Why, then, did this strange hermit choose such an unsuitable spot for his meditations ? An unpleasant occurrence provided the curious explanation.

One day a band of youthful and ignorant hooligans came across the lonely Yogi by chance and began to persecute him. They left the city with reprehensible punctuality to engage in a daily campaign of stone-throwing, dirt-flinging and abusive jeering. The hermit continued to sit quietly, and patiently endured his trials, although he was stalwart enough to be able to give them a sound thrashing. He did not even rebuke them because he was under a vow of silence.

Nothing stopped the young brutes until a man happened to pass by when they were busy with their usual persecution of the Yogi. The stranger was shocked at seeing a holy man so ill-treated. He went back to Madras and gave information to the police, from whom he demanded help on behalf of the voiceless Yogi. The help was forthcoming and the despicable band was dispersed with severe warnings.

After this event a police officer decided to make some enquiries about the hermit, but he was unable to find a single person who knew anything about him. So he was compelled to question the Yogi, which he did with all the authority of the law. After much hesitation the Yogi wrote a brief statement upon a slate. This is what he scribbled :

" I am a pupil of Marakayar. My master directed me to cross the plains and go south to Madras. He described this piece of ground and explained where I would be able to find it. He told me to take up my abode here and to continue in the steady practise of Yoga until I have made myself perfect in it. I have given up the worldly life and desire only to be left alone.

I have no interest in the affairs of Madras and seek nothing more than to follow my spiritual path."

The police officer was quite satisfied that the man was a genuine faqueer of a superior type, so he withdrew after promising protection against the hooligans. He recognized the name of Marakayar as being that of a famous Muhammedan faqueer who had recently died.

"Out of evil cometh good," runs the old proverb. The upshot of this unpleasant affair was that the presence of the recluse became known to a wealthy and pious citizen of Madras. The latter endeavoured to tempt him into the city with the lure of residence in a fine house, but the hermit would not disobey his master's instructions. In the end the newly-found patron had to build a stone-and-timber bungalow near the ground which the Yogi refused to leave. The latter consented to occupy it and, as it was properly roofed, he was thenceforth adequately protected against the inclemencies of changing seasons.

His patron also appointed a personal attendant for the Yogi. It was now no longer necessary for the latter to beg, as all his food was brought to him by the attendant. Whether his master Marakayar had foreseen such a pleasant consequence of an unpleasant experience or not, it remained that the last condition of his pupil was much better than the first.

I learn that the Sage Who Never Speaks has not even one pupil. He seeks none and accepts none. He is one of those solitaries who prefer to live in isolation in order to achieve their own "spiritual liberation." If there is any value in the latter, then their attitude is apparently a selfish one, judged by our Western lights. And yet, when one remembers the Sage's profound considerateness towards the drunkard and his refusal to retaliate against the young hooligans, one wonders whether he can be so very selfish after all.

§

Accompanied by two other persons, I make my second attempt to interview the Sage Who Never Speaks. One is my interpreter, while the second man is none other than the Yogi who has taught me so much—Brama, "the Adyar anchorite," as I affectionately call him. Brama never cares to enter the city, but when I make known the object of my visit and desire him to accompany me, he agrees without demur.

At the compound we meet another visitor, who has left a large car on the roadside and walked across the fields to the same objective. He, too, is desirous of seeing the silent Sage. He tells me during a brief conversation that he is a brother of the Queen of Gadwal, a small state which is tributary to the Nizam of Hyderabad. He informs me that he also is a patron of the Sage, inasmuch as he insists on making a regular contribution towards the cost of maintaining the shelter. He has come on a brief visit to Madras, but cannot leave the town without paying his respects to the Sage, and perchance receiving his blessing. What the latter is worth, I learn from a story which the visitor narrates.

A lady at the Court of Gadwal had a child who suffered from some dread ailment. By some odd coincidence she heard of the existence of the Sage Who Never Speaks. Such is her anxiety that she journeys to Madras and begs the hermit to grant his blessing and heal the little boy. The blessing is given and from that date the child makes a marvellous recovery. The incident comes to the notice of the Queen, who also visits the hermit. Her Highness presents him with a purse of six hundred rupees, which he refuses to accept. She presses him until he writes a message saying that the money can be used to improve his shelter by fixing a fence around the cottage, so that he shall secure more privacy. The Queen arranges to have this done and thus the bamboo fence comes into being.

The attendant again admits us into the cottage, where we find the recluse sunk in the same trance-like condition which he maintained throughout my first visit.

We squat upon the floor in silence and wait patiently before the tall, majestic, black-bearded figure on the marble dais. About half-way through the second hour we perceive the first signs of returning activity in the Sage's body. His breathing becomes deeper and then more audible. The eyelids move, the eyeballs roll alarmingly upwards until the whites glare and then come down to normal. A slight swaying movement becomes perceptible in his trunk.

Five minutes later the expression in the Sage's eyes changes in such a way that we know he has become aware of his physical environment. He looks attentively at the interpreter, turns his head abruptly and looks at Brama and then at the other visitor, turns it again and looks at me.

I seize the opportunity and place a pencil and a pad of paper at his feet. He hesitates awhile, takes up the pencil and writes in large flourishing Tamil characters :

" Who came here the other day and tried to take pictures ? "

I am compelled to admit to this activity. As a matter of fact, the effort had been useless, for I had under-exposed the films.

He writes again :

" When you go again to Yogis who are in deep trance, never disturb them by such actions. Do not attempt to break in abruptly upon their meditations. In my own case it did not matter, but I tell you this to guide your future actions when you try to see other Yogis. Such interruption may be dangerous to them and they might put a curse upon you."

It is evidently looked upon as a minor act of sacrilege to penetrate the solitude of such a man, so I express my regrets.

The Queen of Gadwal's brother now proffers his devotion to the Sage. When he has finished I venture to introduce myself as one deeply interested in the ancient wisdom of India. I have heard across the seas, I inform him, that India still possesses a few men who have made remarkable attainments in Yoga and I seek to discover them. Will the Sage give me such enlightenment as he thinks fit ?

The hermit remains statuesque, impassive ; his face betrays no responsive change of expression. For fully ten minutes he gives no sign that he has heard my request. I begin to fear that I have drawn a blank, that he regards the materialistic Westerner as unfit even for the slightest degree of enlightenment. Possibly my clumsy outrage with the camera has repelled him. Am I not expecting too much, when I expect this reserved member of a reclusive species to break his trance for the sake of an infidel member of an alien race ? A sense of chagrin rises up in me.

My disappointment is too premature. The Sage takes the pencil at length and scrawls something upon the paper. When he has finished I lean over and push the pad to our interpreter.

" What is there to understand ? " he slowly translates. The writing is difficult to decipher.

" The universe is full of problems ? " I rejoin, disconcerted.

I fancy that a slightly derisive smile now begins to play around the lips of the Sage.

" Since you do not understand even your own self," he asks, " how can you hope to understand the universe ? "

He looks straight into my eyes. I feel that behind his steady gaze there is some deep knowledge, some store of secrets which he is guarding with relentless care. I cannot account for this queer impression.

"Yet I am much bewildered," is all I can bring myself to say next.

"Why, then, do you go about like a bee which sucks mere drops of the honey of knowledge, when the heavy mass of pure honey awaits you?"

This answer tantalizes me. It is, no doubt, all-sufficient to an Oriental mind. Its mystic vagueness charms me as a piece of poetry, but blurs me when I look for a useful contribution that will solve some of life's problems.

"But where shall one look?"

"Seek your own self, and you shall know the Truth which is deep hidden therein," comes the reply.

"But I find only the emptiness of ignorance," I persist.

"The ignorance exists within your thoughts alone," he writes laconically.

"Pardon me, master, but your answer plunges me into still further ignorance!"

The Sage actually smiles at my temerity. He hesitates awhile, screws up his eyebrows, and then writes:

"You have thought yourself into your present ignorance; now think yourself back into wisdom, which is the same as self-understanding. Thought is like a bullock cart which carries a man into the darkness of a mountain tunnel. Turn it backwards and you will be carried back to the light again."

I ruminate over his words, which still puzzle me a little. Seeing this, the Sage beckons for the pad, poises the pencil in the air for a few moments, and explains:

"This backward-turning of thought is the highest Yoga. Now do you understand?"

A very dim light begins to dawn on me. I feel that, given sufficient time in which to meditate on the matter, we shall be able to understand each other; therefore, I resolve not to press the point too much.

I am so intent on watching him that I have not noticed the arrival of a fresh visitor, who has taken advantage of the opened gate to enter and join us. I become aware of his presence only when he breathes a strange remark into my ear, for he is sitting immediately behind me. Whilst I am puzzling over a reply of the Sage, feeling slightly disappointed at the cryptic character of his words, a mysterious murmur reaches me, its words phrased in excellent English:

"My master can give you the answer for which you are waiting."

I turn my head and look at the intruder.

He is a man not older than forty, dressed in the ochre-coloured robe of a wandering Yogi. The skin of his face shines like polished brass. He is well built and broad shouldered—a powerful looking figure. His nose is thin, prominent and beaked like a parrot's. His eyes are small and seem to be wrinkled in perpetual laughter. He squats upon his haunches and grins broadly at me when our eyes meet.

But I cannot perpetrate the rude action of entering into desultory conversation with the stranger, so I turn back and fix my attention again upon the Sage.

Another question comes to the forefront of my mind. It is possibly too daring or too impertinent.

" Master, the world needs help. Is it right for the wise ones, such as yourself, to be lost to it in solitary retirement ? "

A quizzical expression crosses the calm face of the hermit.

" My son," he replies, " when you do not know yourself, how can you dream of understanding me ? It is of little avail to discuss the things of the spirit. Strive to enter into your inner self through the practice of Yoga. You must work hard upon this path. Then your problems will solve themselves of their own accord."

I make a last attempt to draw him.

" The world needs a deeper light than it possesses. I would like to find it and share it. What shall I do ? "

" When you know the Truth you will know exactly what to do to serve mankind best, nor will you lack the power to do so. If a flower possesses the honey, the bee will find it out of its own accord. If a man possesses spiritual wisdom and strength, he need not go in search of people ; they will come unasked to him. Cultivate your inner self until you know it fully. No other instruction is necessary. This is the only thing to do."

He then informs us that he wishes to close the interview, so as to resume his trance.

I ask for a final message.

The silent Sage gazes over my head into seeming space. A minute later he pencils a reply and pushes the pad towards me. We read :

" I am very pleased because you came here. Take this as my initiation."

I hardly finish taking in the purport of his answer when I suddenly feel a strange force entering my body. It pours through my spinal column and stiffens the neck and draws up the head. The power of will seems raised to a superlative degree. I become conscious of a dynamic urge to conquer myself and make the body obey the will to realize one's deepest ideals. And I feel intuitively that those ideals are but voices of my best self, which alone can promise me lasting happiness.

A queer thought comes to me that some current is being projected to me from the Sage, some invisible telepathic current. Can it be that he is thus vouchsafing to me an inkling of his own attainment ?

The eyes of the recluse become fixed and the far-off look again enters them. His body becomes taut as he settles down more firmly into his familiar posture. I plainly perceive that he is withdrawing his attention into depths which may possibly be deeper than thought, that he is plunging his consciousness into inner recesses which he loves better than this world.

Is he then a true Yogi ? Is he engaged on mysterious inward explorations which, I begin to suspect, may be fraught with some meaning to humanity ? Who knows ?

When we emerge from the compound, Brama, the Adyar anchorite, turns to me and says, in a quiet voice :

" This Yogi has reached a high state, although not the final goal. He possesses occult gifts, but is keener to perfect his spirituality. His fine bodily condition I attribute to his long practice of the Yoga of Body Control, though I now observe that he has advanced into the art of Mind Control. I knew him before."

" When ? "

" I discovered him some years ago near here, when he lived in the open field without a cottage. I recognized him for what he was—a practising Yogi following my path. I shall also tell you that he informed me—through writing, of course—that in early life he was a Sepoy in the army. After his period of service came to an end, he wearied of this worldly life and embraced solitude. It was then that he met the renowned faqueer Marakayar and became his disciple."

We proceed in silence across the fields and then rejoin the dusty road. I do not mention to anyone the unexpected and inexplicable experience which came to me in the cottage. I want to muse over it while its echoes are yet sounding fresh within me.

I never see the Sage again. He does not wish me to intrude upon his secluded life and I must respect his wish. I leave him to his lonely meditations, wrapped in his mantle of impenetrability. He has no desire to found a school or collect a following, and his ambitions seem to stretch no farther than passing unobtrusively through life. He has nothing to add to what he has already said to me. He does not make an art of conversation for its own sake, as we do in the West.

THE GREAT TEMPLE OF ARUNACHALA AND THE HILL OF THE HOLY BEACON

" Here is no stone building whose columned beauty stays one's emotions in a few minutes of silent wonder, as do those courts of the deities near Athens, but rather a gloomy sanctuary of dark mysteries."

YOGIS' CAVES HEWN OUT OF SOLID MOUNTAIN ROCK

" Go to some place over which the mighty Himalayas keep eternal guard. There you will find a totally different class of men. They live in humble huts or caves, eat little food and constantly pray to God. They, too, are called Yogis."

(*Above*) THE CAVE HOME OF SHRI SADGURU MEHER BABA
(*Below*) THE "NEW MESSIAH"
" This Parsee holy man is doubtless a great lover of Nature, for he has set his retreat in a scene of aloof, untroubled peace."

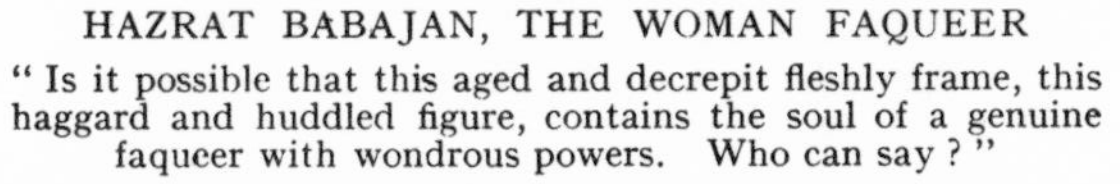

HAZRAT BABAJAN, THE WOMAN FAQUEER

" Is it possible that this aged and decrepit fleshly frame, this haggard and huddled figure, contains the soul of a genuine faqueer with wondrous powers. Who can say ? "

UPASANI MAHARAJ

" And so, when Meher came face to face with Upasani Maharaj, he felt that he had found his master."

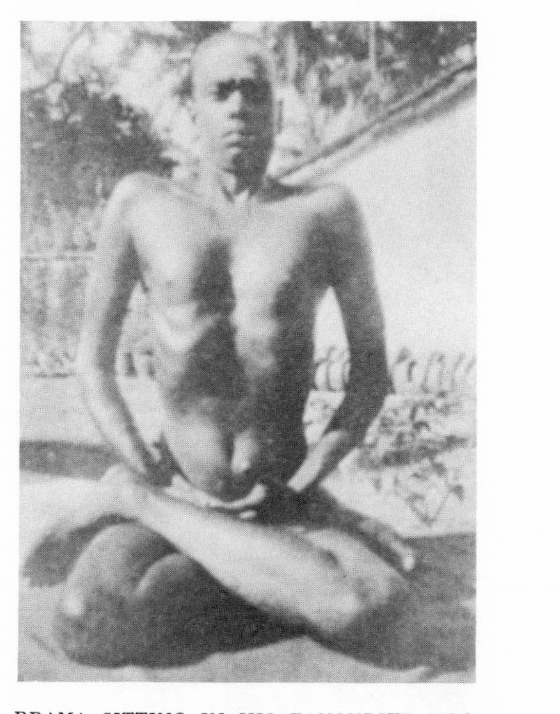

BRAMA SITTING IN HIS FAVOURITE YOGA POSTURE

"If a Yogi enters into such a posture and then practises a certain breathing exercise, he will become more youthful."

THE ANCHORITE OF THE ADYAR RIVER

"One gathers the impression that the mind behind those eyes is pondering over some matter."

SHRI SHANKARA, THE SPIRITUAL HEAD OF SOUTH INDIA
His noble face, pictured in grey and brown, takes an honoured place in the long portrait gallery of my memory."

By courtesy Indian Railways Bureau, London

INTERIOR OF DILWARA TEMPLE

" The tradition of my office requires that I give a spiritual discourse in the local temple."

By courtesy Indian Railways Bureau, London

IN THE MUHAMMEDAN MOSQUE

" Something inside me always thrills to the graceful arches of a mosque and to the delicate beauty of cupolas. Once again I remove my shoes and enter the charming white building."

THE MASTER MAHASAYA

"A patriarch has stepped from the pages of the Bible, and a figure from Mosaic times has turned to flesh."

SARADA DEVI, "THE HOLY MOTHER"

She was the wife of Ramakrishna. The latter was the spiritual guide of Mahasaya, and was one of the last of India's Rishees, or spiritual supermen.

BADREENATH SATHU

A faqueer who claims extraordinary occult powers. Here he is seen in a mystic trance wherein the eyeballs turn upon their axes. Note the chin-rest.

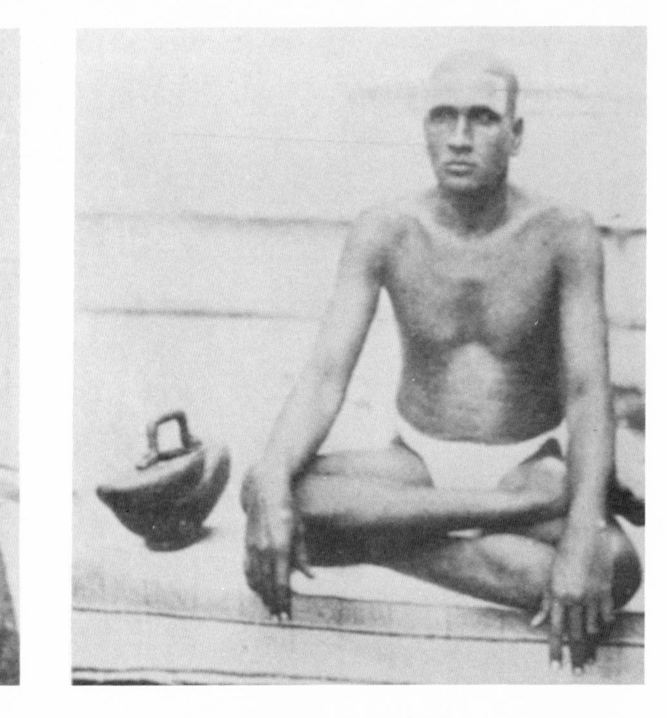

EESWARA SWAMI

Once a pupil of the Maharishee, but now an adept in his own turn, lives in a temple and instructs his own group of disciples.

By courtesy Indian Railways Bureau, London

(*Above*) WANDERING SNAKE CHARMERS
(*Below*) COMMON FAQUEERS OF AN INFERIOR ORDER AT BENARES

THE RIVER BANK AT BENARES

"The feet of many centuries have worn down the steps until they are rugged and uneven."

VISHUDHANANDA THE MAGICIAN

"His venerable appearance and seat of honour are enough to inform me that here is the object of my quest."

By courtesy Indian Railways Bureau, London

TWILIGHT OVER THE JUMNA

"The river reflects the last red light of sunset. All nature, dumb at the lovely sight, seems to have come to momentary rest."

SAHABJI MAHARAJ

" Master of over one hundred thousand people who practise a mysterious form of Yoga."

By courtesy Indian Railways Bureau, London

THE GATEWAY TO JEHANGIR'S PALACE, AGRA

" We explore colourful edifices where once the seductive favourites of kings flaunted their olive-skinned beauty upon marble balconies and in golden baths."

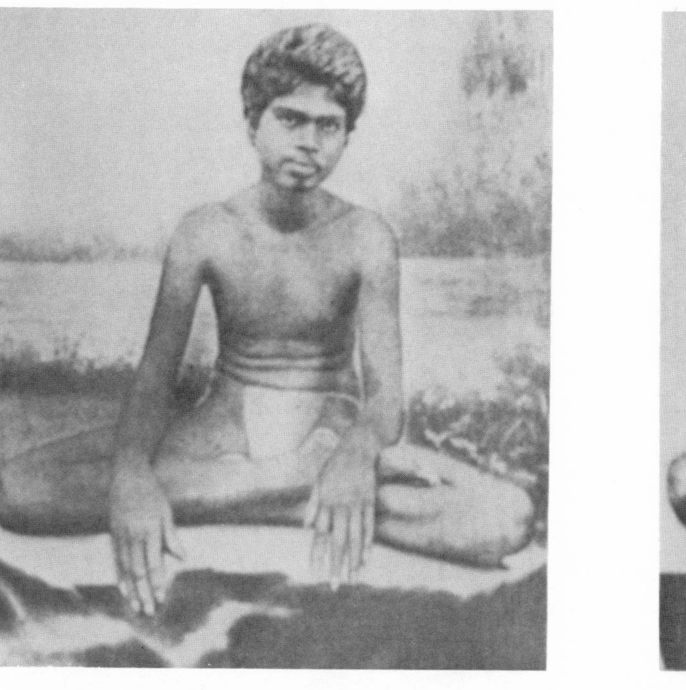

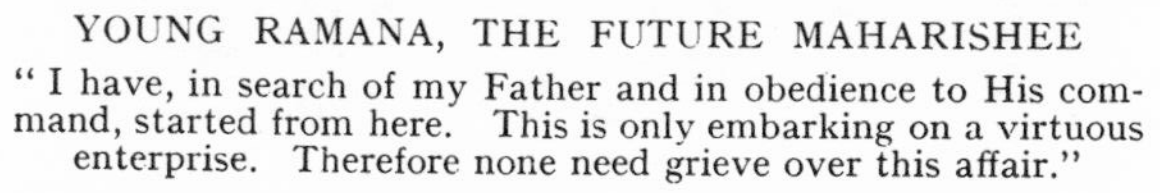

YOUNG RAMANA, THE FUTURE MAHARISHEE

" I have, in search of my Father and in obedience to His command, started from here. This is only embarking on a virtuous enterprise. Therefore none need grieve over this affair."

THE MAHARISHEE OR GREAT SAGE

" He gazes out towards the jungle-covered hills which stretch to the horizon and remains motionless. It is impossible to be in frequent contact with him without becoming lit up inwardly, as it were, by a ray from his spiritual orb."

YOGI RAMIAH

"I meet him at the pool, whither he has come with a brass pitcher for water. His darkly mysterious, but benignant, countenance again attracts me."

RAMIAH'S QUAINT ABODE

"He stays in a small stone shelter which he has had constructed under the shadow of some huge boulders."

CHAPTER VIII

WITH THE SPIRITUAL HEAD OF SOUTH INDIA

SOMEONE draws up to my side before we reach the end of the road which is to take us into Madras. I turn my head. The yellow robed Yogi—for it is he—rewards me with a majestic grin. His mouth stretches almost from ear to ear, and his eyes wrinkle into narrow slits.

"You wish to speak to me ?" I enquire.

"I do, sir," he replies quickly, and with a good accent to his English. "May I ask what you are doing in our country ?"

I hesitate before this inquisitiveness, and decide to give a vague reply.

"Oh ! just travelling around."

"You are interested in our holy men, I believe ?"

"Yes—a little."

"I am a Yogi, sir," he informs me.

He is the heftiest-looking Yogi I have ever seen.

"How long have you been one ?"

"Three years, sir."

"Well, you look none the worse for it, if you will pardon my saying so !"

He draws himself proudly together and stands at attention. Since his feet are naked, I take the click of his heels for granted.

"For seven years I was a soldier of His Majesty the King-Emperor !" he exclaims.

"Indeed !"

"Yes, sir. I served with the ranks in the Indian Army during the Mesopotamian campaign. After the war I was put into the Military Accounts Department because of my superior intelligence !"

I am compelled to smile at this unsolicited testimonial to himself.

"I left the service on account of family trouble and went through a period of great distress. This induced me to take to the spiritual path and become a Yogi."

I hand him a card.

" Shall we exchange names ? " I suggest.

" My personal name is Subramanya ; my caste name is Aiyar," he quickly announces.

" Well, Mr. Subramanya, I am waiting for an explanation of your whispered remark in the house of the silent Sage."

" And I have been waiting all this time to give it to you ! Take your questions to my master, for he is the wisest man in India, wiser even than the Yogis. "

" So ? And have you travelled throughout all India ? Have you met all the great Yogis, that you can make such a statement ? "

" I have met several of them, for I know the country from Cape Comorin to the Himalayas."

" Well ? "

" Sir, I have never met anyone like him. He is a great soul. And I want you to meet him."

" Why ? "

" Because he has led me to you ! It is his power which has drawn you to India ! "

This bombastic statement strikes me as being too exaggerated and I begin to recoil from the man. I am always afraid of the rhetorical exaggerations of emotional persons, and it is obvious that the yellow-robed Yogi is highly emotional. His voice, gesture, appearance and atmosphere plainly reveal it.

" I do not understand," is my cold reply.

He falls into further explanations.

" Eight months ago I came into touch with him. For five months I was permitted to stay with him and then I was sent forth on my travels once more. I do not think you are likely to meet with another such man as he. His spiritual gifts are so great that he will answer your unspoken thoughts. You need only be with him a short time to realize his high spiritual degree."

" Are you sure he would welcome my visit ? "

" Oh, sir ! Absolutely. It is his guidance which sent me to you."

" Where does he live ? "

" On Arunachala—the Hill of the Holy Beacon."

" And where is that ? "

" In the North Arcot territory, which lies farther south. I will constitute myself your guide. Let me take you there. My master will solve your doubts and remove your problems, because he knows the highest truth."

" That sounds quite interesting," I admit reluctantly, " but I regret that the visit is impossible at present. My trunks are packed and I shall soon be leaving for the North-east. There are two important appointments to be fulfilled, you see."

" But this is more important."

" Sorry. We met too late. My arrangements are made and they cannot be easily altered. I may be back in the South later, but we must leave this journey for the present."

The Yogi is plainly disappointed.

" You are missing an opportunity, sir, and——"

I foresee a useless argument, so cut him short.

" I must leave you now. Thanks, anyway."

" I refuse to accept your refusal," he obstinately declares. " To-morrow evening I shall call upon you and I hope then to hear that you have changed your mind."

Our conversation abruptly finishes. I watch his strong, well-knit, yellow-robed figure start across the road.

When I reach home, I begin to feel that it is possible I have made an error of judgment. If the master is worth half the disciple's claims, then he is worth the troublesome journey into the southern tip of the peninsula. But I have grown somewhat tired of enthusiastic devotees. They sing pæans of praise to their masters, who prove on investigations to fall lamentably short of the more critical standards of the West. Furthermore, sleepless nights and sticky days have rendered my nerves less serene than they should be ; thus, the possibility that the journey might prove a wild goose chase looms larger than it should.

Yet argument fails to displace feeling. A queer instinct warns me that there may be some real basis for the Yogi's ardent insistence on the distinctive claims of his master. I cannot keep off a sense of self-disappointment.

§

About the time of tiffin, that is, tea and biscuits, the servant announces a visitor. The latter proves to be a fellow member of the ink-stained fraternity, to wit, the writer Venkataramani.

Several letters of introduction lie where I have thrown them, at the bottom of my trunk. I have no desire to use them. This is in response to a curious whim that it might be better to tempt whatever gods there be to do their best—or worst. However, I used one in Bombay, preparatory to beginning my quest, and I used another in Madras because I have been charged to deliver a personal message with it. And thus, this second note has brought Venkataramani to my door.

He is a member of the Senate of Madras University, but he is better known as the author of talented essays and novels of village life. He is the first Hindu writer in Madras Presidency, who uses the medium of English, to be publicly presented with an inscribed ivory shield because of his services to literature. He writes in a delicate style of such merit as to win high commendation from Rabindranath Tagore in India and from the late Lord Haldane in England. His prose is piled with beautiful metaphors, but his stories tell of the melancholy life of neglected villages.

As he enters the room I look at his tall, lean person, his small head with its tiny tuft of hair, his small chin and bespectacled eyes. They are the eyes of a thinker, an idealist and a poet combined. Yet the sorrows of suffering peasants are reflected in their sad irises.

We soon find ourselves on several paths of common interest. After we have compared notes about most things, after we have contemptuously pulled politics to pieces and swung the censers of adoration before our favourite authors, I am suddenly impressed to reveal to him the real reason of my Indian visit. I tell him with perfect frankness what my object is; I ask him about the whereabouts of any real Yogis who possess demonstrable attainments; and I warn him that I am not especially interested in meeting dirt-besmeared ascetics or juggling faqueers.

He bows his head and then shakes it negatively.

" India is no longer the land of such men. With the increasing materialism of our country, its wide degeneration on one hand and the impact of unspiritual Western culture on the other, the men you are seeking, the great masters, have all but disappeared. Yet I firmly believe that some exist in retirement, in lonely forests perhaps, but unless you devote a whole lifetime to the search, you will find them with the greatest difficulty. When my fellow Indians undertake such a quest as yours, they have to roam far and wide nowadays. Then how much harder will it be for a European ? "

" Then you hold out little hope ? " I ask.

" Well, one cannot say. You may be fortunate."

Something moves me to put a sudden question :

" Have you heard of a master who lives in the mountains of North Arcot ? "

He shakes his head.

Our talk wanders back to literary topics.

I offer him a cigarette, but he excuses himself from smoking. I light one for myself and while I inhale the fragrant smoke of the Turkish weed, Venkataramani pours out his heart in passionate praise of the fast disappearing ideals of old Hindu culture. He makes reference to such ideas as simplicity of living, service of the community, leisurely existence and spiritual aims. He wants to lop off parasitic stupidities which grow on the body of Indian society. The biggest thing in his mind, however, is his vision of saving the half-million villages of India from becoming mere recruiting centres for the slums of large industrialized towns. Though this menace is more remote than real, his prophetic insight and memory of Western industrial history sees this as a certain result of present day trends. Venkataramani tells me that he was born in a family with a property near one of the oldest villages of South India, and he greatly lamented the cultural decay and material poverty into which village life had fallen. He loves to hatch out schemes for the betterment of the simple village folk, and he refuses to be happy whilst they are unhappy.

I listen quietly in the attempt to understand his viewpoint. Finally, he rises to go and I watch his tall thin form disappear down the road.

Early next morning I am surprised to receive an unexpected visit from him. His carriage rushes hastily to the gate, for he fears that I might be out.

"I received a message late last night that my greatest patron is staying for one day at Chingleput," he bursts out.

After he has recovered his breath, he continues:

"His Holiness Shri Shankara Acharya of Kumbakonam is the Spiritual Head of South India. Millions of people revere him as one of God's teachers. It happens that he has taken a great interest in me and has encouraged my literary career, and of course he is the one to whom I look for spiritual advice. I may now tell you what I refrained from mentioning yesterday. We regard him as a master of the highest spiritual attainment. But he is not a Yogi. He is the Primate of the Southern Hindu world, a true saint and great religious philosopher. Because he is fully aware of most of the spiritual currents of our time, and because of his own attainment, he has probably an exceptional knowledge of the real Yogis. He travels a good deal from village to village and from city to city, so that he is particularly well informed on such matters. Wherever he goes, the holy men come to him to pay their respects. He could probably give you some useful advice. Would you like to visit him ? "

" That is extremely kind of you. I shall gladly go. How far is Chingleput ? "

" Only thirty-five miles from here. But stay—— ? "

" Yes ? "

" I begin to doubt whether His Holiness would grant you an audience. Of course I shall do my utmost to persuade him. But—— "

" I am a European ! " I finish the sentence for him. " I understand."

" You will take the risk of a rebuff ? " he asks, a little anxiously.

" Certainly. Let us go."

After a light meal we set out for Chingleput. I ply my literary companion with questions about the man I hope to see this day. I learn that Shri Shankara lives a life of almost ascetic plainness as regards food and clothing, but the dignity of his high office requires him to move in regal panoply when travelling. He is followed then by a retinue of mounted elephants and camels, pundits and their pupils, heralds and camp followers generally. Wherever he goes he becomes the magnet for crowds of visitors from the surrounding localities. They come for spiritual, mental, physical and financial assistance. Thousands of rupees are daily laid at his feet by the rich, but because he has taken the vow of poverty, this income is applied to worthy purposes. He relieves the poor, assists education, repairs decaying temples and improves the condition of those artificial rain-fed pools which are so useful in the riverless tracts of South India. His mission, however, is primarily spiritual. At every stopping-place he endeavours to inspire the people to a deeper understanding of their heritage of Hinduism, as well as to elevate their hearts and minds. He usually gives a discourse at the local temple and then privately answers the multitude of querents who flock to him.

I learn that Shri Shankara is the sixty-sixth bearer of the title in direct line of succession from the original Shankara. To get his office and power into the right perspective within my mind, I am forced to ask Venkataramani several questions about the founder of the line. It appears that the first Shankara flourished over one thousand years ago, and that he was one of the greatest of the historical Brahmin sages. He might be described as a rational mystic, and as a philosopher of first rank. He found the Hinduism of his time in a disordered and decrepit state, with its spiritual vitality fast fading. It seems that he was born for a mission. From the age of eighteen he wandered throughout India on foot, arguing with the intelligentsia and the priests of every district through which he passed, teaching the doctrines of his own creation, and acquiring a considerable following. His intellect was so acute that, usually, he was more than a match for those he met. He was fortunate enough to be accepted and honoured as a prophet during his lifetime, and not after the life had flickered out of his throat.

He was a man with many purposes. Although he championed the chief religion of his country, he strongly condemned the pernicious practices which had grown up under its cloak. He tried to bring people into the way of virtue and exposed the futility of mere reliance on ornate rituals, unaccompanied by personal effort. He broke the rules of caste by performing the obsequies at the death of his own mother, for which the priests excommunicated him. This fearless young man was a worthy successor to Buddha, the first famous caste breaker. In opposition to the priests he taught that every human being, irrespective of caste or colour, could attain to the grace of God and to knowledge of the highest Truth. He founded no special creed but held that every religion was a path to God, if sincerely held and followed into its mystic inwardness. He elaborated a complete and subtle system of philosophy in order to prove his points. He has left a large literary legacy, which is honoured in every city of sacred learning throughout the country. The pundits greatly treasure his philosophical and religious bequest, although they naturally quibble and quarrel over its meaning.

Shankara travelled throughout India wearing an ochre robe and carrying a pilgrim's staff. As a clever piece of strategy, he established four great institutions at the four points of the compass. There was one at Badrinath in the North, at Puri in the East, and so on. The central headquarters, together with a temple and monastery, were established in the South, where he began his work. To this day the South has remained the holy of holies of Hinduism. From these institutions there would emerge, when the rainy seasons were over, trained bands of monks who travelled the country to carry Shankara's message. This remarkable man died at the early age of thirty-two, though one legend has it that he simply disappeared.

The value of this information becomes apparent when I learn that his successor, whom I am to see this day, carries on the same work and the same teaching. In this connection, there exists a strange tradition. The first Shankara promised his disciples that he would still abide with them in spirit, and that he would accomplish this by the mysterious process of "overshadowing" his successors. A somewhat similar theory is attached to the office of the Grand Lama of Tibet. The predecessor in office, during his last dying moments, names the one worthy to follow him. The selected person is usually a lad of tender years, who is then taken in hand by the best teachers available and given a thorough training to fit him for his exalted post. His training is not only religious and intellectual, but also along the lines of higher Yoga and meditation practices. This training is then followed by a life of great activity in the service of his people. It is a singular fact that through all the many centuries this line has been established, not a single holder of the title has ever been known to have other than the highest and the most selfless character.

Venkataramani embellishes his narrative with stories of the remarkable gifts which Shri Shankara the Sixty-sixth possesses. There is an account of the miraculous healing of his own cousin. The latter has been crippled by rheumatism and confined to his bed for many years. Shri Shankara visits him, touches his body, and within three hours the invalid is so far better that he gets out of bed ; soon, he is completely cured.

There is the further assertion that His Holiness is credited with the power of reading the thoughts of other persons ; at any rate, Venkataramani fully believes this to be true.

§

We enter Chingleput through a palm-fringed highway and find it a tangle of whitewashed houses, huddled red roofs and narrow lanes. We get down and walk into the centre of the city, where large crowds are gathered together. I am taken into a house where a group of secretaries are busily engaged handling the huge correspondence which follows His Holiness from his headquarters at Kumbakonam. I wait in a chairless anteroom while Venkataramani sends one of the secretaries with a message to Shri Shankara. More than half an hour passes before the man returns with the reply that the audience I seek cannot be granted. His Holiness does not see his way to receiving a European ; moreover, there are two hundred people waiting for interviews already. Many persons have been staying in the town overnight in order to secure their interviews. The secretary is profuse in his apologies.

I philosophically accept the situation, but Venkataramani says that he will try to get into the presence of His Holiness as a privileged friend, and then plead my cause. Several members of the crowd murmur unpleasantly when they become aware of his intention to pass into the coveted house out of his turn. After much talk and babbling explanations, he wins through. He returns eventually, smiling and victorious.

" His Holiness will make a special exception in your case. He will see you in about one hour's time."

I fill the time with some idle wandering in the picturesque lanes which run down to the chief temple. I meet some servants who are leading a train of grey elephants and big buff-brown camels to a drinking-place. Someone points out to me the magnificent animal which carries the Spiritual Head of South India on his travels. He rides in regal fashion, borne aloft in an opulent howdah on the back of a tall elephant. It is finely covered with ornate trappings, rich cloths and gold embroideries. I watch the dignified old creature step forward along the street. Its trunk coils up and comes down again as it passes.

Remembering the time-worn custom which requires one to bring a little offering of fruits, flowers or sweetmeats when visiting a spiritual personage, I procure a gift to place before my august host. Oranges and flowers are the only things in sight and I collect as much as I can conveniently carry.

In the crowd which presses outside His Holiness's temporary residence, I forget another important custom. " Remove your shoes," Venkataramani reminds me promptly. I take them off and leave them out in the street, hoping that they will still be there when I return !

We pass through a tiny doorway and enter a bare anteroom. At the far end there is a dimly lit enclosure, where I behold a short figure standing in the shadows. I approach closer to him, put down my little offering and bow low in salutation. There is an artistic value in this ceremony which greatly appeals to me, apart from its necessity as an expression of respect and as a harmless courtesy. I know well that Shri Shankara is no Pope, for there is no such thing in Hinduism, but he is teacher and inspirer of a religious flock of vast dimensions. The whole of South India bows to his tutelage.

§

I look at him in silence. This short man is clad in the ochre-coloured robe of a monk and leans his weight on a friar's staff. I have been told that he is on the right side of forty, hence I am surprised to find his hair quite grey.

His noble face, pictured in grey and brown, takes an honoured place in the long portrait gallery of my memory. That elusive element which the French aptly term *spirituel* is present in this face. His expression is modest and mild, the large dark eyes being extraordinarily tranquil and beautiful. The nose is short, straight and classically regular. There is a rugged little beard on his chin, and the gravity of his mouth is most noticeable. Such a face might have belonged to one of the saints who graced the Christian Church during the Middle Ages, except that this one possesses the added quality of intellectuality. I suppose we of the practical West would say that he has the eyes of a dreamer. Somehow, I feel in an inexplicable way that there is something more than mere dreams behind those heavy lids.

"Your Holiness has been very kind to receive me," I remark, by way of introduction.

He turns to my companion, the writer, and says something in the vernacular. I guess its meaning correctly.

"His Holiness understands your English, but he is too afraid that you will not understand his own. So he prefers to have me translate his answers," says Venkataramani.

I shall sweep through the earlier phases of this interview, because they are more concerned with myself than with this Hindu Primate. He asks about my personal experiences in the country; he is very interested in ascertaining the exact impressions which Indian people and institutions make upon a foreigner. I give him my candid impressions, mixing praise and criticism freely and frankly.

The conversation then flows into wider channels and I am much surprised to find that he regularly reads English newspapers, and that he is well informed upon current affairs in the outside world. Indeed, he is not unaware of what the latest noise at Westminster is about, and he knows also through what painful travail the troublous infant of democracy is passing in Europe.

I remember Venkataramani's firm belief that Shri Shankara

possesses prophetic insight. It touches my fancy to press for some opinion about the world's future.

" When do you think that the political and economic conditions everywhere will begin to improve ? "

" A change for the better is not easy to come by quickly," he replies. " It is a process which must needs take some time. How can things improve when the nations spend more each year on the weapons of death ? "

" There is nevertheless much talk of disarmament to-day. Does that count ? "

" If you scrap your battleships and let your cannons rust, that will not stop war. People will continue to fight, even if they have to use sticks ! "

" But what can be done to help matters ? "

" Nothing but spiritual understanding between one nation and another, and between rich and poor, will produce goodwill and thus bring real peace and prosperity."

" That seems far off. Our outlook is hardly cheerful, then ? "

His Holiness rests his arm a little more heavily upon his staff.

" There is still God," he remarks gently.

" If there is, He seems very far away," I boldly protest.

" God has nothing but love towards mankind," comes the soft answer.

" Judging by the unhappiness and wretchedness which afflict the world to-day, He has nothing but indifference," I break out impulsively, unable to keep the bitter force of irony out of my voice. His Holiness looks at me strangely. Immediately I regret my hasty words.

" The eyes of a patient man see deeper. God will use human instruments to adjust matters at the appointed hour. The turmoil among nations, the moral wickedness among people and the suffering of miserable millions will provoke, as a reaction, some great divinely inspired man to come to the rescue. In this sense, every century has its own saviour. The process works like a law of physics. The greater the wretchedness caused by spiritual ignorance, materialism, the greater will be the man who will arise to help the world."

" Then do you expect someone to arise in our time, too ? "

" In our century," he corrects. " Assuredly. The need of the world is so great and its spiritual darkness is so thick, that an inspired man of God will surely arise."

" Is it your opinion, then, that men are becoming more degraded ? " I query.

"No, I do not think so," he replied tolerantly. "There is an indwelling divine soul in man which, in the end, must bring him back to God."

"But there are ruffians in our Western cities who behave as though there were indwelling demons in them," I counter, thinking of the modern gangster.

"Do not blame people so much as the environments into which they are born. Their surroundings and circumstances force them to become worse than they really are. That is true of both the East and West. Society must be brought into tune with a higher note. Materialism must be balanced by idealism; there is no other real cure for the world's difficulties. The troubles into which countries are everywhere being plunged are really the agonies which will force this change, just as failure is frequently a sign-post pointing to another road."

"You would like people to introduce spiritual principles into their worldly dealings, then?"

"Quite so. It is not impracticable, because it is the only way to bring about results which will satisfy everyone in the end, and which will not speedily disappear. And if there were more men who had found spiritual light in the world, it would spread more quickly. India, to its honour, supports and respects its spiritual men, though less so than in former times. If all the world were to do the same, and to take its guidance from men of spiritual vision, then all the world would soon find peace and grow prosperous."

Our conversation trails on. I am quick to notice that Shri Shankara does not decry the West in order to exalt the East, as so many in his land do. He admits that each half of the globe possesses its own set of virtues and vices, and that in this way they are roughly equal! He hopes that a wiser generation will fuse the best points of Asiatic and European civilizations into a higher and balanced social scheme.

I drop the subject and ask permission for some personal questions. It is granted without difficulty.

"How long has Your Holiness held this title?"

"Since 1907. At that time I was only twelve years old. Four years after my appointment I retired to a village on the banks of the Cauvery, where I gave myself up to meditation and study for three years. Then only did my public work begin."

"You rarely remain at your headquarters in Kumbakonam I take it?"

"The reason for that is that I was invited by the Maharajah

of Nepal in 1918 to be his guest for a while. I accepted and since then have been travelling slowly towards his state in the far north. But see !—during all those years I have not been able to advance more than a few hundred miles, because the tradition of my office requires that I stay in every village and town which I pass on the route or which invites me, if it is not too far off. I must give a spiritual discourse in the local temple and some teaching to the inhabitants."

I broach the matter of my quest and His Holiness questions me about the different Yogis or holy men I have so far met. After that, I frankly tell him :

" I would like to meet someone who has high attainments in Yoga and can give some sort of proof or demonstration of them. There are many of your holy men who can only give one more talk when they are asked for this proof. Am I asking too much ? "

The tranquil eyes meet mine.

There is a pause for a whole minute. His Holiness fingers his beard.

" If you are seeking initiation into real Yoga of the higher kind, then you are not seeking too much. Your earnestness will help you, while I can perceive the strength of your determination ; but a light is beginning to awaken within you which will guide you to what you want, without doubt."

I am not sure whether I correctly understand him.

" So far I have depended on myself for guidance. Even some of your ancient sages say that there is no other god than that which is within ourselves," I hazard.

And the answer swiftly comes :

" God is everywhere. How can one limit Him to one's own self ? He supports the entire universe."

I feel that I am getting out of my depth and immediately turn the talk away from this semi-theological strain.

" What is the most practical course for me to take ? "

" Go on with your travels. When you have finished them, think of the various Yogis and holy men you have met ; then pick out the one who makes most appeal to you. Return to him, and he will surely bestow his initiation upon you."

I look at his calm profile and admire its singular serenity.

" But suppose, Your Holiness, that none of them makes sufficient appeal to me. What then ? "

" In that case you will have to go on alone until God Himself initiates you. Practise meditation regularly ; contemplate the higher things with love in your heart ; think often of the soul and that will help to bring you to it. The best time to practise is the hour of waking ; the next best time is the hour of twilight. The world is calmer at those times and will disturb your meditations less."

He gazes benevolently at me. I begin to envy the saintly peace which dwells on his bearded face. Surely, his heart has never known the devastating upheavals which have scarred mine ? I am stirred to ask him impulsively :

" If I fail, may I then turn to you for assistance ? "

Shri Shankara gently shakes his head.

" I am at the head of a public institution, a man whose time no longer belongs to himself. My activities demand almost all my time. For years I have spent only three hours in sleep each night. How can I take personal pupils ? You must find a master who devotes his time to them."

" But I am told that real masters are rare, and that a European is unlikely to find them."

He nods his assent to my statement, but adds :

" Truth exists. It can be found."

" Can you not direct me to such a master, one who you know is competent to give me proofs of the reality of higher Yoga ? "

His Holiness does not reply till after an interval of protracted silence.

" Yes. I know of only two masters in India who could give you what you wish. One of them lives in Benares, hidden away in a large house, which is itself hidden among spacious grounds. Few people are permitted to obtain access to him ; certainly, no European has yet been able to intrude upon his seclusion. I could send you to him, but I fear that he may refuse to admit a European."

" And the other——? " My interest is strangely stirred.

" The other man lives in the interior, farther south. I visited him once and know him to be a high master. I recommend that you go to him."

" Who is he ? "

" He is called the Maharishee.[1] I have not met him, but know him to be a high master. Shall I provide you with full instructions, so that you may discover him ? "

A picture flashes suddenly before my mind's eye.

I see the yellow-robed friar, who has vainly persuaded me to

[1] The title is derived from Sanskrit. *Maha* means great : *Rishee* means sage or seer. Hence, the Great Sage.

accompany him to his teacher. I hear him murmuring the name of a hill. It is : " The Hill of the Holy Beacon."

" Many thanks, Your Holiness," I rejoin, " but I have a guide who comes from the place."

" Then you will go there ? "

I hesitate.

" All arrangements have been made for my departure from the South to-morrow," I mutter uncertainly.

" In that case I have a request to make."

" With pleasure."

" Promise me that you will not leave South India before you have met the Maharishee."

I read in his eyes a sincere desire to help me. The promise is given.

A benignant smile crosses his face.

" Do not be anxious. You shall discover that which you seek."

A murmur from the crowd which is in the street penetrates the house.

" I have taken up too much of your valuable time," I apologize. " I am indeed sorry."

Shri Shankara's grave mouth relaxes. He follows me into the ante-room and whispers something into the ear of my companion. I catch my name in the sentence.

At the door I turn to bow in farewell salutation. His Holiness calls me back to receive a parting message :

" You shall always remember me, and I shall always remember you ! "

And so, hearing these cryptic and puzzling words, I reluctantly withdraw from this interesting man, whose entire life has been dedicated to God from childhood. He is a pontiff who cares not for worldly power, because he has renounced all and resigned all. Whatever material things are given to him, he at once gives again to those who need them. His beautiful and gentle personality will surely linger in my memory.

I wander about Chingleput till evening, exploring its artistic, old-world beauty, and then seek a final glimpse of His Holiness before returning home.

I find him in the largest temple of the city. The slim, modest, yellow-robed figure is addressing a huge concourse of men, women and children. Utter silence prevails among the large audience. I cannot understand his vernacular words, but I can understand that he is holding the deep attention of all present, from the intellectual Brahmin to the illiterate peasant. I do not know, but I hazard the guess that he speaks on the profoundest topics in the simplest manner, for such is the character I read in him.

And yet, though I appreciate his beautiful soul, I envy the simple faith of his vast audience. Life, apparently, never brings them deep moods of doubt. God *is ;* and there the matter ends. They do not appear to know what it means to go through dark nights of the soul, when the world seems like the grim scene of a jungle-like struggle ; when God recedes into shadowy nothingness ; and when man's own existence seems nothing more than a fitful passage across this small, transient fragment of the universe which we call Earth.

We drive out of Chingleput under an indigo sky gemmed with stars. I listen to palms majestically waving their branches over the water's edge in an unexpected breeze.

My companion suddenly breaks the silence between us.

" You are indeed lucky ! "

" Why ? "

" Because this is the first interview which His Holiness has granted to a European writer."

" Well——? "

" That brings his blessing upon you ! "

§

It is nearly midnight when I return home. I take a last glimpse overhead. The stars stud the vast dome of the sky in countless myriads. Nowhere in Europe can one see them in such overwhelming numbers. I run up the steps leading to the veranda, flashing my pocket torch.

Out of the darkness, a crouching figure rises and greets me.

" Subramanya ! " I exclaim, startled. " What are you doing here ? " The ochre-robed Yogi indulges in one of his tremendous grins.

" Did I not promise to visit you, sir ? " He reminds me reproachfully.

" Of course ! "

In the large room, I fire a question at him.

" Your master—is he called the Maharishee ? "

It is now his turn to draw back, astonished.

" How do you know, sir ? Where could you have learnt this ? "

" Never mind. To-morrow we both start for his place. I shall change my plans."

" This is joyful news, sir."

" But I shall not stay there long, though. A few days, maybe."

I fling a few more questions at him during the next half-hour, and then, thoroughly tired, go to bed. Subramanya is quite content to sleep on a piece of palm matting which lies on the floor. He wraps himself up in a thin cotton cloth, which serves at once as a mattress, sheet and blanket, and disdains my offer of more comfortable bedding.

The next thing of which I am aware is suddenly awakening. The room is totally dark. I feel my nerves strangely tense. The atmosphere around me seems like electrified air. I pull my watch from under the pillow and, by the glow of its radium-lit dial, discover the time to be a quarter to three. It is then that I become conscious of some bright object at the foot of the bed. I immediately sit up and look straight at it.

My astounded gaze meets the face and form of His Holiness Shri Shankara. It is clearly and unmistakably visible. He does not appear to be some ethereal ghost, but rather a solid human being. There is a mysterious luminosity around the figure which separates it from the surrounding darkness.

Surely the vision is an impossible one ? Have I not left him at Chingleput ? I close my eyes tightly in an effort to test the matter. There is no difference and I still see him quite plainly !

Let it suffice that I receive the sense of a benign and friendly presence. I open my eyes and regard the kindly figure in the loose yellow robe.

The face alters, for the lips smile and seem to say :

" Be humble and then you shall find what you seek ! "

Why do I feel that a living human being is thus addressing me ? Why do I not regard it as a ghost, at least ?

The vision disappears as mysteriously as it has come. It leaves me feeling exalted, happy and unperturbed by its supernormal nature. Shall I dismiss it as a dream ? What matters it ?

There is no more sleep for me this night. I lie awake pondering over the day's meeting, over the memorable interview with His Holiness Shri Shankara of Kumbakonam, the Hierarch of God to the simple people of South India.

CHAPTER IX

THE HILL OF THE HOLY BEACON

AT the Madras terminus of the South Indian Railway, Subramanya and I board a carriage on the Ceylon boat train. For several hours we roll onwards through the most variegated scenes. Green stretches of growing rice alternate with gaunt red hills, shady plantations of stately coconut trees are followed by scattered peasants toiling in the paddy fields.

As I sit at the window, the swift Indian dusk begins to blot out the landscape and I turn my head to muse of other things. I begin to wonder at the strange things which have happened since I have worn the golden ring which Brama has given me. For my plans have changed their face ; a concatenation of unexpected circumstances has arisen to drive me farther South, instead of going farther East as I have intended. Is it possible, I ask myself, that these golden claws hold a stone which really possesses the mysterious power which the Yogi has claimed for it ? Although I endeavour to keep an open mind, it is difficult for any Westerner of scientifically trained mind to credit the idea. I dismiss the speculation from my mind, but do not succeed in driving away the uncertainty which lurks at the back of my thoughts. Why is it that my footsteps have been so strangely guided to the mountain hermitage whither I am travelling ? Why is it that two men, who both wear the yellow robe, have been coupled as destiny's agents to the extent of directing my reluctant eyes towards the Marishee ? I use this word destiny, not in its common sense, but because I am at a loss for a better one. Past experience has taught me full well that seemingly unimportant happenings sometimes play an unexpected part in composing the picture of one's life.

We leave the train, and with it the main line, forty miles from Pondicherry, that pathetic little remnant of France's territorial possessions in India. We go over to a quiet, little-used branch railroad which runs into the interior, and wait for nearly two hours in the semi-gloom of a bleak waiting-room. The holy man paces along the bleaker platform outside, his tall figure looking half-ghost, half-real in the starlight. At last the ill-timed train, which puffs infrequently up and down the line, carries us away. There are but few other passengers.

I fall into a fitful, dream-broken sleep which continues for some hours until my companion awakens me. We descend at a little wayside station and the train screeches and grinds away into the silent darkness. Night's life has not quite run out and so we sit in a bare and comfortless little waiting-room, whose small kerosene lamp we light ourselves.

We wait patiently while day fights with darkness for supremacy. When a pale dawn emerges at last, creeping bit by bit through a small barred window in the back of our room, I peer out at such portion of our surroundings as becomes visible. Out of the morning haze there rises the faint outline of a solitary hill, apparently some few miles distant. The base is of impressive extent and the body of ample girth, but the head is not to be seen, being yet thick-shrouded in the dawn mists.

My guide ventures outside, where he discovers a man loudly snoring in his tiny bullock cart. A shout or two brings the driver back to this mundane existence, thus making him aware of business waiting in the offing. When informed of our destination, he seems but too eager to transport us. I gaze somewhat dubiously at his narrow conveyance—a bamboo canopy balanced on two wheels. Anyway, we clamber aboard and the man bundles the luggage after us. The holy man manages to compress himself into the minimum space which a human being can possibly occupy; I crouch under the low canopy with legs dangling out in space; the driver squats upon the shaft between his bulls with his chin almost touching his knees, and the problem of accommodation being thus solved more or less satisfactorily, we bid him be off.

Our progress is anything but rapid, despite the best efforts of a pair of strong, small, white bullocks. These charming creatures are very useful as draught animals in the interior of India, because they endure heat better than horses and are less fastidious in the matter of diet. The customs of the quiet villages and small townships of the interior have not changed very much in the course of centuries. The bullock carts which transported the traveller from place to place in B.C. 100, transport him still, two thousand years after.

Our driver, whose face is the colour of beaten bronze, has

taken much pride in his animals. Their long, beautifully curved horns are adorned with shapely gilt ornaments ; their thin legs have tinkling brass bells tied to them. He guides them by means of a rein threaded through their nostrils. While their feet merrily jog away upon the dust-laden road, I watch the quick tropic dawn come on apace.

An attractive landscape shapes itself both on our right and left. No drab flat plain this, for heights and hillocks are not long absent from the eyes whenever one searches the horizon's length. The road traverses a district of red earth dotted with terrains of scrubby thorn-bush and a few bright emerald paddy fields.

A peasant with toil-worn face passes us. No doubt, he is going out to his long day's work in the fields. Soon we overtake a girl with a brass water pitcher mounted upon her head. A single vermilion robe is wrapped around her body, but her shoulders are left bare. A blood-coloured ruby ornaments one nostril, and a pair of gold bracelets gleam on her arms in the pale morning sunlight. The blackness of her skin reveals her as a Dravidian—as indeed most of the inhabitants of these parts probably are, save the Brahmins and Muhammedans. These Dravidian girls are usually gay and happy by nature. I find them more talkative than their brown countrywomen and more musical in voice.

The girl stares at us with unfeigned surprise and I guess that Europeans rarely visit this part of the interior.

And so we ride on until the little township is reached. Its houses are prosperous-looking and arranged into streets which cluster around two sides of an enormous temple. If I am not mistaken, the latter is a quarter of a mile long. I gather a rough conception of its architectural massiveness a while later when we reach one of its spacious gateways. We halt for a minute or two and I peer inside to register some fleeting glimpses of the place. Its strangeness is as impressive as its size. Never before have I seen a structure like this. A vast quadrangle surrounds the enormous interior, which looks like a labyrinth. I perceive that the four high enclosing walls have been scorched and coloured by hundreds of years of exposure to the fierce tropical sunshine. Each wall is pierced by a single gateway, above which rises a queer superstructure consisting of a giant pagoda. The latter seems strangely like an ornate, sculptured pyramid. Its lower part is built of stone, but the upper portion seems to be thickly-plastered brickwork. The pagoda is divided into many storeys, but the entire surface is profusely decorated with a variety of figures and carvings. In addition to these four entrance towers, I count no less than five others which rise up within the interior of the temple. How curiously they remind one of Egyptian pyramids in the similarity of outline!

My last glimpse is of long roofed cloisters, of serried ranks of flat stone pillars in large numbers, of a great central enclosure, of dim shrines and dark corridors and many little buildings. I make a mental note to explore this interesting place before long.

The bullocks trot off and we emerge into open country again. The scenes which we pass are quite pretty. The road is covered with red dust; on either side there are low bushes and occasional clumps of tall trees. There are many birds hidden among the branches, for I hear the flutter of their wings, as well as the last notes of that beautiful chorus which is their morning song all over the world.

Dotted along the route are a number of charming little wayside shrines. The differences of architectural style surprise me, until I conclude that they have been erected during changing epochs. Some are highly ornate, over-decorated and elaborately carved in the usual Hindu manner, but the larger ones are supported by flat-surfaced pillars which I have seen nowhere else but in the South. There are even two or three shrines whose classical severity of outline is almost Grecian.

I judge that we have now travelled about five or six miles, when we reach the lower slopes of the hill whose vague outline I had seen from the station. It rises like a reddish-brown giant in the clear morning sunlight. The mists have now rolled away, revealing a broad skyline at the top. It is an isolated upland of red soil and brown rock, barren for the most part, with large tracts almost treeless, and with masses of stone split into great boulders tossed about in chaotic disorder.

"Arunachala! The sacred red mountain!" exclaims my companion, noticing the direction of my gaze. A fervent expression of adoration passes across his face. He is momentarily rapt in ecstasy, like some medieval saint.

I ask him, "Does the name mean anything?"

"I have just given you the meaning," he replies with a smile. "The name is composed of two words, 'Aruna' and 'Achala,' which mean red mountain, and since it is also the name of the presiding deity of the temple, its full translation should be 'sacred red mountain.'"

"Then where does the holy beacon come in?"

"Ah! Once a year the temple priests celebrate their central festival. Immediately that occurs within the temple, a huge fire blazes out on top of the mountain, its flame being fed with vast quantities of butter and camphor. It burns for many days and can be seen for many miles around. Whoever sees it, at once prostrates himself before it. It symbolizes the fact that this mountain is sacred ground, overshadowed by a great deity."

The hill now towers over our heads. It is not without its rugged grandeur, this lonely peak patterned with red, brown and grey boulders, thrusting its flat head thousands of feet into the pearly sky. Whether the holy man's words have affected me or whether for some unaccountable cause, I find a queer feeling of awe arising in me as I meditate upon the picture of the sacred mountain, as I gaze up wonderingly at the steep incline of Arunachala.

"Do you know," whispers my companion, "that this mountain is not only esteemed holy ground, but the local traditions dare to assert that the gods placed it there to mark the spiritual centre of the world!"

This little bit of legend forces me to smile. How naïve it is!

At length I learn that we are approaching the Maharishee's hermitage. We turn aside from the road and move down a rough path which brings us to a thick grove of coconut and mango trees. We cross this until the path suddenly comes to an abrupt termination before an unlocked gate. The driver descends, pushes the gate open, and then drives us into a large unpaved courtyard. I stretch out my cramped limbs, descend to the ground, and look around.

The cloistered domain of the Maharishee is hemmed in at the front by closely growing trees and a thickly clustered garden; it is screened at the back and side by hedgerows of shrub and cactus, while away to the West stretches the scrub jungle and what appears to be dense forest. It is most picturesquely placed on a lower spur of the hill. Secluded and apart, it seems a fitting spot for those who wish to pursue profound themes of meditation.

Two small buildings with thatched roofs occupy the left side of the courtyard. Adjoining them stands a long, modern structure, whose red-tiled roof comes sharply down into overhanging eaves. A small veranda stretches across a part of the front.

The centre of the courtyard is marked by a large well. I watch a boy, who is naked to the waist and dark-skinned to the point of blackness, slowly draw a bucket of water to the surface with the aid of a creaking hand windlass.

The sound of our entry brings a few men out of the buildings into the courtyard. Their dress is extremely varied. One is garbed in nothing but a ragged loin-cloth, but another is prosperously attired in a white silk robe. They stare questioningly at us. My guide grins hugely, evidently enjoying their astonishment. He crosses to them and says something in Tamil. The expression on their faces changes immediately, for they smile in unison and beam at me with pleasure. I like their faces and their bearing.

" We shall now go into the hall of the Maharishee," announces the holy man of the yellow robe, bidding me follow him. I pause outside the uncovered stone veranda and remove my shoes. I gather up the little pile of fruits which I have brought as an offering, and pass into an open doorway.

§

Twenty brown-and-black faces flash their eyes upon us. Their owners are squatting in half-circles on a red-tiled floor. They are grouped at a respectful distance from the corner which lies farthest to the right hand of the door. Apparently everyone has been facing this corner just prior to our entry. I glance there for a moment and perceive a seated figure upon a long white divan, but it suffices to tell me that here indeed is the Maharishee.

My guide approaches the divan, prostrates himself prone on the floor, and buries his eyes under folded hands.

The divan is but a few paces away from a broad high window in the end wall. The light falls clearly upon the Maharishee and I can take in every detail of his profile, for he is seated gazing rigidly through the window in the precise direction whence we have come this morning. His head does not move, so, thinking to catch his eye and greet him as I offer the fruits, I move quietly over to the window, place the gift before him, and retreat a pace or two.

A small brass brazier stands before his couch. It is filled with burning charcoal, and a pleasant odour tells me that some aromatic powder has been thrown on the glowing embers. Close by is an incense burner filled with joss sticks. Threads of bluish grey smoke arise and float in the air, but the pungent perfume is quite different.

I fold a thin cotton blanket upon the floor and sit down, gazing expectantly at the silent figure in such a rigid attitude upon the couch. The Maharishee's body is almost nude, except for a thin, narrow loin-cloth, but that is common enough in these parts. His skin is slightly copper-coloured, yet quite fair in comparison with that of the average South Indian. I judge him to be a tall man; his age somewhere in the early fifties. His head, which is covered with closely cropped grey hair, is well formed. The high and broad expanse of forehead gives intellectual distinction to his personality. His features are more European than Indian. Such is my first impression.

The couch is covered with white cushions and the Maharishee's feet rest upon a magnificently marked tiger skin.

Pin-drop silence prevails throughout the long hall. The sage remains perfectly still, motionless, quite undisturbed at our arrival. A swarthy disciple sits on the floor at the other side of the divan. He breaks into the quietude by beginning to pull at a rope which works a punkah-fan made of bamboo matting. The fan is fixed to a wooden beam and suspended immediately above the sage's head. I listen to its rhythmic purring, the while I look full into the eyes of the seated figure in the hope of catching his notice. They are dark brown, medium-sized and wide open.

If he is aware of my presence, he betrays no hint, gives no sign. His body is supernaturally quiet, as steady as a statue. Not once does he catch my gaze, for his eyes continue to look into remote space, and infinitely remote it seems. I find this scene strangely reminiscent. Where have I seen its like? I rummage through the portrait gallery of memory and find the picture of the Sage Who Never Speaks, that recluse whom I visited in his isolated cottage near Madras, that man whose body seemed cut from stone, so motionless it was. There is a curious similarity in this unfamiliar stillness of body which I now behold in the Maharishee.

It is an ancient theory of mine that one can take the inventory of a man's soul from his eyes. But before those of the Maharishee I hesitate, puzzled and baffled.

The minutes creep by with unutterable slowness. First they mount up to a half-hour by the hermitage clock which hangs on a wall; this too passes by and becomes a whole hour. Yet no one in the hall seems to stir; certainly no one dares to speak. I reach a point of visual concentration where I have forgotten the existence of all save this silent figure on the couch. My offering of fruits remains unregarded on the small carved table which stands before him.

My guide has given me no warning that his master will receive me as I had been received by the Sage Who Never Speaks. It has come upon me abruptly, this strange reception characterized by complete indifference. The first thought which would come into the mind of any European, " Is this man merely posing for the benefit of his devotees ? " crosses my mind once or twice but I soon rule it out. He is certainly in a trance condition, though my guide has not informed me that his master indulges in trances. The next thought which occupies my mind, " Is this state of mystical contemplation nothing more than meaningless vacancy ? " has a longer sway but I let it go for the simple reason that I cannot answer it.

There is something in this man which holds my attention as steel filings are held by a magnet. I cannot turn my gaze away from him. My initial bewilderment, my perplexity at being totally ignored, slowly fade away as this strange fascination begins to grip me more firmly. But it is not till the second hour of the uncommon scene that I become aware of a silent, resistless change which is taking place within my mind. One by one, the questions which I have prepared in the train with such meticulous accuracy drop away. For it does not now seem to matter whether they are asked or not, and it does not seem to matter whether I solve the problems which have hitherto troubled me. I know only that a steady river of quietness seems to be flowing near me, that a great peace is penetrating the inner reaches of my being, and that my thought-tortured brain is beginning to arrive at some rest.

How small seem those questions which I have asked myself with such frequency ! How petty grows the panorama of the lost years ! I perceive with sudden clarity that the intellect creates its own problems and then makes itself miserable trying to solve them. This is indeed a novel concept to enter the mind of one who has hitherto placed such high value upon intellect.

I surrender myself to the steadily deepening sense of restfulness until two hours have passed. The passage of time now provokes no irritation, because I feel that the chains of mind-made problems are being broken and thrown away. And then, little by little, a new question takes the field of consciousness.

" Does this man, the Maharishee, emanate the perfume of spiritual peace as the flower emanates fragrance from its petals ? "

I do not consider myself a competent person to apprehend

spirituality, but I have personal reactions to other people. This dawning suspicion that the mysterious peace which has arisen within me must be attributed to the geographical situation in which I am now placed, is my reaction to the personality of the Maharishee. I begin to wonder whether, by some radio-activity of the soul, some unknown telepathic process, the stillness which invades the troubled waters of my own soul really comes from him. Yet he remains completely impassive, completely unaware of my very existence, it seems.

Comes the first ripple. Someone approaches me and whispers in my ear, " Did you not wish to question the Maharishee ? "

He may have lost patience, this quondam guide of mine. More likely, he imagines that I, a restless European, have reached the limit of my own patience. Alas, my inquisitive friend ! Truly I came here to question your master, but now . . . I, who am at peace with all the world and with myself, why should I trouble my head with questions ? I feel that the ship of my soul is beginning to slip its moorings ; a wonderful sea waits to be crossed ; yet you would draw me back to the noisy port of this world, just when I am about to start the great adventure !

But the spell is broken. As if this infelicitous intrusion is a signal, figures rise from the floor and begin to move about the hall, voices float up to my hearing, and—wonder of wonders! —the dark brown eyes of the Maharishee flicker once or twice. Then the head turns, the face moves slowly, very slowly, and bends downward at an angle. A few more moments, and it has brought me into the ambit of its vision. For the first time the sage's mysterious gaze is directed upon me. It is plain that he has now awakened from his long trance.

The intruder, thinking perhaps that my lack of response is a sign that I have not heard him, repeats his question aloud. But in those lustrous eyes which are gently staring at me, I read another question, albeit unspoken.

" Can it be—is it possible—that you are still tormented with distracting doubts when you have now glimpsed the deep mental peace which you—and all men—may attain ? "

The peace overwhelms me. I turn to the guide and answer :

" No. There is nothing I care to ask now. Another time——"

I feel now that some explanation of my visit is required of me, not by the Maharishee himself but by the little crowd which has begun to talk so animatedly. I know from the accounts of my guide that only a handful of these people are resident disciples, and that the others are visitors from the country around. Strangely enough, at this point my guide himself arises and makes the required introduction. He speaks energetically in Tamil, using a wealth of gesture while he explains matters to the assembled company. I fear that his explanation is mixing a little fable with his facts, for it draws cries of wonder.

§

The midday meal is over. The sun unmercifully raises the afternoon temperature to a degree I have never before experienced. But then, we are now in a latitude not so far from the Equator. For once I am grateful that India is favoured with a climate which does not foster activity, because most of the people have disappeared into the shady groves to take a siesta. I can therefore approach the Maharishee in the way I prefer, without undue notice or fuss.

I enter the large hall and sit down near him. He half-reclines upon some white cushions placed on the divan. An attendant pulls steadily at the cord which operates the punkah-fan. The soft burr of the rope and the gentle swish of the fan as it moves through the sultry air sound pleasantly in my ears.

The Maharishee holds a folded manuscript book in his hands; he is writing something with extreme slowness. A few minutes after my entry he puts the book aside and calls a disciple. A few words pass between them in Tamil and the man tells me that his master wishes to reiterate his regrets at my inability to partake of their food. He explains that they live a simple life, and never having catered for Europeans before do not know what the latter eat. I thank the Maharishee, and say that I shall be glad to share their unspiced dishes with them; for the rest, I shall procure some food from the township. I add that I regard the question of diet as being far less important than the quest which has brought me to his hermitage.

The sage listens intently, his face calm, imperturbable and non-committal.

"It is a good object," he comments at length.

This encourages me to enlarge upon the same theme.

"Master, I have studied our Western philosophies and sciences, lived and worked among the people of our crowded cities, tasted their pleasures and allowed myself to be caught up into their ambitions. Yet I have also gone into solitary places and wandered there amid the loneliness of deep thought. I have questioned the sages of the West; now I have turned my face towards the East. I seek more light."

The Maharishee nods his head, as if to say, "Yes, I quite understand."

"I have heard many opinions, listened to many theories. Intellectual proofs of one belief or another lie piled up all around me. I am tired of them, sceptical of anything which cannot be proved by personal experience. Forgive me for saying so, but I am not religious. Is there anything beyond man's material existence. If so, how can I realize it for myself?"

The three or four devotees who are gathered around us stare in surprise. Have I offended the subtle etiquette of the hermitage by speaking so brusquely and boldly to their master? I do not know; perhaps I do not care. The accumulated weight of many years' desire has unexpectedly escaped my control and passed beyond my lips. If the Maharishee is the right kind of man, surely he will understand and brush aside mere lapses from convention.

He makes no verbal reply but appears to have dropped into some train of thought. Because there is nothing else to do and because my tongue has now been loosened, I address him for the third time:

"The wise men of the West, our scientists, are greatly honoured for their cleverness. Yet they have confessed that they can throw but little light upon the hidden truth behind life. It is said that there are some in your land who can give what our Western sages fail to reveal. Is this so? Can you assist me to experience enlightenment? Or is the search itself a mere delusion?"

I have now reached my conversational objective and decide to await the Maharishee's response. He continues to stare thoughtfully at me. Perhaps he is pondering over my questions. Ten minutes pass in silence.

At last his lips open and he says gently:

"You say I. '*I* want to know.' Tell me, who is that *I*?"

What does he mean? He has now cut across the services of the interpreter and speaks direct to me in English. Bewilderment creeps across my brain.

"I am afraid I do not understand your question," I reply blankly.

"Is it not clear. Think again!"

I puzzle over his words once more. An idea suddenly

flashes into my head. I point a finger towards myself and mention my name.

"And do you know him?"

"All my life!" I smile back at him.

"But that is only your body! Again I ask, 'Who are *you?*'"

I cannot find a ready answer to this extraordinary query.

The Maharishee continues:

"Know first that *I* and then you shall know the truth."

My mind hazes again. I am deeply puzzled. This bewilderment finds verbal expression. But the Maharishee has evidently reached the limit of his English, for he turns to the interpreter and the answer is slowly translated to me:

"There is only one thing to be done. Look into your own self. Do this in the right way and you shall find the answer to all your problems."

It is a strange rejoinder. But I ask him:

"What must one do? What method can I pursue?"

"Through deep reflection on the nature of one's self, and through constant meditation, the light can be found."

"I have frequently given myself up to meditation upon the truth, but I see no signs of progress."

"How do you know that no progress has been made? It is not easy to perceive one's progress in the spiritual realm."

"Is the help of a master necessary?"

"It might be."

"Can a master help a man to look into his own self in the way you suggest?"

"He can give the man all that he needs for this quest. Such a thing can be perceived through personal experience."

"How long will it take to get some enlightenment with a master's help?"

"It all depends on the maturity of the seeker's mind. The gunpowder catches fire in an instant, while much time is needed to set fire to the coal."

I receive a queer feeling that the sage dislikes to discuss the subject of masters and their methods. Yet my mental pertinacity is strong enough to override this feeling, and I address a further question on the matter to him. He turns a stolid face toward the window, gazes out at the expanse of hilly landscape beyond, and vouchsafes no answer. I take the hint and drop the subject.

"Will the Maharishee express an opinion about the future of the world, for we are living in critical times?"

"Why should you trouble yourself about the future?" demands the sage. "You do not even properly know about the present! Take care of the present; the future will then take care of itself."

Another rebuff! But I do not yield so easily on this occasion, for I come from a world where the tragedies of life press far more heavily on people than they do in this peaceful jungle retreat.

"Will the world soon enter a new era of friendliness and mutual help, or will it go down into chaos and war?" I persist.

The Maharishee does not seem at all pleased, but nevertheless he makes a reply.

"There is One who governs the world, and it is His look-out to look after the world. He who has given life to the world, knows how to look after it also. He bears the burden of this world, not you."

"Yet if one looks around with unprejudiced eyes, it is difficult to see where this benevolent regard comes in," I object.

The sage appears to be still less pleased. Yet his answer comes:

"As you are, so is the world. Without understanding yourself, what is the use of trying to understand the world? This is a question that seekers after truth need not consider. People waste their energies over all such questions. First, find out the truth behind yourself; then you will be in a better position to understand the truth behind the world, of which yourself is a part."

There is an abrupt pause. An attendant approaches and lights another incense stick. The Maharishee watches the blue smoke curl its way upwards and then picks up his manuscript book. He unfolds its pages and begins to work on it again, thus dismissing me from the field of his attention.

This renewed indifference of his plays like cold water upon my self-esteem. I sit around for another quarter of an hour, but I can see that he is in no mood to answer my questions. Feeling that our conversation is really at an end, I rise from the tiled floor, place my hands together in farewell, and leave him.

§

I have sent someone to the township with orders to fetch a conveyance, for I wish to inspect the temple. I request him to find a horsed carriage, if there is one in the place, for a bullock cart is picturesque to look at, but hardly as rapid and comfortable as one could wish.

I find a two-wheeled pony carriage waiting for me as I enter the courtyard. It possesses no seat, but such an item no longer troubles me. The driver is a fierce-looking fellow with a soiled red turban on his head. His only other garment is a long piece of unbleached cloth made into a waistband, with one end passing between his thighs and then tucking into his waist.

A long, dusty ride and then at last the entrance to the great temple, with its rising storeys of carved reliefs, greets us. I leave the carriage and begin a cursory exploration.

"I cannot say how old is the temple of Arunachala," remarks my companion in response to a question, "but as you can see its age must extend back hundreds of years."

Around the gates and in the approaches to the temple are a few little shops and gaudy booths, set up under overhanging palms. Beside them sit humbly dressed vendors of holy pictures and sellers of little brass images of Shiva and other gods. I am struck by the preponderance of representations of the former deity, for in other places Krishna and Rama seem to hold first place. My guide offers an explanation.

"According to our sacred legends, the god Shiva once appeared as a flame of fire on the top of the sacred red mountain. Therefore the priests of the temple light the large beacon once a year in memory of this event, which must have happened thousands of years ago. I suppose the temple was built to celebrate it, as Shiva still overshadows the mountain."[1]

A few pilgrims are idly examining the stalls, where one can buy, not only these little brass deities, but also gaudy chromolithographs picturing some event from the sacred stories, books of a religious character, blotchily printed in Tamil and Telegu languages, and coloured paints wherewith to mark on one's forehead the fitting caste or sect symbol.

A leprous beggar comes hesitatingly towards me. The flesh of his limbs is crumbling away. He is apparently not certain whether I shall have him driven off, poor fellow, or whether he will be able to touch my pity. His face is rigid with his terrible disease. I feel ashamed as I place some alms on the ground, but I fear to touch him.

The gateway, which is shaped into a pyramid of carven figures, next engages my attention. This great towered portico

[1] We Westerners may regard these deities as fantastic personifications of religious ideas, but the Hindus themselves do not doubt they really exist as real beings.

looks like some pyramid out of Egypt with its pointed top chopped off. Together with its three fellows, it dominates the countryside. One sees them miles away long before one approaches them.

The face of the pagoda is lined with profuse carvings and quaint little statues. The subjects have been drawn from sacred myth and legend. They represent a queer jumble. One perceives the solitary forms of Hindu divinities entranced into devout meditation, or observes their intertwined shapes engaged in amorous embraces, and one wonders. It reminds one that there is something in Hinduism for all tastes, such is the all-inclusive nature of this creed.

I enter the precincts of the temple, to find myself in part of an enormous quadrangle. The vast structure encloses a labyrinth of colonnades, cloisters, galleries, shrines, rooms, corridors, covered and uncovered spaces. Here is no stone building whose columned beauty stays one's emotions in a few minutes of silent wonder, as do those courts of the deities near Athens, but rather a gloomy sanctuary of dark mysteries. The vast recesses awe me with their chill air of aloofness. The place is a maze, but my companion walks with confident feet. Outside, the pagodas have looked attractive with their reddish stone colouring, but inside the stonework is ashen grey.

We pass through a long cloister with solid walls and flat, quaintly carved pillars supporting the roofs. We move into dim corridors and dark chambers and eventually arrive at a vast portico which stands in the outer court of this ancient fane.

"The Hall of a Thousand Pillars!" announces my guide as I gaze at the time-greyed structure. A serried row of flat, carved, gigantic stone columns stretches before me. The place is lonely and deserted; its monstrous pillars loom mysteriously out of the semi-gloom. I approach them more closely to study the old carvings which line many of their faces. Each pillar is composed of a single block of stone, and even the roof which it supports is composed of large pieces of flat stone. Once again I see gods and goddesses disporting themselves with the help of the sculptor's art; once again the carved faces of animals familiar and unfamiliar stare at me.

We wander on across the flagstones of these pillared galleries, pass through dark passages lit here and there by small bowl-lamps, whose wicks are sunk in castor oil, and thus arrive near a central enclosure. It is pleasant to emerge once again in the bright sunshine as we cross over to the enclosure. One can now observe the five shorter pagodas which dot the interior of the temple. They are formed precisely like the pyramidal towers which mark the entrance gateways in the high-walled quadrangle. I examine the one which stands near us and arrive at the conclusion that it is built of brick, and that its decorated surface is not really stone-carved, but modelled out of baked clay or some durable plaster. Some of the figures have evidently been picked out with paint, but the colours have now faded.

We enter the enclosure and after wandering through some more long, dark passages in this stupendous temple, my guide warns me that we are approaching the central shrine, where European feet may not walk. But though the holy of holies is forbidden to the infidel, yet the latter is allowed to catch a glimpse from a dark corridor which leads to the threshold. As if to confirm his warning I hear the beating of drums, the banging of gongs and the droning incantations of priests mingling into a monotonous rhythm that sounds rather eerie in the darkness of the old sanctuary.

I take my glimpse, expectantly. Out of the gloom there rises a golden flame set before an idol, two or three dim altar lights, and the sight of a few worshippers engaged in some ritual. I cannot distinguish the forms of the priestly musicians, but now I hear the conch horn and the cymbal add their harsh, weird notes to the music.

My companion whispers that it would be better for me not to stay any longer, as my presence will be decidedly unwelcome to the priests. Thereupon we withdraw into the somnolent sanctity of the outer parts of the temple. My exploration is at an end.

When we reach the gateway once more, I have to step aside because an elderly Brahmin sits on the ground in the middle of the path with a little brass water-jug beside him. He paints a gaudy caste mark on his forehead, holding a broken bit of mirror in his left hand. The red-and-white trident which presently appears upon his brow—sign of an orthodox Hindu of the South—gives him, in Western eyes, the grotesque appearance of a clown. A shrivelled old man, who sits in a booth by the temple gates and sells little images of holy Shiva, raises his eyes to meet mine and I pause to buy something at his unuttered request.

Somewhere in the far end of the township I espy the gleaming whiteness of a marble minaret, so I leave the temple and drive to the local mosque. Something inside me always thrills to the graceful arches of a mosque and to the delicate beauty of cupolas. Once again I remove my shoes and enter the charming white building. How well it has been planned, for its vaulted height inevitably elevates one's mood! There are a few worshippers present; they sit, kneel or prostrate themselves upon their small, colourful prayer rugs. There are no mysterious shrines here, no gaudy images, for the Prophet has written that nothing shall come between a man and God—not even a priest! All worshippers are equal before the face of Allah. There is neither priest nor pundit, no hierarchy of superior beings to interpose themselves in a man's thoughts when he turns towards Mecca.

As we return through the main street I note the money-changers' booths, the sweetmeat stalls, the cloth merchant's shop and the sellers of grain and rice—all existing for the benefit of pilgrims to the ancient sanctuary which has called the place into being.

I am now eager to get back to the Maharishee, and the driver urges his pony to cover the distance which lies before us at a rapid pace. I turn my head and take a final glimpse of the temple of Arunachala. The nine sculptured towers rise like pylons into the air. They speak to me of the patient toil in the name of God which has gone into the making of the old temple, for it has undoubtedly taken more than a man's lifetime to construct. And again that queer reminiscence of Egypt penetrates my mind. Even the domestic architecture of the streets possesses an Egyptian character in the low houses and thick walls.

Shall a day ever come when these temples will be abandoned and left, silent and deserted, to crumble slowly into the red and grey dust whence they have emerged? Or will man find new gods and build new fanes wherein to worship them?

While our pony gallops along the road towards the hermitage which lies on one of the slopes of yonder rock-strewn hill, I realize with a catch in my breath that Nature is unrolling an entire pageant of beauty before our eyes. How often have I waited for this hour in the East, when the sun, with much splendour, goes to rest upon its bed of night! An Oriental sunset holds the heart with its lovely play of vivid colours. And yet the whole event is over so quickly, an affair of less than half an hour.

Those lingering autumnal evenings of Europe are almost unknown here. Out in the west a great flaming ball of fire begins its visible descent into the jungle. It assumes the most striking orange hue as a prelude to its rapid disappearance from the vault of heaven. The sky around it takes on all the colours of the spectrum, providing our eyes with an artistic feast which no painter could ever provide. The fields and groves around us have entered into an entranced stillness. No more can the chirruping of little birds be heard. The chatter of wild monkeys has come to an end. The giant circle of red fire is quickly fading into some other dimension. Evening's curtain falls thicker yet and soon the whole panorama of thrusting tongues of flame and outspread colours sinks away into darkness.

The calmness sinks into my thoughts, the loveliness of it all touches my heart. How can one forget these benign minutes which the fates have portioned us, when they make us play with the thought that, under the cruel face of life, a benevolent and beautiful Power may yet be hiding? These minutes put our commonplace hours to shame. Out of the dark void they come like meteors, to light a transient trail of hope and then to pass away from our ken.

§

Fireflies whirl about the hermitage garden, drawing strange patterns of light on the background of darkness, as we drive into the palm-fringed courtyard. And when I enter the long hall and drop to a seat on the floor, the sublime silence appears to have reached this place and pervaded the air.

The assembled company squats in rows around the hall, but among them there is no noise and no talk. Upon the corner couch sits the Maharishee, his feet folded beneath him, his hands resting unconcernedly upon his knees. His figure strikes me anew as being simple, modest; yet withal it is dignified and impressive. His head is nobly poised, like the head of some Homeric sage. His eyes gaze immovably towards the far end of the hall. That strange steadiness of sight is as puzzling as ever. Has he been merely watching through the window the last ray of light fade out of the sky, or is he so wrapt in some dreamlike abstraction as to see naught of this material world at all?

The usual cloud of incense floats among the wooden rafters of the roof. I settle down and try to fix my eyes on the Maharishee, but after a while feel a delicate urge to close them. It is not long before I fall into a half sleep, lulled by the intangible peace which, in the sage's proximity, begins to penetrate me more deeply. Ultimately there comes a gap in my consciousness and then I experience a vivid dream.

It seems that I become a little boy of five. I stand on a rough path which winds up and around the sacred hill of Arunachala, and hold the Maharishee's hand; but now he is a great towering figure at my side, for he seems to have grown to giant's size. He leads me away from the hermitage and, despite the impenetrable darkness of the night, guides me along the path which we both slowly walk together. After a while the stars and the moon conspire to bestow a faint light upon our surroundings. I notice that the Maharishee carefully guides me around fissures in the rocky soil and between monstrous boulders that are shakily perched. The hill is steep and our ascent is slow. Hidden in narrow clefts between the rocks and boulders or sheltered by clusters of low bushes, tiny hermitages and inhabited caves come into view. As we pass by, the inhabitants emerge to greet us and, although their forms take on a ghostly appearance in the starlight, I recognize that they are Yogis of varying kinds. We never stop for them, but continue to walk until the top of the peak is reached. We halt at last, my heart throbbing with a strange anticipation of some momentous event about to befall me.

The Maharishee turns and looks down into my face; I, in turn, gaze expectantly up at him. I become aware of a mysterious change taking place with great rapidity in my heart and mind. The old motives which have lured me on begin to desert me. The urgent desires which have sent my feet hither and thither vanish with incredible swiftness. The dislikes, misunderstandings, coldnesses and selfishness which have marked my dealings with many of my fellows collapse into the abyss of nothingness. An untellable peace falls upon me and I know now that there is nothing further that I shall ask from life.

Suddenly the Maharishee bids me turn my gaze away to the bottom of the hill. I obediently do so and to my astonishment discover that the Western hemisphere of our globe lies stretched out far below. It is crowded with millions of people; I can vaguely discern them as masses of forms, but the night's darkness still enshrouds them.

The sage's voice comes to my ears, his words slowly uttered:

"When you go back there, you shall have this peace which you now feel. But its price will be that you shall henceforth cast aside the idea that you are this body or this brain. When this peace will flow into you, then you shall have to forget your own self, for you will have turned your life over to THAT!"

And the Maharishee places one end of a thread of silver light in my hand.

I awaken from that extraordinarily vivid dream with the sense of its penetrating sublimity yet upon me. Immediately the Maharishee's eyes meet mine. His face is now turned in my direction, and he is looking fixedly into my eyes.

What lies behind that dream? For the desires and bitternesses of personal life fade for a while into oblivion. That condition of lofty indifference to self and profound pity for my fellows which I have dreamt into being, does not take its departure even though I am now awake. 'Tis a strange experience.

But if the dream has any verity in it, then the thing will not last; it is not yet for me.

How long have I been sunk in dream? For everyone in the hall now begins to rise and to prepare for sleep. I must perforce follow the example.

It is too stuffy to sleep in that long, sparsely ventilated hall, so I choose the courtyard. A tall, grey-bearded disciple brings me a lantern and advises me to keep it burning throughout the night. There is a possibility of unwelcome visitors, such as snakes and even cheetahs, but they are likely to keep clear of a light.

The earth is baked hard and I possess no mattress, with the result that I do not fall asleep for some hours. But no matter —I have enough to think over, for I feel that in the Maharishee I have met the most mysterious personality whom life has yet brought within the orbit of my experience.

The sage seems to carry something of great moment to me, yet I cannot easily determine its precise nature. It is intangible, imponderable, perhaps spiritual. Each time I think of him to-night, each time I remember that vivid dream, a peculiar sensation pierces me and causes my heart to throb with vague, but lofty expectations.

§

During the ensuing days I endeavour to get into closer contact with the Maharishee, but fail. There are three reasons for this failure. The first arises naturally out of his own reserved nature, his obvious dislike of argument and discussion, his stolid indifference to one's beliefs and opinions. It becomes perfectly obvious that the sage has no wish to convert anyone to his own ideas, whatever they may be, and no desire to add a single person to his following.

The second cause is certainly a strange one, but nevertheless it exists. Since the evening of that peculiar dream, I feel a great awe whenever I enter his presence. The questions which would otherwise have come chatteringly from my lips are hushed, because it seems almost sacrilege to regard him as a person with whom one can talk and argue on an equal plane, so far as common humanity is concerned.

The third cause of my failure is simple enough. Almost always there are several other persons present in the hall, and I feel disinclined to bring out my private thoughts in their presence. After all, I am a stranger to them and a foreigner in this district. That I voice a different language to some of them is a fact of little import, but that I possess a cynical, sceptical outlook unstirred by religious emotion is a fact of much import when I attempt to give utterance to that outlook. I have no desire to hurt their pious susceptibilities, but I have also no desire to discuss matters from an angle which makes little appeal to me. So, to some extent, this thing makes me tongue-tied.

It is not easy to find a smooth way across all three barriers ; several times I am on the point of putting a question to the Maharishee, but one of the three factors intervenes to cause my failure.

My proposed week-end quickly passes and I extend it to a week. The first conversation which I have had with the Maharishee worthy of the name is likewise the last. Beyond one or two quite perfunctory and conventional scraps of talk, I find myself unable to get to grips with the man.

The week passes and I extend it to a fortnight. Each day I sense the beautiful peace of the sage's mental atmosphere, the serenity which pervades the very air around him.

The last day of my visit arrives and yet I am no closer to him. My stay has been a tantalizing mixture of sublime moods and disappointing failures to effect any worth-while personal contact with the Maharishee. I look around the hall and feel a slight despondency. Most of these men speak a different language, both outwardly and inwardly ; how can I hope to come closer to them ? I look at the sage himself. He sits there on Olympian heights and watches the panorama of life as one apart. There is a mysterious property in this man which differentiates him from all others I have met. I feel, somehow, that he does not belong to us, the human race, so much as he belongs to Nature, to the solitary peak which rises abruptly behind the hermitage, to the rough tract of jungle which stretches away into distant forests, and to the impenetrable sky which fills all space.

Something of the stony, motionless quality of lonely Arunachala seems to have entered into the Maharishee. I have learnt that he has lived on the hill for thirty years and refuses to leave it, even for a single short journey. Such a close association must inevitably have its effects on a man's character. I know that he loves this hill, for someone has translated a few lines of a charming but pathetic poem which the sage has written to express this love. Just as this isolated hill rises out of the jungle's edge and rears its squat head to the sky, so does this strange man raise his own head in solitary grandeur, nay, in uniqueness, out of the jungle of common humanity. Just as Arunachala, Hill of the Sacred Beacon, stands aloof, apart from the irregular chain of hills which girdles the entire landscape, so does the Maharishee remain mysteriously aloof even when surrounded by his own devotees, men who have loved him and lived near him for years. The impersonal, impenetrable quality of all Nature—so peculiarly exemplified in this sacred mountain—has somehow entered into him. It has segregated him from his weaker fellows, perhaps for ever. Sometimes I catch myself wishing that he would be a little more human, a little more susceptible to what seems so normal to us, but so like feeble failings when exhibited in his impersonal presence. And yet, if he has really attained to some sublime realization beyond the common, how can one expect him to do so without passing beyond man, without leaving his laggard race behind for ever ? Why is it that under his strange glance I invariably experience a peculiar expectancy, as though some stupendous revelation will soon be made to me ?

Yet beyond the moods of palpable serenity and the dream which stars itself in the sky of memory, no verbal or other revelation has been communicated to me. I feel somewhat desperate at the pressure of time. Almost a fortnight gone and only a single talk that means anything ! Even the abruptness in the sage's voice has helped, metaphorically, to keep me off. This unwonted reception is also unexpected, for I have not forgotten the glowing inducements to come here with which the yellow-robed holy man plied me. The tantalizing thing is that I want the sage, above all other men, to loosen his tongue for me, because a single thought has somehow aken possession of my mind. I do not obtain it by any process of ratiocination ; it comes unbidden, entirely of its own accord.

" This man has freed himself from all problems, and no woe can touch him."

Such is the purport of this dominating thought.

I resolve to make a fresh attempt to force my questions into voice and to engage the Maharishee in answer to them. I go out to one of his old disciples, who is doing some work in the adjoining cottage and who has been exceedingly kind to me, and tell him earnestly of my wish to have a final chat with his master. I confess that I feel too shy to tackle the sage myself. The disciple smiles compassionately. He leaves me and soon returns with the news that his master will be very pleased to grant the interview.

I hasten back to the hall and sit down conveniently near the divan. The Maharishee turns his face immediately, his mouth relaxing into a pleasant greeting. Straightway, I feel at ease and begin to question him.

" The Yogis say that one must renounce this world and go off into secluded jungles or mountains, if one wishes to find truth. Such things can hardly be done in the West ; our lives are so different. Do you agree with the Yogis ? "

The Maharishee turns to a Brahmin disciple of courtly countenance. The latter translates his answer to me.

" The life of action need not be renounced. If you will meditate for an hour or two every day, you can then carry on with your duties. If you meditate in the right manner, then the current of mind induced will continue to flow even in the midst of your work. It is as though there were two ways of expressing the same idea ; the same line which you take in meditation will be expressed in your activities."

" What will be the result of doing that ? "

" As you go on you will find that your attitude towards people, events and objects will gradually change. Your actions will tend to follow your meditations of their own accord."

" Then you do not agree with the Yogis ? " I try to pin him down.

But the Maharishee eludes a direct answer.

" A man should surrender the personal selfishness which binds him to this world. Giving up the false self is the true renunciation."

" How is it possible to become selfless while leading a life of worldly activity ? "

" There is no conflict between work and wisdom."

" Do you mean that one can continue all the old activities in one's profession, for instance, and at the same time get enlightenment ? "

" Why not ? But in that case one will not think that it is the old personality which is doing the work, because one's consciousness will gradually become transferred until it is centred in That which is beyond the little self."

" If a person is engaged in work, there will be little time left for him to meditate."

The Maharishee seems quite unperturbed at my poser.

" Setting apart time for meditation is only for the merest spiritual novices," he replies. " A man who is advancing will begin to enjoy the deeper beatitude, whether he is at work or not. While his hands are in society, he keeps his head cool in solitude."

" Then you do not teach the way of Yoga ? "

" The Yogi tries to drive his mind to the goal, as a cowherd drives a bull with a stick, but on this path the seeker coaxes the bull by holding out a handful of grass ! "

" How is that done ? "

" You have to ask yourself the question, Who am I ? This investigation will lead in the end to the discovery of something within you which is behind the mind. Solve that great problem, and you will solve all other problems thereby."

There is a pause as I try to digest his answer. From the square-framed and barred hole in the wall which does duty as a window, as it does in so many Indian buildings, I obtain a fine view of the lower slopes of the sacred hill. Its strange outline is bathed in the early morning sunlight.

The Maharishee addresses me again :

" Will it be clearer if it is put in this way ? All human beings are ever wanting happiness, untainted with sorrow. They want to grasp a happiness which will not come to an end. The instinct is a true one. But have you ever been struck by the fact that they love their own selves most ? "

" Well ? "

" Now relate that to the fact that they are ever desirous of attaining happiness through one means or another, through drink or through religion, and you are provided with a clue to the real nature of man."

" I fail to see——."

The tone of his voice becomes higher.

" Man's real nature *is* happiness. Happiness is inborn in

the true self. His search for happiness is an unconscious search for his true self. The true self is imperishable; therefore, when a man finds it, he finds a happiness which does not come to an end."

"But the world is so unhappy?"

"Yes, but that is because the world is ignorant of its true self. All men, without exception, are consciously or unconsciously seeking for it."

"Even the wicked, the brutal and the criminal?" I ask.

"Even they sin because they are trying to find the self's happiness in every sin which they commit. This striving is instinctive in man, but they do not know that they are really seeking their true selves, and so they try these wicked ways first as a means to happiness. Of course, they are wrong ways, for a man's acts are reflected back to him."

"So we shall feel lasting happiness when we know this true self?"

The other nods his head.

A slanting ray of sunshine falls through the unglazed window upon the Maharishee's face. There is serenity in that unruffled brow, there is contentment around that firm mouth, there is a shrine-like peace in those lustrous eyes. His unlined countenance does not belie his revelatory words.

What does the Maharishee mean by these apparently simple sentences? The interpreter has conveyed their outward meaning to me in English, yes, but there is a deeper purport which he cannot convey. I know that I must discover that for myself. The sage seems to speak, not as a philosopher, not as a pundit trying to explain his own doctrine, but rather out of the depth of his own heart. Are these words the marks of his own fortunate experience?

"What exactly is this self of which you speak? If what you say is true, then there must be another self in man."

His lips curve in a smile for a moment.

"Can a man be possessed of two identities, two selves?" he makes answer. "To understand this matter it is first necessary for a man to analyse himself. Because it has long been his habit to think as others think, he has never faced his 'I' in the true manner. He has not a correct picture of himself; he has too long identified himself with the body and the brain. Therefore, I tell you to pursue this enquiry, Who am I?"

He pauses to let these words soak into me. I listen eagerly to his next sentences.

" You ask me to describe this true self to you. What can be said ? It is That out of which the sense of the personal ' I ' arises, and into which it shall have to disappear."

" Disappear ? " I echo back. " How can one lose the feeling of one's personality ? "

" The first and foremost of all thoughts, the primeval thought in the mind of every man, is the thought ' I.' It is only after the birth of this thought that any other thoughts can arise at all. It is only after the first personal pronoun ' I ' has arisen in the mind, that the second personal pronoun ' You ' can make its appearance. If you could mentally follow the ' I ' thread until it leads you back to its source, you would discover that, just as it is the first thought to appear, so is it the last to disappear. This is a matter which can be experienced."

" You mean that it is perfectly possible to conduct such a mental investigation into oneself ? "

" Assuredly ! It is possible to go inwards until the last thought ' I ' gradually vanishes."

" What is left ? " I query. " Will a man then become quite unconscious, or will he become an idiot ? "

" Not so ! On the contrary, he will attain that consciousness which is immortal, and he will become truly wise, when he has awakened to his true self, which is the real nature of man."

" But surely the sense of ' I ' must also pertain to that ? " I persist.

" The sense of ' I ' pertains to the person, the body and brain," replies the Maharishee calmly. " When a man knows his true self for the first time, something else arises from the depths of his being and takes possession of him. That something is behind the mind ; it is infinite, divine, eternal. Some people call it the kingdom of heaven, others call it the soul, still others name it Nirvana, and we Hindus call it Liberation ; you may give it what name you wish. When this happens a man has not really lost himself ; rather, he has found himself."

As the last word falls from the interpreter's lips, there flashes across my mind those memorable words which were uttered by a wandering Teacher in Galilee, words which have puzzled so many good persons : *Whosoever shall seek to save his life shall lose it ; and whosoever shall lose his life shall preserve it.*

How strangely similar are the two sentences ! Yet the

Indian sage has arrived at the thought in his own non-Christian way, through a psychological path which seems exceedingly difficult and appears unfamiliar.

The Maharishee speaks again, his words breaking into my thoughts.

"Unless and until a man embarks upon this quest of the true self, doubt and uncertainty will follow his footsteps throughout life. The greatest kings and statesmen try to rule others, when in their heart of hearts they know that they cannot rule themselves. Yet the greatest power is at the command of the man who has penetrated to his inmost depth. There are men of giant intellects who spend their lives gathering knowledge about many things. Ask these men if they have solved the mystery of man, if they have conquered themselves, and they will hang their heads in shame. What is the use of knowing about everything else when you do not yet know who you are? Men avoid this enquiry into the true self, but what else is there so worthy to be undertaken?"

"That is such a difficult, a superhuman task," I comment.

The sage gives an almost imperceptible shrug of his shoulders.

"The question of its possibility is a matter of one's own experience. The difficulty is less real than you think."

"For us, who are active, practical Westerners, such introspections——?" I begin doubtfully and leave my sentence trailing in mid-air.

The Maharishee bends down to light a fresh joss stick, which will replace one whose red spark is dying out.

"The realization of truth is the same for both Indians and Europeans. Admittedly the way to it may be harder for those who are engrossed in worldly life, but even then one can and must conquer. The current induced during meditation can be kept up by habit, by practising to do so. Then one can perform his work and activities in that very current itself; there will be no break. Thus, too, there will be no difference between meditation and external activities. If you meditate on this question, Who am I?—if you begin to perceive that neither the body nor the brain nor the desires are really you, then the very attitude of enquiry will eventually draw the answer to you out of the depths of your own being; it will come to you of its own accord as a deep realization."

Again I ponder his words.

"Know the real self," he continues, "and then the truth will shine forth within your heart like sunshine. The mind will become untroubled and real happiness will flood it, for happiness and the true self are identical. You will have no more doubts once you attain this self-awareness."

He turns his head and fixes his gaze at the far end of the hall. I know then that he has reached his conversational limit. Thus ends our last talk and I congratulate myself that I have drawn him out of the shell of taciturnity before my departure.

§

I leave him and wander away to a quiet spot in the jungle, where I spend most of the day among my notes and books. When dusk falls I return to the hall, for within an hour or two a pony-carriage or bullock-cart will arrive to bear me away from the hermitage.

Burning incense makes the air odorous. The Maharishee has been half-reclining under the waving punkah as I enter but he soon sits up and assumes his favourite attitude. He sits with legs crossed, the right foot placed on the left thigh and the left foot merely folded beneath the right thigh. I remember being shown a similar position by Brama, the Yogi who lives near Madras, who called it "The Comfortable Posture." It is really a half-Buddha posture and quite easy to do. The Maharishee, as is his wont, holds his chin with his right hand and rests the elbow on a knee; next he gazes attentively at me but remains quite silent. On the floor beside him I notice his gourd-shell water-jug and his bamboo staff. They are his sole earthly possessions, apart from the strip of loin-cloth. What a mute commentary on our Western spirit of acquisitiveness!

His eyes, always shining, steadily become more glazed and fixed; his body sets into a rigid pose; his head trembles slightly and then comes to rest. A few more minutes and I can plainly see that he has re-entered the trance-like condition in which he was when I first met him. How strange that our parting shall repeat our meeting! Someone brings his face close to mine and whispers in my ear, "The Maharishee has gone into holy trance. It is useless now to talk."

A hush falls upon the little company. The minutes slowly pass but the silence only deepens. I am not religious but I can no more resist the feeling of increasing awe which begins to grip my mind than a bee can resist a flower in all its luscious bloom. The hall is becoming pervaded with a subtle, intangible and indefinable *power* which affects me deeply. I feel, without doubt and without hesitation, that the centre of this mysterious power is no other than the Maharishee himself.

His eyes shine with astonishing brilliance. Strange sensations begin to arise in me. Those lustrous orbs seem to be peering into the inmost recesses of my soul. In a peculiar way, I feel aware of everything he can see in my heart. His mysterious glance penetrates my thoughts, my emotions and my desires; I am helpless before it. At first this disconcerting gaze troubles me; I become vaguely uneasy. I feel that he has perceived pages that belong to a past which I have forgotten. He knows it all, I am certain. I am powerless to escape; somehow, I do not want to, either. Some curious intimation of future benefit forces me to endure that pitiless gaze.

And so he continues to catch the feeble quality of my soul for a while, to perceive my motley past, to sense the mixed emotions which have drawn me this way and that. But I feel that he understands also what mind-devastating quest has impelled me to leave the common way and seek out such men as he.

There comes a perceptible change in the telepathic current which plays between us, the while my eyes blink frequently but his remain without the least tremor. I become aware that he is definitely linking my own mind with his, that he is provoking my heart into that state of starry calm which he seems perpetually to enjoy. In this extraordinary peace, I find a sense of exaltation and lightness. Time seems to stand still. My heart is released from its burden of care. Never again, I feel, shall the bitterness of anger and the melancholy of unsatisfied desire afflict me. I realize deeply that the profound instinct which is innate in the race, which bids man look up, which encourages him to hope on, and which sustains him when life has darkened, is a true instinct, for the essence of being is good. In this beautiful, entranced silence, when the clock stands still and the sorrows and errors of the past seem like trivialities, my mind is being submerged in that of the Maharishee and wisdom is now at its perihelion. What is this man's gaze but a thaumaturgic wand, which evokes a hidden world of unexpected splendour before my profane eyes?

I have sometimes asked myself why these disciples have been staying around the sage for years, with few conversations, fewer comforts and no external activities to attract them. Now I begin to understand—not by thought but by lightning-like illumination

—that through all those years they have been receiving a deep and silent reward.

Hitherto, everyone in the hall has been hushed to a deathlike stillness. At length, someone quietly rises and passes out. He is followed by another, and then another, until all have gone.

I am alone with the Maharishee! Never before has this happened. His eyes begin to change; they narrow down to pin-points. The effect is curiously like the "stopping-down" in the focus of a camera lens. There comes a tremendous increase in the intense gleam which shines between the lids, now almost closed. Suddenly, my body seems to disappear, and we are both out in space!

It is a crucial moment. I hesitate—and decide to break this enchanter's spell. Decision brings power and once again I am back in the flesh, back in the hall.

No word passes from him to me. I collect my faculties, look at the clock, and rise quietly. The hour of departure has arrived.

I bow my head in farewell. The sage silently acknowledges the gesture. I utter a few words of thanks. Again, he silently nods his head.

I linger reluctantly at the threshold. Outside, I hear the tinkle of a bell. The bullock-cart has arrived. Once more I raise my hands, palms touching.

And so we part.

CHAPTER X

AMONG THE MAGICIANS AND HOLY MEN

SPACE and time, those defiant enemies of man, hurry this pen again. My feet must once more take giant strides on this eastward trek, while my pen sets down a few salient things that are worth a written memorial.

It is true that the faqueer of a few tricks, the magician of the streets, holds for me, as for everyone else, a natural interest. Yet mine is only a fleeting interest, for he can throw little light on the great mysteries of human life which are alone worthy of a man's deepest thought. Still, his presence is a diversion and I turn aside on occasions to enquire after him.

I want to picture a few of the types who come into the orbit of my wandering, to point my pen at widely differing men. One of them looms up in memory, though he is but an insignificant trickster whom I meet at Rajahmundry, a quiet town in the north-eastern part of Madras Presidency.

An aimless stroll takes me through a place where my shoes sink into the soft sand which covers the ground. Eventually I arrive at a narrow street which leads to a bazaar. As I walk along in the sultry air, old men squat in open doorways, children play amid the dirt, and a stark-naked youngster dives out of a house—only to disappear again on catching sight of the stranger.

In the long, bustling bazaar itself, elderly merchants sit in their little shops and stroke their beards expectantly while I pass ; the sellers of food and grain squat beside their open booths, while an army of flies is busy attacking their wares. In course of time I come to the somewhat gaudy structure of a temple, where a little group of men and women stirs out of the dust at my approach. The leprous, the crippled and the destitute make their rendezvous near the temples and the stations of most Indian cities, that they may gather alms of the pious and the strangers. Worshippers walk noiselessly into the building, their bare feet treading the dust on the stones. Shall

I, too, wander into the building and watch the ministrations of the priests? I debate the question and decide in the negative.

I proceed on my protracted ramble until I observe a youth striding along before me. He is dressed in a European shirt worn, as is the custom, back to front, and a flowing waistband, while his right arm clasps a bundle of cloth-bound books. When I overtake him, he instinctively turns his head; our eyes meet—and our acquaintance begins!

The exigencies of my profession have taught me to serve the conventions whenever one can, but to dispense with them whenever they stand between one and an objective. I like travel, but usually in an unconventional way; hence my Indian wanderings will hardly be a model for the Cook's tourist or unbohemian traveller.

The youth proves to be a student at a large local college, and he possesses an air of general intelligence which is quite attractive. Moreover, he seems to have a care for the ancient culture of his land, and when I tell him of my interest in the subject, his delight knows no bounds. I discover, too, that he he has not yet succumbed to the hysteria for politics which has attacked most of the young students in the towns, though India is now in the throes of the long turmoil which Gandhi has aroused into being in his effort to disturb the relations between white rulers and brown ruled.

Half an hour later he is guiding me to an open space where a little crowd has gathered in expectant mood. There is a man in the centre who is bawling something at the top of his voice. The youth informs me that this loud declaration consists mainly of a list of wonderful Yogic powers which the man claims to possess.

The self-proclaimed Yogi is powerfully built; he has an elongated head, thick-set shoulders, and an abdomen which has begun to bulge through the piece of cotton cloth wrapped about his loins which constitutes part of his dress. For the rest he wears a long loose white robe. I feel that there is a little too much bravado about the man, but when he offers to perform the mango-tree feat, if sufficient financial inducement is forthcoming, I join with a few others in throwing some coins at his feet.

He begins by placing a capacious earthenware pot in front of him and then proceeds to squat on the ground. The pot is filled with reddish brown earth. He shows us a little mango stone and plants it in the earth. After that he produces a large cloth out of his travelling bag, and spreads it over the pot, his folded knees and his thighs.

For several minutes we are treated to some mystic incantations, which the Yogi chants in a monotonous voice, and then he withdraws the cloth. The first bud of a mango plant peeps its head above the earth !

Once again he covers both pot and legs, picks up a reed pipe, and emits a weird noise which is presumably to be taken for music. After some more minutes, he takes up the cloth to show us that the little plant has grown a few inches higher. This procedure of covering and uncovering, with due intervals of pipe music, is repeated until a small mango bush has emerged from the earth. It is about nine or ten inches high. Hardly a tree ! But nevertheless a small yellowish gold mango fruit hangs from the top of the plant.

" All this tree has sprung from the seed which you saw me bury in the earth ! " announces the Yogi triumphantly.

My mental constitution does not permit me to accept his statement too readily. I feel, somehow, that the feat was a piece of mere jugglery.

The young man delivers his opinion :

" Sahib, that man is a Yogi. Such men can do wonderful things."

But I am not satisfied. Trying to comprehend the mystery, I decide that the man is more likely a member of the Maskelyne and Devant fraternity. Yet how can one be certain about the matter ?

The Yogi closes his bag and continues to crouch on his hams, while watching the crowd slowly disperse.

An idea comes suddenly. When we are alone, I approach the Yogi, pull out a five-rupee note, and say to the student :

" Tell him that he can have this money, if he will show me how the thing is done."

The youth obediently translates my request. The man makes a show of refusal, but I catch the gleam of desire in his eyes.

" Offer him seven rupees, then."

Still the crouching man scorns my attempt to negotiate.

" Very well, tell him that we bid him farewell."

We proceed to walk away, though I purposely take slow steps. Within a few seconds the Yogi shouts and recalls us.

" If the sahib will give one hundred rupees, the Yogi promises to tell all."

" No ! Seven—or he can keep his secret. Come ! "

Once again we move away. Soon there is another shout. We return.

" The Yogi says he will accept the seven rupees." And the explanation duly comes forth.

The man opens his travelling bag and produces the paraphernalia with which his mystifying feat has been performed. It consists of a mango stone in bud and three slips of mango plant, each longer than the previous one.

He compresses the shortest slip into a mussel shell. The plant bends round into this cramping position, the shell is closed and buried in the earth. To produce the first bud, the man has only to dig his fingers into the earth and remove the lid of the shell, when the plant will once more stand erect.

The longer slips of plant are hidden within his cotton waist-wrap. During the intervals of waiting, chanting and music making, he raises the cloth cover once or twice to see how the growth is proceeding, without however permitting anyone else to do the same. Under cover of these movements, he deftly takes a longer slip from his waist-cloth, plants it in the earth, removes the shorter plant and replaces it in his dress. Thus the illusion of a growing plant is created.

I walk away a little wiser, 'tis true, but I begin to wonder whether my last illusions about these Yogis will fall from me like bronze leaves rustled off the trees in autumn.

And then I remember the warning given me by Brama, the Yogi of the Adyar river, that faqueers of a low order and pseudo Yogis give performances in the streets that are nothing but conjuring feats. Such men bring the name of Yogi into discredit with the younger people and educated classes, he has informed me.

This man who makes mangoes grow in less than half an hour is no real Yogi ; he is a pretender.

§

Nevertheless the faqueers who practise a true magic do exist. One comes to me during a halt at Berhampur, while I go to a second at Puri.

In this town of Berhampur, where the old customs and dusty ways of Hindu life refuse to be dislodged, I have taken temporary quarters in a rest-house which possesses a widely roofed veranda. One broiling afternoon I seek refuge from the stifling heat in the pleasant shade of this veranda. From my long chair I watch the play of sunshine upon the luxuriant foliage of some tropical plants in the garden.

There comes the almost silent patter of naked feet and a rather wild-looking man, carrying a small bamboo basket approaches the compound gate. He has long, black, tangled locks and I notice that his eyes are a little bloodshot. He comes closer, deposits his basket in the dust, and momentarily raises his hands to cover his face as a salute. He addresses me in a mixture of vernacular and faintly recognizable English. I fancy that the vernacular is Telegu, though I am not sure. The accent of his English is so execrable that I am unable to grasp the meaning of more than three or four words. I retaliate by trying some sentences in English on him, but his command of the language is totally insufficient to enable him to understand me. My command of Telegu, however, is even more insufficient to enable me to understand him. We both discover this fact after we have attempted utterances which are nothing more than long strings of sound to the other. Finally, he attempts to devise a language of gesture and facial expression until I gather that he has something of importance in the basket to show me.

I dive into the bungalow and call for the servant, who knows a sprinkling of English—just about enough to sprinkle some intelligibility upon his own vernacular verbosity. I bid him do what he can to translate.

" He wishes show you faqueer's magic, master."

" Excellent. Let him show it, then. How much money does he want ? "

" He says master can give what he pleases."

" Go ahead ! "

The faqueer's unkempt appearance and unknown origin alternately intrigue and repel me. It is difficult to fathom the expression on this man's countenance. There is something almost sinister about it, yet I do not feel the presence of evil. What I sense around him is an aura of strange forces, unfamiliar powers.

He makes no attempt to mount the veranda steps, but squats down under a banyan tree, whose long, rambling branches form a low canopy which trails over his head and sinks to the ground. Out of the bamboo basket he draws forth a venomous-looking scorpion, which he holds by means of a pair of rudely made wooden pincers.

The unpleasant-looking insect tries to run away. Immediately the faqueer draws a circle around it in the dust, using his index finger. Thereafter, it continues to run round and round. Each time it reaches the circle it hesitates, as though confronting some visible barrier, and then goes off in another direction. I watch the thing closely in that hard brilliant tropical light.

After two or three minutes of this peculiar exhibition, I raise my hand in a gesture of satisfaction and the faqueer replaces the scorpion in his basket, from which he next draws out two sharp, thin, pointed iron skewers.

He closes his somewhat terrifying, reddened eyes and seems to wait for an appropriate moment to perform his next piece of magic. At length he opens his optical organs, takes one of the skewers and puts it into his mouth, point foremost. He forces it through his cheek until most of its length protrudes strangely outside his face. As if not satisfied with this slightly gruesome feat, he repeats it by forcing the second skewer through his other cheek. Mingled sensations of repulsion and wonder flow through me.

When he imagines that I have seen enough, he withdraws each of the skewers in turn and proffers a salute. I descend the veranda steps and closely examine his face. Beyond a few insignificant drops of blood and two tiny holes in the skin, both wounds are hardly noticeable !

The man makes a gesture to bid me occupy my chair again. When I am once more reclining on the veranda, he quietly composes himself for two or three minutes as though in further preparation for some striking feat.

Calmly, with the detachment with which one might pull a button from a jacket, the faqueer's right hand ascends to his eyes, seizes the right eyeball and gradually pulls it out of its socket !

I start back, astonished.

There is a few seconds' interval and he draws the organ a little farther out, so that it hangs loosely on his cheek, suspended by protruding muscles and veins.

A feeling of nausea overwhelms me at the ghastly sight. I remain uneasy until he replaces the dislodged eyeball in its socket.

I have had enough of his magic and reward him with some silver rupees. Half-heartedly, I ask the servant to enquire if the man is willing to explain how he performs these anatomical horrors.

" Promise no tell, master. Father teach son only. Only family know."

His unwillingness does not disturb me. After all, it is a

matter more for the investigation of surgeons and doctors than for errant writers.

The faqueer covers his face with his hands in a parting salute, retreats through the gates of the compound, and soon disappears down the dusty road.

§

The quiet ripple of the waves at Puri comes to my ears. It is pleasant to catch the tang of a faint breeze which blows in from the Bay of Bengal. I walk upon a deserted part of the shore, where yellowish white sands stretch away in a broad expanse and where one sees the horizon through the hot, shimmering haze which fills the air. The sea is like liquid sapphire.

My watch glitters in the glaring sunlight as I draw it out of a pocket. Retracing my steps to the town, I walk right into an inexplicable performance which is destined to provide me with a standing puzzle.

I discover a gaudily dressed man surrounded by a mixed crowd. His turban and pyjama trousers reveal him as a Muhammedan. I reflect on the anachronism that a Muhammedan should be so prominent in a town which is so pronouncedly Hindu. The man piques my curiosity and arouses my interest. He has a little, tame monkey which is quaintly dressed in coloured clothes. He puts it through its paces and each time it unerringly obeys the commands of its master with an intelligence which is almost human.

Espying me, the man says something to the creature, which straightaway hops through the crowd and accosts me with a plaintive cry. It then removes its hat and holds it out before me, as though begging for baksheesh. I throw in a four anna piece. The monkey politely bows its head, makes a sort of curtsy, and then returns to its master.

Its next performance is to execute an amazing dance in perfect time to the music pressed out of an old accordion by the man. It possesses an artistic grace and exquisite sense of rhythm worthy of a better stage.

When the show comes to an end, the man addresses a few words in Urdu to his assistant—a young Muhammedan—who approaches me and asks me to enter a tent which stands at the rear, as his master has something special to show me.

While the youth remains outside to keep back the press of people, I enter the tent with the gaudily dressed man. I discover inside that the structure is really a cloth partition flung around four upright posts, and that it is quite roofless. One can see, therefore, almost as well inside it as out. A plain, light wooden table occupies the centre.

The man opens a linen wrap and takes out several tiny dolls, each about two inches high. The heads are made of coloured wax and the legs of stiff straw shod with flat, iron buttons. The man then places the tiny figures on the table, so that each one stands quite erect upon its iron buttons.

He withdraws about a yard from the table and begins to issue commands in Urdu. Within a minute or two, the dolls commence to stir around the table and then to dance!

He waves a short wand, much as an orchestra conductor wields his baton to beat time, and the coloured little figures dance away in perfect rhythm with his flourishes!

They move all over the table's surface, but carefully avoid falling over the edge. I see this amazing display in full daylight at about four o'clock in the afternoon. Suspecting some trick, I move nearer the table and examine it thoroughly, even moving my arms above the figures and below the table in quest of strands of thread, but I can find nothing untoward. Is the man not a mere conjuror but a faqueer of some kind?

He then proceeds to indicate, by means of signs and words, that I should point out different parts of the table. I do so and on each occasion the dolls mass themselves together and dance in a body towards the precise direction which I indicate!

Lastly he shows me a rupee piece and utters something which I intuitively divine as a request to produce such a coin. I take one out of my pocket and place it on the table. Almost immediately the silver coin commences to dance across the surface towards the faqueer. When it reaches the farther edge of the table, it falls off and rolls over to his feet, where it suddenly stops. The man picks it up and keeps it, making some courtly salaams in acknowledgment.

Am I witnessing some remarkable piece of conjuring or a feat of real Yogi magic? My doubts must be clearly writing themselves upon my face, for the faqueer calls in his young assistant. The latter asks me whether I wish to see some more of his master's power. I reply in the affirmative, whereupon he hands the old accordion to the faqueer and then requests me to place my ring on the table. I take the ring off my finger and obey him. It is the same ring which Brama, the anchorite of the Adyar river, presented me as a farewell gift. I watch its golden claws and greenish stone, the while the faqueer withdraws a few paces away and issues command after command in Urdu. At each word the ring rises into the air and falls again ! The man makes an appropriate gesture with his right hand synchronously with his commands ; his left hand still holds the accordion.

Now he begins to play the instrument and, before my astounded gaze, the ring starts to dance upon the table in harmony with the music ! The man has not approached it, has not even touched it. I do not know what to make of this remarkable performance. How is it possible to transform so mysterious a piece of inanimate matter, and to make it into an object that responds to verbal commands ?

When the assistant returns my ring I examine it closely, but can find no trace of any mark.

Once again the faqueer unwraps his cotton package. This time he draws out a rusty, flat iron bar. It is about two and a half inches long and a half inch in width. He is about to place it on the table, when I intervene and request the assistant to let me examine it. They raise no objection and I carefully scrutinize it. There are no threads attached to it. I return it and look over the table, but find nothing suspicious.

The bar rests on the table top. The faqueer vigorously rubs the palms of his hands together for about one minute. Then he bends his trunk slightly forward and holds his hands a few inches above the iron bar. I watch him attentively. He begins to draw his hands slowly backward, still pointing his fingers toward the bar, when my startled eyes see the rusty object follow him. It moves over the table-top of its own accord, parallel to the faqueer's backward movement !

The distance between the man's fingers and the bar is about five inches. When his hands hover above the table's edge, the bar likewise rests there. Once again I ask to be allowed to examine it. Permission is readily granted. I pick it up immediately, but find nothing wrong ; it is just a scrap of old iron.

The faqueer repeats the same feat with a small, steel-handled knife.

I reward him liberally for these unusual displays and then endeavour to obtain some explanation of them. The faqueer vouchsafes the information that it is usually essential for the object to be made of, or to contain, iron, because iron possesses a peculiar psychic quality ; now, he has so perfected himself in this art that he can perform the same feat with objects made of gold.

I seek in mind for a solution of his secret. Almost at once, it occurs to me that a long thin hair, looped at one end, could catch the bar in its loop and yet remain practically invisible. And then I remember my dancing ring, the fact that the faqueer's both hands were occupied with the accordeon, and that he stood several paces away. Neither can the assistant be accused of complicity, for he stood outside the tent during the movements of the dolls. However, in order to test the matter still further, I praise the man as being a clever conjurer and juggler.

His brow darkens and he vehemently denies being one.

"What are you then?" I press home my enquiry.

"I am a true faqueer," he answers proudly through the assistant, "a practiser of the art of ——." I am unable to catch the last word, which is some Urdu name.

I tell him of my interest in these things.

"Yes, I observed that even before you reached the crowd," he replies, disconcertingly. "That is why I invited you to this tent."

"Indeed."

"Yes, do not imagine that I am collecting money through greed. It is because I need a certain sum to build a mausoleum for my late master. I have set my heart upon this work and I shall not rest until it is built."

I beg him to tell me a little more about his life. Very reluctantly, he yields to the request.

"When I was a boy of thirteen I was occupied in taking care of a herd of goats for my father. One day there came to our village a lean ascetic whose thinness was almost terrifying. The bones seemed to be sticking up out of his skin. He asked for a night's food and shelter, which was readily given him by my father, who always treated holy men with respect and regard. However, instead of staying for a single night, his stay extended for more than a year; such was the liking which our family formed for him, that my father continually pressed him to remain and enjoy our hospitality. He was a wonderful man and we early discovered that he possessed strange powers. One evening, as we sat at our simple meal of rice and vegetables, he looked at me several times very closely and I wondered why. The following morning he came to the place where I was tending the goats and sat down by my side.

"'My child,' he said, 'would you like to become a faqueer?'"

"I did not have a very clear idea of what that sort of life

was like, but its freedom and strangeness appealed greatly to me. So I told him that I would be glad to become one. He spoke to my parents and said that he would return when I was three years older, and then he would take me away with him. Strangely enough, both my parents died during that time so that when he came I was quite free to accompany him. Thereafter we roamed the land, going from village to village; I as his disciple, he as my master. All the marvels which you have seen to-day are really his, for he taught me how to do them."

"Is it possible to learn these things easily?" I ask.

The faqueer laughs.

"Only by many years of hard practices can a man master such things."

Somehow, I feel that his story rings true. He seems a pleasant, sincere sort of man. Though I am sceptical by temperament, yet I keep my scepticism on a leash.

As I stagger out of the tent, uncertain whether I have lived through an extraordinary dream, the pleasant breeze revives me. I hear it stir a row of graceful coconut trees which shadow a distant compound. The farther I walk away, the more incredible those feats appear to me. I would like to suspect some trick on the faqueer's part, yet I feel that his character is more honest than not. But how can one explain this amazing art of moving material objects without visible contact? I do not understand how anyone can alter natural laws at his mere whim. Perhaps we do not know as much about the nature of things as we think we do.

§

Puri is one of the sacred cities of India. Monasteries and temples have found a home here since antiquity. Pilgrims pour into the town during certain years of festival, and help to pull the gigantic Car of Juggernaut on its two-mile journey. I take the opportunity to study the holy men who pass through the place, and in the result have to modify my earlier unfavourable impressions.

One wandering holy man, who speaks broken but understandable English, proves to be quite a fine character when I get into closer acquaintance with him. He is on the right side of forty and wears a thin necklace of berries around his throat. He tells me that he roams from shrine to shrine upon pilgrimage, and from monastery to monastery. Wearing only a single robe and begging his food, his ambition is to visit the chief sacred places of the East and South. I help him with a little alms. In return he shows me a small book printed in Tamil. It is so yellow-stained and weather-worn as to appear nearly a century old. It contains several quaint woodcuts. Slowly and carefully he cuts out two of the pictures and presents them to me.

My encounter with the Literary Sadhu, as I name him, is more amusing. It happens one morning when I sit upon the sands, reading the rose-scented pages of Omar Khayyám. *The Rubá'iyát* is a poem which always fascinates me, but since the day when a young Persian writer initiated me into its deeper meaning, I find a twofold pleasure in drinking the wine of its quatrains. This delight which the poem holds for me accounts, perhaps, for the fact that I am so absorbed in it as not to notice the figure which walks across the sands towards me. It is only when raising my eyes from the printed pages at last that I see this unexpected visitor squatting on folded legs beside me.

He wears a holy man's yellow robe and on the ground he has placed a walking-staff and a small linen bundle. I notice the edges of some books peeping out of the latter.

" Pardon me, sir," says the man in excellent English as he introduces himself, " but I, too, am a student of your literature." He begins to untie the knot of his linen bundle. " Please do not be offended, sir. I could not resist talking to you."

" Offended ? Not at all ! " I smile back at him.

" You are a tourist ? "

" Hardly that."

" But you have not lived long in our country ? " he persists.

I make a nodding assent.

He unrolls the bundle and displays three cloth-bound books with worn-looking covers and tattered corners, some paper-wrapped pamphlets and some writing paper.

" Observe, sir, here I have *Essays*, by Lord Macaulay. A wonderful literary style, sir, a great intellect—but what a materialist ! "

So I have stumbled across a budding literary critic, I reflect.

" This book is *A Tale of Two Cities*, by Mr. Charles Dickens. What sentiment, what tear-bringing pathos, sir ! "

After that the holy man quickly wraps his treasures together and turns to address me once more.

" If it is not too impertinent, may I inquire the title of the book you are reading, sir ? "

" I am reading a book by Khayyám."

" Mr. Khayyám ? I have not heard of him. Is he one of your novelists ? "

I laugh at the question.

" No—a poet."

There is an interval of silence.

" You are very inquisitive," I remark. " Is it alms that you want ? "

" I did not come for money, sir," he answers slowly. " What I really want, what I hope for, is that you will present me with a book. I am so fond of reading, you see."

" Yes, you shall have a book. When I return to the bungalow you may accompany me, and I shall find you something slow and early Victorian that will be sure to please you."

" My deep gratitude, sir."

" Wait a moment. Before I give you the present I want you to tell me something. What is the third book in your bundle ? "

" Ah, sir ! it is a most uninteresting volume."

" Quite possibly. But I would like to know its title."

" It is most unworthy of mention, sir."

" Do you still want the book I have promised you ? "

The other man becomes a little panic-stricken.

" I do, indeed, sir. I must tell you, since you force me. It is called *Mammonism and Materialism : A Study of the West*, by a Hindu Critic."

I pretend to look shocked.

" Oh, ho ! So that is the kind of literature you study ? "

" It was given to me by a merchant in the town," he excuses himself in a weak, apologetic manner.

" Let me see it, then."

I run my eyes over the chapter headings of his tattered volume and read a page here and there. It is written in declamatory style by some Bengali babu and published in Calcutta—probably at its author's expense. On the strength of the two degrees tacked on to the end of his name, but without any first-hand acquaintance with his subject, the writer luridly pictures Europe and America as a kind of new inferno, full of suffering and gloom, and peopled by tortured working-classes and sybaritic plutocrats engaged in debased pleasures.

I return the book without comment. The holy man hastily puts it away and produces one of his pamphlets.

" This contains a short biography of an Indian saint, but it is printed in Bengalee," he informs me.

" Now tell me—do you agree with the writer of *Mammonism*," I ask.

" Just a little, sir ; just a little ! It is my ambition to travel to the West one day ; then I shall see it for myself."

" And what will you do there ? "

" I shall deliver lectures to transform the darkness of peoples' minds into light. I would like to follow in the footsteps of our great Swami Vivekananda, who gave such captivating orations in the great cities of your lands. Alas, that he died so young ! What a golden tongue died with him ! "

" Well, you are a strange kind of holy man," I remark.

He raises a forefinger to the side of his nose and replies, with a sapient air :

" The Supreme Playwright has set the stage. What are we but actors who make our entrances and exits, as your world-renowned Shakespeare says ! "

§

I come now to the realization that India's holy men are an extremely mixed lot. Many are good, inoffensive people for the most part, even though they seem anæmic from the angle of power or wisdom. Others are either failures in worldly life or just men looking for an easy living. One of these men approaches me and begs for baksheesh. His matted hair, ash-smeared body and rascally face give him a repulsive appearance. I decide to resist his importunities, if only to study the result. Resistance merely increases his persistence. When, finally, he tries a new tack by offering to sell me his bead rosary—to which dirty-looking object he attaches reverential importance, if I am to judge by the exorbitant price he demands—I bid him begone.

Less common are those foolish ascetics who publicly display their efforts at self-torture. The man who holds an arm aloft in the air until his nails are half a yard long may be matched by the man who stands on one leg for years. What either hopes to gain from these unattractive exhibitions—aside from the few annas he may collect in the begging bowl which rests at his side—it is not easy to determine.

A few seem to practise a sinister sorcery quite openly. They are the voodoo men of India and work mainly in the villages. For a small fee, they will injure your enemy, dispose of an unfavoured wife or clear the path of your ambition by striking your rival down with mysterious sickness. One hears dark and astonishing tales concerning these black magicians. Yet they, too, rejoice in the name of Yogi or faqueer.

Remains a cultured remnant of holy men who condemn themselves to long years of distracted search, to periods of painful self-denial, and to ostracism from the conventional world of organized society, because they have gone forth in search of truth. They possess an instinct which plainly says —whether rightly or wrongly—that to attain to truth is to attain to lasting happiness. We may question the Indian's stereotyped, religious and world-renouncing way of conducting this search, but the urge which sends him forth is less open to question.

The average man in the West has no time for such a quest. He possesses a good excuse for accepting the prevailing mood of indifference, because he knows that if he errs, then he errs in company with a whole continent. For this sceptical age treats the search after truth as a trifle, while spending its own energy upon the serious pursuit of what our best moments reveal as trifles. Somehow it never occurs to us that the few whose lives are spent in the passionate quest of life's real meaning, are more likely to form correct opinions on the problems of the passing hour, than those who spend their energies upon a dozen different interests and have given barely a single thought to the discovery of truth.

A Westerner once came down into the Punjab plains on a mission other than mine, but some folk he encountered there caused him to strike off at an unexpected tangent, until he came dangerously near to forgetting his primal purpose. Alexander the Great was looking for a vaster land than his own to put under his sceptre. He came as a soldier but it seemed that he might finish as a philosopher.

I often speculate about the thoughts which ran through Alexander's brain as he drove his chariot homeward across icy mountains and parched deserts. It is not difficult to perceive that the Macedonian king, who fell under the spell of the sages and Yogis he encountered and spent days at a time eagerly questioning them and warmly discussing their philosophy, needed only a few more years' sojourn in their midst to startle the West with new departures in policy.

The holy men of to-day still contain some among their ranks who do much to keep alive what there is of idealism and spirituality in the country. That the undesirables are in the majority is possible ; if so, it is the inevitable result of time's degenerating activity, but it need not blind us to the presence of the saving remnant, who shine out all the more. One meets such a bewildering variety that it does not seem advisable to affix a label, either of praise or blame, upon the whole race. I understand the attitude of those hot-headed students of the towns who assure me that the extermination of these " parasitic holy men " will constitute a great blessing on India. I equally understand those milder spirits who, older in years and residents of quieter towns, inform me that if Indian society can no longer provide for its holy men, then it is doomed.

The problem is important to India in other directions, for economic distress is compelling certain revaluations. The holy man fulfils no useful economic function in the country. Swarms of ignorant and untaught persons wander through the villages and attend the periodic religious fairs in certain cities. They become bogy-men to the children, and impertinent, importunate beggars to adults. They are a burden to society, for they have nothing to give in return for that which they receive. Yet there exist also really noble men who have thrown up good positions or given away their property, in order to go forth and find God. Wherever they go they endeavour to exalt those with whom they come in contact. If character counts, then their efforts to uplift themselves and others is surely worth the bit of bread or plate of rice they receive.

One can only say, in conclusion, that one must strip the spiritual skin off a man, whether he be vain humbug or saintly wanderer, if his real worth is to be rightly estimated.

§

The black mantilla of night descends upon the ample shoulders of this earth, the while I wander through narrow, overcrowded lanes in old Calcutta.

My mind is still haunted by a gruesome sight of the morning. Our train puffs into Howrah Station bearing a ghastly cargo on its cow-catcher. The line runs for many miles through a dangerous jungle where princely panthers roam freely. During the night our engine hits a beast, kills it instantly, and carries the broken body into the station. The panther's torn, jagged flesh is not easily dislodged from the iron frame.

But in the onward-rushing train I have picked up another thread of guidance in this quest. Like most main-line trains in India, it is packed to the point of fullness. The compartment in which I have been fortunate enough to find a berth—for all trains carry sleeping berths, except in the lowest class—contains a mixed crew. They discuss their affairs so openly that soon one learns who and what they are. There is a venerable son of Islam who is attired in a long, black silk coat, which is buttoned around his neck. A round black cap, neatly embroidered in gold, rests on his thinly thatched head. White pyjama trousers are gathered around his legs, while his shoes provide an artistic finish to his dress for they are daintily made with red and green threadwork. There is a beetle-browed Mahratti from Western India ; a gold-turbaned Marwari who, like many members of his race, is a moneylender ; and a stout Brahmin lawyer from the South. They are all men of some wealth for they are attended by personal servants who dart out of their third-class carriages at most stopping-places, to enquire after their masters' welfare.

The Muhammedan gives me a single glance, closes his eyes, and drifts off into vacuous sleep. The Mahratti busies himself in conversation with the Marwari. The Brahmin has recently entered the train ; he has yet to settle down.

I am in one of my talkative moods, but there is no one to whom I can talk. The invisible barrier between West and East seems to divide me from all the others. I feel cheered, therefore, when the rubicund Brahmin pulls out a book whose English title, *Life of Ramakrishna*, I cannot help seeing, so boldly is it printed upon the cover. I seize the bait and bring him into conversation. Has not someone once told me that Ramakrishna was the last of the Rishees, those spiritual supermen ? Upon this point I engage my fellow-traveller, and he is eager to respond. We ascend the heights of philosophical discussion and descend into talk on the homelier aspects of Indian life.

Whenever he mentions the name of the Rishee, his voice fills with love and awe and his eyes light up. The reality of his devotion to this long-passed man is indubitable. Within two hours I learn that the Brahmin has a master who is one of the two or three surviving disciples of the great Ramakrishna himself. This master of his is nearly eighty years old and lives, not in some lonely retreat, but in the heart of Calcutta's Indian quarter.

Of course, I beg for the address and it is freely given.

" You will need no introduction other than your own desire to see him," says the lawyer.

And so I am now in Calcutta itself, searching for the house of the Master Mahasaya, the aged disciple of Ramakrishna.

Passing through an open courtyard which adjoins the street, I reach a steep flight of steps leading into a large, rambling old house. I climb up a dark stairway and pass through a low door on the top storey. I find myself in a small room, which opens out on to the flat, terraced roof of the house. Two of its walls are lined with low divans. Save for the lamp and a small pile of books and papers, the room is otherwise bare. A young man enters and bids me wait for the coming of his master, who is on a lower floor.

Ten minutes pass. I hear the sound of someone stirring from a room on the floor below out into the stairway. Immediately there is a tingling sensation in my head and the idea suddenly grips me that that man downstairs has fixed his thoughts upon me. I hear the man's footsteps going up the stairs. When at last—for he moves with extreme slowness—he enters the room, I need no one to announce his name. A venerable patriarch has stepped from the pages of the Bible, and a figure from Mosaic times has turned to flesh. This man with bald head, long white beard, and white moustache, grave countenance, and large, reflective eyes ; this man whose shoulders are slightly bent with the burden of nearly eighty years of mundane existence, can be none other than the master Mahasaya.

He takes his seat on a divan and then turns his face towards mine. In that grave, sober presence I realize instantly that there can be no light persiflage, no bandying of wit or humour, no utterance even of the harsh cynicism and dark scepticism which overshadow my soul from time to time. His character, with its commingling of perfect faith in God and nobility of conduct, is written in his appearance for all to see.

He addresses me in perfectly accented English.

" You are welcome here."

He bids me come closer and take my seat on the same divan. He holds my hand for a few moments. I deem it expedient to introduce myself and explain the object of my visit. When I have concluded speaking, he presses my hand again in a kindly manner and says :

" It is a higher power which has stirred you to come to India, and which is bringing you in contact with the holy men of our land. There is a real purpose behind that, and the future will surely reveal it. Await it patiently."

"Will you tell me something about your master Ramakrishna?"

"Ah, now you raise a subject about which I love best to talk. It is nearly half a century since he left us, but his blessed memory can never leave me; always it remains fresh and fragrant in my heart. I was twenty-seven when I met him and was constantly in his society for the last five years of his life. The result was that I became a changed man; my whole attitude towards life was reversed. Such was the strange influence of this god-man Ramakrishna. He threw a spiritual spell upon all who visited him. He literally charmed them, fascinated them. Even materialistic persons who came to scoff became dumb in his presence."

"But how can such persons feel reverence for spirituality—a quality in which they do not believe?" I interpose, slightly puzzled.

The corners of Mahasaya's mouth pull up in a half smile. He answers:

"Two persons taste red pepper. One does not know its name; perhaps he has never even seen it before. The other is well acquainted with it and recognizes it immediately. Will it not taste the same to both? Will not both of them have a burning sensation on the tongue? In the same way, ignorance of Ramakrishna's spiritual greatness did not debar materialistic persons from 'tasting' the radiant influence of spirituality which emanated from him."

"Then he really was a spiritual superman?"

"Yes, and in my belief even more than that. Ramakrishna was a simple man, illiterate and uneducated—he was so illiterate that he could not even sign his name, let alone write a letter. He was humble in appearance and humbler still in mode of living, yet he commanded the allegiance of some of the best-educated and most-cultured men of the time in India. They had to bow before his tremendous spirituality which was so real that it could be felt. He taught us that pride, riches, wealth, worldly honours, worldly position are trivialities in comparison with that spirituality, are fleeting illusions which deceive men. Ah, those were wonderful days! Often he would pass into trances of so palpably divine a nature that we who were gathered around him then would feel that he was a god, rather than a man. Strangely, too, he possessed the power of inducing a similar state in his disciples by means of a single touch; in this state they could understand the deep mysteries of God by means of direct perception. But let me tell you how he affected me.

"I had been educated along Western lines. My head was filled with intellectual pride. I had served in Calcutta colleges as Professor of English Literature, History and Political Economy, at different times. Ramakrishna was living in the temple of Dakshineswar, which is only a few miles up the river from Calcutta. There I found him one unforgettable spring day and listened to his simple expression of spiritual ideas born of his own experience. I made a feeble attempt to argue with him but soon became tongue-tied in that sacred presence, whose effect on me was too deep for words. Again and again I visited him, unable to stay away from this poor, humble but divine person, until Ramakrishna one day humorously remarked:

"'A peacock was given a dose of opium at four o'clock. The next day it appeared again exactly at that hour. It was under the spell of opium and came for another dose.'

"That was true, symbolically speaking. I had never enjoyed such blissful experiences as when I was in the presence of Ramakrishna, so can you wonder why I came again and again? And so I became one of his group of intimate disciples, as distinguished from merely occasional visitors. One day the master said to me:

"'I can see from the signs of your eyes, brow and face that you are a Yogi. Do all your work then, but keep your mind on God. Wife, children, father and mother, live with all and serve them as if they are your own. The tortoise swims about in the waters of the lake, but her mind is fixed to where her eggs are laid on the banks. So, do all the work of the world but keep the mind in God.'

"And so, after the passing away of our master, when most of the other disciples voluntarily renounced the world, adopted the yellow robe, and trained themselves to spread Ramakrishna's message through India, I did not give up my profession but carried on with my work in education. Nevertheless, such was my determination not to be of the world although I was in it, that on some nights I would retire at dead of night to the open veranda before the Senate House and sleep among the homeless beggars of the city, who usually collected there to spend the night. This used to make me feel, temporarily at least, that I was a man with no possessions.

"Ramakrishna has gone, but as you travel through India

you will see something of the social, philanthropic, medical and educational work being done throughout the country under the inspiration of those early disciples of his, most of whom, alas! have now passed away too. What you will not see so easily is the number of changed hearts and changed lives primarily due to this wonderful man. For his message has been handed down from disciple to disciple, who have spread it as widely as they could. And I have been privileged to take down many of his sayings in Bengali; the published record has entered almost every household in Bengal, while translations have also gone into other parts of India. So you see how Ramakrishna's influence has spread far beyond the immediate circle of his little group of disciples."

Mahasaya finishes his long recital and relapses into silence. As I look at his face anew, I am struck by the non-Hindu colour and cast of his face. Again I am wafted back to a little kingdom in Asia Minor, where the children of Israel find a temporary respite from their hard fortunes. I picture Mahasaya among them as a venerable prophet speaking to his people. How noble and dignified the man looks! His goodness, honesty, virtue, piety and sincerity are transparent. He possesses that self-respect of a man who has lived a long life in utter obedience to the voice of conscience.

"I wonder what Ramakrishna would say to a man who cannot live by faith alone, who must satisfy reason and intellect?" I murmur questioningly.

"He would tell the man to pray. Prayer is a tremendous force. Ramakrishna himself prayed to God to send him spiritually inclined people, and soon after that those who later became his disciples or devotees began to appear."

"But if one has never prayed—what then?"

"Prayer is the last resort. It is the ultimate resource left to man. Prayer will help a man where the intellect may fail."

"But if someone came to you and said that prayer did not appeal to his temperament. What counsel would you give him?" I persist gently.

"Then let him associate frequently with truly holy men who have had real spiritual experience. Constant contact with them will assist him to bring out his latent spirituality. Higher men turn our minds and wills towards divine objects. Above all, they stimulate an intense longing for the spiritual life. Therefore, the society of such men is very important as the first step, and often it is also the last, as Ramakrishna himself used to say."

Thus we discourse of things high and holy, and how man can

find no peace save in the Eternal Good. Throughout the evening different visitors make their arrival until the modest room is packed with Indians—disciples of the master Mahasaya. They come nightly and climb the stairs of this four-storeyed house to listen intently to every word uttered by their teacher.

And for a while I, too, join them. Night after night I come, less to hear the pious utterances of Mahasaya than to bask in the spiritual sunshine of his presence. The atmosphere around him is tender and beautiful, gentle and loving; he has found some inner bliss and the radiation of it seems palpable. Often I forget his words, but I cannot forget his benignant personality. That which drew him again and again to Ramakrishna seems to draw me to Mahasaya also, and I begin to understand how potent must have been the influence of the teacher when the pupil exercises such a fascination upon me.

When our last evening comes, I forget the passage of time, as I sit happily at his side upon the divan. Hour after hour has flown by; our talk has had no interlude of silence, but at length it comes. And then the good master takes my hand and leads me out to the terraced roof of his house where, in the vivid moonlight, I see a circling array of tall plants growing in pots and tubs. Down below a thousand lights gleam from the houses of Calcutta.

The moon is at its full. Mahasaya points up towards its round face and then passes into silent prayer for a brief while. I wait patiently at his side until he finishes. He turns, raises his hand in benediction and lightly touches my head.

I bow humbly before this angelic man, unreligious though I am. After a few more moments of continued silence, he says softly:

"My task has almost come to an end. This body has nearly finished what God sent it here to do. Accept my blessing before I go."[1]

He has strangely stirred me. I banish the thought of sleep and wander through many streets. When, at length, I reach a great mosque and hear the solemn chant, "*God is most great!*" break forth upon the midnight stillness, I reflect that if anyone could free me from the intellectual scepticism to which I cling and attach me to a life of simple faith, it is undoubtedly the master Mahasaya.

[1] Before long I was apprised of his death.

§

" You have missed him. Perhaps it was destined that you should not meet. Who can tell ? "

The speaker is Dr. Bandyopadhya, House Surgeon to one of the Calcutta hospitals. He is one of the most skilful surgeons in the city ; his hands have performed six thousand operations ; his name possesses a string of degrees trailing after it ; and I have derived much pleasure in carefully and critically examining with him some of the knowledge of the Yoga of Body Control which I have picked up. His scientific training in medicine and his expert knowledge of anatomy have proved helpful in my endeavour to lift the subject of Yoga to a purely rational plane.

" I know almost nothing of Yoga," he has confessed. " What you tell me is new to me. I have not even met a Yogi, that is, a real one, save Narasingha Swami, who came to Calcutta not long ago."

It is then that I enquire after the latter's whereabouts, only to receive this disappointing answer.

" Narasingha Swami flashed into Calcutta, created a sensation, and then went off I know not where. I understood that he emerged suddenly out of retirement in the interior, before he came here, so he may have returned there."

" I would like to know what happened."

" He was the talk of the town for a short time. He was discovered by Dr. Neoghy, who is Professor of Chemistry at the Presidency College of Calcutta University, a month or two before at Madhupore. Dr. Neoghy saw him lick a few drops of poisonous acid, and also stuff glowing charcoal into his mouth and keep it there until it stopped glowing. The doctor's interest was aroused and the Yogi was persuaded to come to Calcutta. The University arranged to have a public demonstration of Narasingha Swami's powers before an audience composed exclusively of scientists and medical men. I was among those invited to be present. It was held in the Physics Theatre of the Presidency College. We were a fairly critical lot and, as you know, I have given very little thought to matters of religion, Yoga, and suchlike things, because my attention has been centred on professional studies.

" The Yogi stood in the centre of the theatre and he was handed poisons which had been taken from the college laboratory stock. We gave him a bottle of sulphuric acid first. He poured a few drops into his palm and licked them up with his tongue. He was then given strong carbolic acid, and he licked that up too. We tried him with that deadly poison, potassium cyanide, but he swallowed it without turning a hair ! The feat was astounding, unbelievable even, yet we had to accept the evidence of our own eyes. He had taken enough potassium cyanide to kill any other man within three minutes at most, yet there he stood smiling and apparently unharmed.

"After that, a thick glass bottle was broken and the pieces were ground down to a powder. Narasingha Swami swallowed the powder, which can slowly kill. Three hours after swallowing this strange meal, one of our Calcutta doctors applied a stomach pump to the Yogi and the contents of his stomach were taken out. The poisons were still there. And on the following day the powdered glass was discovered in his stool.

"The thoroughness of our test was beyond dispute. The strength of the sulphuric acid was shown by its destructive effect on a copper coin. Among those present at the demonstration was Sir C. V. Raman, the famous scientist and winner of the Nobel prize, who described the performance as a challenge to modern science. When we asked Narasingha Swami how he was able to take such liberties with his body, he told us that immediately on his return home he would go into a Yoga trance and, by an intense concentration of the mind, counteract the deadly effect of the poisons."[1]

"Can you offer any explanation based on your medical knowledge ?"

The doctor shakes his head.

"No, I can offer none. It completely baffles me."

When I return home, I hunt through a trunk for the notebook in which I have recorded my conversations with Brama, the Yogi of the Adyar river. I turn the pages rapidly until I find this note :

"Poisons cannot harm the adept who has practised the Grand Exercise, no matter how violent they be. This exercise is a combination of certain posture, breathing, will-power and mind concentration exercises. According to our tradition, it confers upon the adept the power of absorbing any object he chooses, even poisons, without being inconvenienced. It is an

[1] Narasingha Swami reappeared in Calcutta some time later, and then proceeded to Rangoon, Burma. Here he gave a similar demonstration, but, owing to a press of unexpected visitors, omitted to follow his usual practice of entering the Yoga trance on arrival home. The result was that he died with tragic swiftness.

exceedingly difficult practice and must be regularly done if it is to keep its merit. A very old man once told me of a Yogi who lived in Benares and who could drink large quantities of poison without being harmed. This Yogi's name was Trailingya Swami; he was very well known in the town in those days, but he died many years ago. Trailingya was a great adept who was very learned in the Yoga of Body Control. He sat almost clothes-less on the banks of the Ganges for years, but no one could hold converse with him because he had imposed a vow of silence upon himself."

Incredible and impossible I had deemed this immunity to poison, when Brama had brought the subject within the line of my vision for the first time. But now, my preconceived ideas of the limits of what is possible have become a little shaky. Sometimes I have wondered at the unbelievable and almost incomprehensible tasks which these Yogis set themselves, yet who knows—perhaps they possess secrets which we Westerners are vainly trying to discover through a thousand laboratory experiments?

CHAPTER XI

THE WONDER-WORKER OF BENARES

MY wanderings in Bengal must hasten into the limbo of unrecorded experience, and my unexpected contacts near Buddha-Gaya with three Tibetan lamas, who proffer an invitation to their mountain monastery, must likewise follow suit, for I am eager to enter the sacred city of Benares.

The train thunders across the great iron bridge near the city, its noise heralding, no doubt, modernity's further invasion of an antiquated and static form of society. The holy Ganges can hardly remain holy much longer when alien and infidel men send snorting fire-chariots across its greyish-green waters.

So this is Benares !

A huge crowd of pilgrims jostle each other while I pass out of the station and step into a waiting carriage. As we drive along the dusty road I become aware of a new element in the atmosphere. I try to ignore it but, with increasing insistence, it forces itself upon my attention.

So this is India's holiest city ! Well, it possesses a most unholy smell ! Benares is reputed to be the oldest populated town in India. Its odour fully confirms its reputation. The unsavoury air seems insupportable. I begin to lose courage. Shall I order the driver to take me back to the station ? Is it not better to be an arrant infidel and breathe clean air than acquire piety at such a monstrous price ? And then I reflect that time will somehow acclimatize one even to this air, as it acclimatizes one to more unfamiliar things still in this stale land. But Benares ! you may be the hub of Hindu culture, yet please learn something from the infidel whites and temper your holiness with a little hygiene !

I learn that the stench arises partly because the roads are paved with a mixture of cow-dung and earth, and partly because the old moat which surrounds the city has been used by the people of many generations as a convenient refuse heap.

If Indian chronicles can be credited, Benares was an established city as long ago as twelve hundred years before the Christian Era. Just as pious Englishmen journeyed to the holy city of Canterbury in the Middle Ages, so have Indians flocked from every part of their country to the holy city of Benares. Hindus come in their wealthy state or poverty-stricken condition to receive its blessing, while the ailing come to eke out their last days, for death here will take the soul straight into Paradise.

The next day I wander afoot through old Kashi—as the Hindus prefer to call their city—and explore the labyrinth of crooked streets which compose it. There is a purpose behind my aimless wandering, for I bear in my pocket a paper which describes the location of the house of a Yogi wonder-worker, whose disciple I met in Bombay.

I pass through stuffy streets along which a carriage would be too wide to pass. I make my way through crowded bazaars, where seethe the people of a dozen different races, and where mangy dogs and innumerable flies add to the bustle. Old women with grey hair and shrunken breasts; young women with supple figures and smooth, brown limbs; pilgrims fingering their rosaries and muttering the same sacred words which they have already repeated perhaps fifty thousand times; the gaunt figures of ash-besmeared elderly ascetics; all these and other types throng the narrow ways. Among a tangle of streets which are full of turmoil, noise and colour, I come accidentally upon the Golden Temple, which is famed among the orthodox throughout India. Ash-bedabbled ascetics, whose uncouth appearance is repellent to Western eyes, crouch around the entrance. Worshippers flow in and out in an endless stream. Several carry lovely flower garlands and thus give a gay colour to the scene. The pious touch the stone door-posts with their foreheads as they leave the temple and then, turning, start in momentary surprise on beholding the white infidel. I become conscious again of the invisible barrier between these men and myself, the profound barrier between white and brown skin.

Two domes, made of thick sheets of gold, glisten in the quivering sunlight; screeching parrots swarm on the nearest tower. The Golden Temple is given over to the god Shiva. Where is he now, I wonder, this god to whom these Hindus cry, before whom they pray, and to whose stone representations I have seen them offer scented flowers and cooked rice?

I move on and stand near the threshold of another temple,

where I watch the god Krishna being worshipped. Lighted camphor burns before a golden idol; the temple bells peal out their insistent calls for his attention; and the sounds of conch horns stray up to his unhearing ears. A lean and austere priest comes out and looks questioningly at me, and I proceed upon my way.

Who can count the multitude of images and idols which teem within the temples and houses of Benares? Who can explain these serious-looking Hindus—so often childish, yet sometimes so profoundly philosophical?

Through the dark alleys I thread my way, afoot and alone, seeking the house of the wonder-worker. At length I emerge from the swarming streets into wider roads. A straggling, ragged column of little boys, thin youths and a few men, swing past me in single file. Their leader carries a makeshift banner, with something indecipherable inscribed upon the flag. They shout queer catchwords and occasional snatches of song. They look at me with hostile faces and scowling eyes as they go by, so that I sense the political nature of this motley procession. Last night, in a packed bazaar, with no European or policeman anywhere in sight, someone behind me hisses out a threat to shoot me. At once I wheel round—only to behold a crowd of bland faces, for the young fanatic (I guess his youth by the sound of his voice) has disappeared around a corner into the darkness. And so I gaze with pity upon this ragged procession which now disappears down the road. Politics, that deceptive siren who promises everybody everything, has gathered a few more victims into her insidious arms.

I come at last to a street where the houses are large and well built and where the compounds are spacious and trimly kept. I quicken my pace until I reach a gate, upon whose post the name VISHUDHANANDA is inscribed on a stone tablet. I enter the compound, for this is the house which I seek, and approach someone who lounges on the veranda. He is a young man with an unintelligent face. I ask him in Hindustani: "Where is the teacher?" but he shakes his head and gives me to understand that no such person is known here. I utter the teacher's name, but again receive a negative reply. The result is disappointing, but I am determined not to be beaten. An inward monitor warns me that the young man thinks no European can possibly have any business here, and that he has jumped to the conclusion I am really seeking some other house. I look again at his face and write him down as stupid. Ignoring his gesticulations, I walk straight into the house.

In an inner room I come upon a semicircle of dark faces. A group of well-dressed Indians squat around the floor. A bearded old man reclines upon a couch at the far end of the room. His venerable appearance and seat of honour are enough to inform me that here is the object of my quest. I raise my hands in salutation, palms touching.

"Peace, master!" I make the conventional Hindustani greeting.

I proffer my introduction and present myself as a writer travelling in India, yet withal a student of their native philosophy and mysticism. I make it clear that the disciple whom I encountered was careful to explain that his teacher never made a public exhibition of his wonderful powers, and that even under the shadow of privacy he rarely displayed them to strangers. Nevertheless, in view of my deep interest in their ancient wisdom, I crave their indulgence and beg to be treated as an exception.

The students stare blankly at each other and then turn towards the teacher, as if in wonderment at his response. Vishudhananda is a man of more than seventy years of age, I judge. A short nose and a long beard adorn his face. I am struck by the large size of his eyes, which are deeply pouched. The sacred thread of a Brahmin hangs around his neck.

The old man fixes his eyes coldly upon me, as though I were a specimen to be studied under a microscope. I feel something weird and uncanny touch my heart. Indeed, some strange force seems to pervade the whole room, and I feel slightly uneasy.

At length he addresses some words, in a dialect which I recognize as Bengalee, to a disciple, who turns and informs me that no audience can be granted unless I bring Pundit Kavirj, who is Principal of the Government Sanskrit College, to act as interpreter. The pundit's perfect knowledge of English, combined with his long standing as a disciple of Vishudhananda, perfectly fits him to act as a medium between us.

"Come with him to-morrow afternoon," says the teacher. "I shall expect you at the hour of four."

I am forced to retreat. On the road I hail a passing carriage and drive through the winding streets to the Sanskrit College. The Principal is not there. Someone thinks he may be at home, so I drive on for another half-hour until I find him at last in a tall, ancient house with a projecting upper storey, whose appearance is strangely like that of a medieval Italian building.

The pundit sits on the floor of a top room, surrounded on every side by small hills of books, papers and scholastic paraphernalia. He has the Brahmin's typical high brow, thin long nose and lighter complexion. His face is refined and scholarly. I explain my errand ; there is a slight hesitation on his part ; and then he agrees to accompany me next day. The appointment fixed, I withdraw.

I ride down to the Ganges and dismiss the carriage. I saunter along the river bank which, for the benefit of bathing pilgrims, is built into long rows of stone steps. The feet of many centuries have worn down the steps until they are rugged and uneven. How untidy and irregular is the water-front of Benares ! Temples tumble into the water ; glistening domes are neighbours to squat, square, decorated palaces which rise to varying heights ; while the whole hotch-potch of buildings mingles the ancient and the modern indiscriminately.

Priests and pilgrims swarm everywhere. I come across some pundits teaching their pupils in small, open rooms. The walls are plainly whitewashed ; the teachers sit on rugs ; and the pupils squat respectfully around, absorbing the cobwebbed doctrines of their creed.

A bearded ascetic's appearance causes me to make enquiries. He has rolled over and over in the dust for four hundred miles. A strange way to make one's pilgrimage to Benares ! Farther on I meet another weird-looking individual. He has held one arm aloft for years. The sinews and ligaments of his unfortunate limb have almost withered, while the flesh which covers it has shrivelled to parchment. How account for such futile austerities, unless, indeed, the unending tropical sun has made the minds of these men a trifle mad ? It may be that existence in a temperature of one hundred and twenty degrees in the shade has helped to unbalance these unfortunate members of a race which is already so prone to religious hysteria.

§

The next day, precisely at four o'clock, Pundit Kavirj and I drive into the courtyard of the teacher's house. We enter the large room and greet him. About six other disciples are present.

Vishudhananda asks me to come a little closer, so I squat down a few feet away from his couch.

" Do you desire to see one of my wonders ? " is his first question.

" If the master wishes to grant this favour, I shall be extremely pleased."

" Give me your handkerchief, then. If you have a silk one, so much the better," translates the Pundit. " Any scent which you desire will be created for you, with nothing but a lens and the sun's rays as equipment."

Fortunately I do carry a silk handkerchief and pass it to the wonder-worker. He takes out a small burning lens and then explains that he wishes to concentrate the sun's rays but, owing to the orb's present position and the sheltered aspect of the room, that cannot be done with directness. The difficulty will easily be overcome, however, by sending one of the disciples outside into the courtyard. The man will use a hand mirror, catch the rays, and then reflect them through an open window into the room.

" I shall now create a scent for you out of the air ! " announces Vishudhananda. " Which would you like ? "

" Can you produce white jasmine ? "

He takes up my handkerchief in his left hand and holds the burning lens above it. For the brief space of two seconds, a gleaming ray of sunlight hovers upon the silken fabric ; then he puts down the lens and hands back the handkerchief. I put it to my nose, and am rewarded with the delightful fragrance of white jasmine !

I examine the handkerchief but can discover no trace of moisture, no evidence that some liquid perfume has been dropped on it. I am puzzled and look half-suspiciously at the old man. He offers to repeat the demonstration.

The second time I choose attar of roses. I watch him narrowly during the further experiment. Every move which he makes, every bit of space around him is scrutinized with all the care I can muster. I examine his puffy hands and his spotless white robe with critical eyes, but can detect nothing suspicious. He repeats his former procedure and evokes the perfume of attar of roses, which strongly impregnates another corner of the handkerchief.

My third choice is violets. Here again he is equally successful.

Vishudhananda is quite emotionless about his triumph. He treats the whole demonstration as a sort of everyday affair, as a mere minor event. His grave face never once relaxes.

" And now *I* shall choose the scent," he unexpectedly declares. " I shall create the perfume of a flower which grows only in Tibet." He concentrates some sunlight upon the last, unscented corner of the handkerchief and lo ! it is done ; he has evoked a fourth perfume, which I fail to recognize.

Slightly bewildered, I put the piece of white silk into my pocket. The feat appears to border on the miraculous. Has he concealed the perfumes upon his person ? Has he hidden them in his robe ? Then he would need to carry a formidable stock because, until I spoke, he could not know which scent I should choose. His simple robe could hardly contain such an ample stock as would be requisite. Besides, not once has his hand disappeared into the folds of his robe.

I ask for permission to inspect the lens. The latter proves to be quite an ordinary magnifying glass, set in a wire frame with a small wire handle. I can see nothing suspicious about it.

There is an additional safeguard, for what it is worth, in the fact that Vishudhananda is being watched, not only by me but also by the half-dozen disciples around us. The Pundit has already informed me that, without a single exception, they are all men of high standing, good education and responsibility.

Hypnotism offers a possible explanation. The value of this explanation can be simply tested. When I return to my quarters, I shall show the handkerchief to other persons.

Vishudhananda has another and greater piece of wonder-working to show me. It is one he seldom performs, though. He tells me that he needs strong sunlight for this second feat ; now, the sun is sinking and evening is approaching. So I am to come again at high noon of a later day of the week. He will then display his amazing feat of temporarily restoring life to the dead !

I leave him and drive home, where I show the handkerchief to three persons. Each one finds that it still bears strong traces of the perfumes. The feat, therefore, cannot be accounted for on the hypothesis of hypnotism. Nor is it much easier to regard the whole affair as a piece of trickery.

§

Once again I am in the house of the magician. The latter tells me that he can restore life only to a small animal ; usually he experiments with a bird.

A sparrow is strangled and left exposed to our gaze for about an hour, so that we can assure ourselves that it is really dead. Its eyes are motionless, its body sad and stiff ; I cannot discover a single sign which might betray the presence of life in the little creature.

The magician picks up his magnifying glass and concentrates a ray of sunlight into an eye of the bird. I wait while a few minutes pass uneventfully. The old man sits bent over his strange task, his large eyes fixed in a glassy stare, his face cold, emotionless and non-committal. Suddenly, his lips open and his voice breaks out into a weird, crooning chant in some language which is unknown to me. A little later the bird's body begins to twitch. I have seen a dog twitch its suffering frame in the same manner, when the spasms of approaching death have overtaken it. Then comes a slight fluttering of the feathers and within a few minutes the sparrow is on its legs, hopping around the floor. Truly the dead have come to life!

During its next phase of this strange existence, the bird gathers sufficient strength to fly up into the air, where it busies itself for a while in finding new perching points as it flies around the room. The thing seems so incredible that I pull body and wits together, in an effort to reassure myself that everything and everyone surrounding me is real, tangible and not hallucinatory.

A tense half-hour passes, while I watch the fluttering efforts of the revived creature. At last a sudden climax provides me with a fresh surprise. The poor sparrow falls through the air and lies motionless at our feet. It remains there without stirring. An examination reveals it as breathless and quite dead.

"Could you have prolonged its life still further?" I ask the magician.

"That is the most I can show you at present," he replies, with a slight shrug. The Pundit whispers that greater things are hoped for from future experiments. There are other things his master can do, though I must not over-use his indulgence and make him play the part of a street showman. What I have seen already must satisfy me. I feel once again the pervading sense of mystery which fills the place. The stories of Vishudhananda's other powers only heighten this feeling.

I learn that he can bring fresh grapes seemingly out of the air and deliver sweetmeats out of sheer nothingness; that if he takes a faded flower in his hand it will soon regain its pristine freshness.

§

What is the secret of these apparent miracles? I try to elicit some hint and receive an extraordinary reply. It is one of those explanations which do not really explain. The real secret still remains hidden behind the square forehead of the Benares wonder-worker, and he has so far not revealed it even to his closest disciple.

He tells me that his birthplace was in Bengal. At the age of thirteen he was bitten by a poisonous animal. His condition became so serious that his mother despaired of his life and took him down to the Ganges to die. According to the Hindu religion, there can be no holier or happier death than beside this river. He was carried into the sacred stream while the mourning family gathered on the banks for the funeral ceremonies. He was lowered into the water. And then a miracle happened. The deeper they dipped him, the more the water sank around his body. When he was raised again, the water rose upward in harmony until it reached its normal level. Again and again he was dipped; again and again the waters sank of their own accord. In short, the Ganges refused to receive the boy as its dying guest!

A Yogi sat on the banks of the river and watched the proceedings. He got up and predicted that the boy was reserved to live and achieve greatness, and that his destiny was most fortunate, inasmuch as he would become a famous Yogi. The man then rubbed some herbs on the poisoned wound and went away. Seven days later he returned and told the parents that the boy was now quite cured, and indeed it was so. But, during the interim a strange thing had happened to the child. His entire mentality and character had changed, and instead of being content to remain at home with his parents, he thirsted to become a wandering Yogi. Henceforth he worried his mother constantly until, a few years later, she granted him permission to leave home. He went forth in quest of the Yoga adepts.

He made his way to Tibet, that trans-Himalayan land of mystery, in the hope of finding his destined teacher among its reputed miracle-working hermits. For it is an idea strongly inherent in the Indian mind that the aspirant must become a personal disciple of someone who has himself mastered the mysteries of Yoga, if he is to succeed in the same quest. The young Bengalee sought for such a man among the solitary hermits who dwell in huts or caves, sometimes when the mountains were swept by howling, icy blizzards, but he returned home disappointed.

Years passed uneventfully, yet his desire found no abatement. Once more he crossed the border and wandered the bleak wastes of Southern Tibet. In a simple habitation among the mountain fastnesses he discovered a man who proved to be the long-sought teacher.

I hear, next, one of those incredible statements which might once have moved me to satiric laughter, but now actually startles me. For I am solemnly assured that this Tibetan master is no less than one thousand two hundred years old! The assertion is made as calmly as a prosaic Westerner might mention that he is forty.

This amazing legend of longevity has cropped up at least twice before. Brama, the Yogi of the Adyar river, once told me that his master in Nepal was over four hundred years old, while a holy man whom I encountered in Western India said that there was a Yogi living in an almost inaccessible mountain cave on the Himalayas who was so old—over one thousand years, was the figure given me—that the lids of his eyes actually drooped heavily with age! I had dismissed both these assertions as being too fantastic, but now I must again entertain a repetition of them, for this man before me hints at being on the track of the elixir of life.

The Tibetan teacher initiated young Vishudhananda into the principles and practices of the Yoga of Body Control. Under this rigorous training, the disciple developed powers of body and mind which were supernormal. He was also initiated into a strange art which he calls Solar Science. For twelve years, despite the hardships of life in a snow-bound region, he continued his pupilage at the feet of the Tibetan possessor of immortal life. His training finished, he was sent back to India. He crossed the mountain passes, descended into the plains, and in due course himself became a teacher of Yoga. He settled for a while at Puri, on the Bay of Bengal, where he still maintains a large bungalow. The flock of disciples which gathered around him belong exclusively to the higher class of Hindus. They comprise wealthy merchants, rich landowners, Government officials and even a Rajah. I get the impression—perhaps I am wrong—that humbler folk are not encouraged.

"How did you perform those wonders you showed me?" I ask bluntly.

Vishudhananda crosses his plump hands.

"What you have been shown is not the result of Yoga practice. It is the result of a knowledge of Solar Science. The essence of Yoga is the development of will power and mental concentration on the part of the Yogi, but in Solar Science practice those qualities are not required. Solar Science is merely a collection of secrets and no special training is necessary to make use of them. It can be studied in exactly the same way that any of your Western material sciences are studied."

Pundit Kavirj supplements the hint that this strange art is more akin to the science of electricity and magnetism than to any other.

I feel as much in the dark as before, so the master vouchsafes some further information.

"This Solar Science which now comes from Tibet is nothing new. It was well known to the great Yogis of India in very ancient times. But now, except for a rare few, it has almost been lost to this country. There are life-giving elements in the sun's rays, and if you knew the secret of separating or selecting those elements, you, too, could do wonders. And there are etheric forces in sunlight which have a magic power, once you get control of them."

"Are you teaching these Solar Science secrets to your disciples?"

"Not yet, but I am preparing to do so. Certain disciples will be selected and the secrets imparted to them. Even now we are building a large laboratory where study classes, demonstrations and experiments will be carried on."

"Then what are your disciples learning at present?"

"They are being initiated into Yoga."

The pundit takes me to inspect the laboratory. It is a modern structure several storeys high and distinctly European in design. The walls are built of red brick and large gaps take the place of windows. These gaps await the coming of huge sheets of plate glass, for the research work to be conducted in the laboratory will involve the reflection of sunlight through red, blue, green, yellow and colourless glass.

The pundit tells me that no Indian works can make glass of the size required to form the giant windows, and therefore the edifice cannot be completed. He asks me to make enquiries in England, but emphasizes that Vishudhananda wants his specifications to be adhered to completely. These include the condition that the makers should guarantee their glass to be absolutely free from air bubbles, and that the coloured glass should be quite transparent. Each sheet is to measure twelve feet in length, eight feet in width and one inch in thickness.[1]

The laboratory building is surrounded by spacious gardens, which are girdled and screened from prying eyes by rows of feather-branched palm trees.

I return to the wonder-worker and sit down before him. The disciples have thinned out ; only two or three are left. Pundit Kavirj squats beside me, his study-worn face fixed in devoted regard of his master.

Vishudhananda momentarily glances at me and then studies the floor. Dignity and reserve mingle in his manner ; his face is preternaturally solemn, and the faces of his disciples reflect his solemnity. I attempt to penetrate behind his mask of gravity, but can perceive nothing. The mind of this man is as impenetrable to my Western mentality as is the inmost shrine of the Golden Temple in yonder town. He is steeped in the strange lore of Oriental magic. I feel strongly that though he has shown me his wonders even before I express a second request, nevertheless he has put up a psychic barrier between us which I shall never cross. My welcome is but a surface one ; Western investigators and Western disciples are not wanted here.

He drops an unexpected remark quite suddenly.

" I could not initiate you as my own pupil unless I secure permission beforehand from my Tibetan master. This is a condition under which I have to work."

Has he read the thoughts which run through my brain ? I gaze at him. His slightly bulging forehead betrays a faint pucker. Anyway, I have expressed no desire to become his disciple. I am in no undue hurry to become anyone's disciple. But of one thing I feel sure—such a request would bring forth a negative answer.

" But how can you communicate with your master if he is in far-off Tibet ? " I query.

[1] I wrote to the largest manufacturers of plate glass in Great Britain, but they refused to undertake the task because the technical conditions laid down by Vishudhananda were impossible of fulfilment. They declared that it was beyond the wit of any manufacturer to devise a process which would guarantee the absence of any air bubbles in the sheets ; that the glass could not be coloured without diminishing its transparency to the sun's rays ; that plate glass could not be made satisfactorily thicker than one quarter of an inch ; and that the sheets would have to be made in halves if breakage on the long journey to Benares was to be avoided.

" We are in perfect touch upon the inner planes," he replies. I am conscious of listening, but not of comprehending. Yet his unexpected remark has turned my mind away from his miracles for a while. I fall into a pensive mood. Unwittingly I find myself asking :

" Master, how can one find enlightenment ? "

Vishudhananda does not reply ; instead, he puts me another question.

" Unless you practise Yoga, how can you obtain enlightenment ? "

I think the matter over for a few seconds.

" Yet I am told that without a teacher it is extremely difficult to understand Yoga, let alone practise it successfully. Genuine teachers are hard to find."

His face remains indifferent and imperturbable.

" When the seeker is ready, the master always appears."

I express my doubts. He spreads out a plump hand.

" A man must first make himself ready ; then, no matter where he is, he will eventually find a teacher. And if the master does not come in the flesh, he will appear to the inward eye of the seeker."

" How shall one begin, then ? "

" Mark off a part of your time every day to sit in the simple posture which I shall show you. That will help to prepare you. Take care also to curb anger and control passion."

Vishudhananda proceeds to show me the Lotus posture, with which I am already familiar. Why he calls this a simple posture, with its intertwined and folded legs, I cannot understand.

" What adult European can achieve such a contortion ! " I exclaim.

" The difficulty lies only in the early attempts. It becomes easy if practised every morning and evening. The important thing is to fix an exact time of the day for this Yoga practice, and to keep regularly to that time. At first five minutes' effort is enough. After one month, you can lengthen the time to ten minutes ; after three months, to twenty minutes, and so on. Take care to keep the spine straight. This exercise will enable a man to acquire physical poise and mental calmness. Calmness is necessary for the further practice of Yoga."

" Then you teach the Yoga of Body Control ? "

" Yes. Do not imagine that the Yoga of Mind Control is superior to it. Just as every human being both thinks and acts, so there must be training for both sides of our nature.

The body acts on the mind, and the mind inter-acts on the body; they cannot be separated in practical development."

I become aware once again of an inner reluctance on the part of this man to submit to further questioning. A mental coldness fills the atmosphere. I decide to withdraw soon, but fling a last question at him.

"Have you discovered whether there is any goal, any purpose, in life?"

The disciples break their gravity and smile at my simplicity. Only an infidel, ignorant Westerner could ask such a question. Do not all the sacred Hindu books, without exception, indicate that God holds this world in His hand for His own purpose?

The teacher does not answer me. He relapses into silence, but glances at Kaviraj, who thereupon supplies the answer.

"Certainly, there is a purpose. We have to attain spiritual perfection, to unite with God."

And then, for the next hour, the room remains silent. Vishudhananda fingers the large pages of a thick book, whose paper cover is printed in Bengalee. The disciples stare, sleep or meditate. A soothing, mesmeric influence begins to steal over me. I feel that if I stay long enough, I shall either fall asleep or fall into some kind of a trance, so I pull my faculties together, thank the teacher, and take my departure.

§

After a light meal I pick my way through tortuous alleys in this motley city, which seems to attract saints and sinners alike. It lures the pious from all over the land into its crowded homes, but it also draws the impious, the ruffianly and the vicious, to say nothing of the priestly parasites.

The jingling temple bells along the bank of the Ganges peal out their call to evening worship. Night is advancing rapidly on the greying sky. Sunset adds another to its own sounds, for the muezzins call to the followers of the Prophet to come to prayer.

I sit on the bank of this ancient river, this much-revered Ganges, and listen to the rustling fronds of palms, which sway slightly in the temporary breeze.

An ash-besmeared beggar approaches me. He halts and I gaze at him. He is some sort of holy man, for something that is not of this world glows in his eyes. I begin to realize that I have not succeeded in understanding this old India so well as

I thought. I grope among the few coins in my pocket, wondering the while whether we can leap across the abyss of civilization which separates us. He takes the alms with a quiet dignity, raises his hands to his ash-covered brow in salutation, and withdraws.

I have mused for long over the mystery of the wonder-worker, who plays tricks with the ether and restores fleeting life to dead birds. His plausible but brief exposition of Solar Science does not capture me. Only a thoughtless man would deny that modern science has not fully explored the possibilities latent in the sun's light; but there are features in this case which incline me to look elsewhere for an explanation.

For, in Western India, I had learnt of the existence of two Yogis who could perform one of Vishudhananda's feats, namely, the extraction of different scents from the air. Unfortunately for my investigation, both these persons died towards the close of last century, but the source of my information seemed reliable enough. In both cases a fragrant, oily essence was made to appear on the palm of the Yogi's hand, as though it exuded through the skin. Sometimes the perfume was strong enough to scent the room.

Now, if Vishudhananda possesses the same strange gift, he can easily transfer some scent from his palm to the handkerchief, whilst appearing to fumble with the magnifying lens. In short, the whole performance of concentrating the sunlight may be nothing more than a piece of play-acting to cover the transference of the magically produced scent. Another point which favours this view is the fact that the wonder-worker has failed to reveal the secret to a single one of his disciples so far. Their hopes have been kept up, meanwhile, by the protracted building of costly laboratories. Even this work has come to a standstill because of the impossibility of procuring the giant sheets of glass in India. And so they wait on and hope.

What process has Vishudhananda really used, if the concentration of sunlight is merely a blind? It may be that the production of fragrant odours is another of the Yoga powers which can be developed by personal effort, but I do not know. Nevertheless, though I cannot provide a tenable theory to account for the wonder-worker's feats, I need not jump at the theory of Solar Science which he offers. Why trouble my head further? My duty is but to play the scribe and record these happenings, not to explain the inexplicable. Here is a side of Indian life which must remain sealed, for even if the plump little wonder-worker, or some chosen disciple, demonstrates this strange art to the outside world and engages the astounded attention of scientists, it is unlikely that the secret will be made known. I think I have read so far into his character, at least.

An inner voice asks me : How has he revived the dead bird ? And what about this legend of a perfected Yogi's ability to extend indefinitely the duration of his life ? Have some Eastern men really discovered the secret of protracted age ?

I turn my head away from the inner questioner and wearily look up at the heavens. The imponderable immensity of the star-filled sky awes me. Nowhere are the stars so bright as in the tropical sky. I continue to gaze fixedly at the twinkling points of light. . . . When I look around again at my fellow-creatures and at the amorphous mass of houses, I begin to feel deeply the recondite mystery of this world. Tangible things and ordinary objects recede quickly into unreality, and the blend of shadowy, moving figures, slowly gliding boats and a few bright lamps, turn both night and environment into some enchanted land of the dream world. The old Indian philosophical doctrine that the universe is but phantom-like in its real nature drifts into my mind and begins to abet this destruction of my sense of reality. I become ready for the strangest experiences that this planet, which hurries so swiftly through the abysses of space, can bring me.

But some creature of the earth world breaks rudely into my heavenly dream by giving loud voice to the monotonous rhythm of an Indian song, and I return rapidly to that pot-pourri of uncertain pleasures and unexpected sorrows which men call life.

CHAPTER XII

WRITTEN IN THE STARS !

THE cupolas quiver with light in the dazzling sunshine, the bathers fill the air with the sounds of their matutinal ablution, and the jumbled, Oriental pageant of the water-front at Benares shows itself anew to my alien gaze. I idle down the Ganges in a heavy junk, whose prow is carved like a cobra's head. I sit on the roof of a cabin, while the three rowers who are below pull their quaint oars.

A merchant from Bombay is my companion and, as he sits next to me, he tells me that he intends to retire from trade when he returns to that city. He is an extremely pious but equally practical man. While laying up treasure in heaven, he has not omitted to lay up treasure in the bank. I have known him for about a week and find him an amiable, genial and friendly person.

" I am retiring at the very age which Sudhei Babu predicted it would happen," he says, eager to explain.

This odd remark causes me, metaphorically, to prick up my ears.

" Sudhei Babu—who is he ? "

" Do you not know ? He is the cleverest astrologer in Benares."

" Oh, just an astrologer ! " I grunt back a little scornfully.

For I have seen the breed squatting in the dust of Bombay's great open space, the Maidan ; sitting in sultry booths at Calcutta ; and foregathering wherever travellers pass through every little town I have visited. Most of them are dirty-looking creatures, with wild locks of unkempt hair. The recognizable print of superstition and ignorance rests upon their faces. Their stock-in-trade usually consists of two or three greasy, well-fingered books and some vernacular almanac filled with incomprehensible signs. I have often cynically thought of their eagerness to direct the fortunes of other persons, when they themselves seemed outside the pale of good fortune.

" I am somewhat surprised at you. Is it safe for a business man to trust himself to the twinkling of the stars. Don't you think common sense is a better guide ? " I add, in the tone of one giving good advice.

The other man half-shakes his head and smiles tolerantly at me.

" How, then, do you explain the prediction of my retirement? Who could have guessed that I would give up trade at such an exceptionally early age, for as you know I am only a year past forty ? "

" Coincidence, perhaps."

" Very well ; let me tell you a little story. Some years ago I met a great astrologer in Lahore and started a large business negotiation on his advice. At that time I was in partnership with an older man. My partner asserted that the affair was far too risky and he refused to agree with me. Because he would not enter into the transaction we dissolved partnership. I carried the business through alone. It was a startling success and brought me a small fortune. Yet unless the Lahore astrologer had strongly supported me, I, too, would have feared to enter into the affair."

" Then you hold the opinion that——"

My companion finishes the sentence for me.

" Our lives are ruled by destiny and that destiny is shown by the positions of the stars ! "

I slip my objections to his statement upon the thread of an impatient gesture.

" The astrologers I have seen in India are such an illiterate, stupid-looking lot, that I cannot imagine what beneficial advice they can give anyone."

" Ah, you must not confuse a learned scholar like Sudhei Babu with those ignorant men you have encountered. Truly, those men are charlatans, but he is a highly intelligent Brahmin who lives in a large house of his own. He has made a deep study of the subject for many years and possesses many volumes of great rarity."

It suddenly occurs to me that my companion is no fool. He belongs to that type of modern Hindu who is enthusiastically practical and who does not hesitate to avail himself of the latest resources of Western invention. He is even ahead of me in some ways. He carries a magnificent moving-picture camera on the boat, whereas I can boast of nothing better than a humble pocket Kodak ; his servant produces a thermos flask and pours out a cooling drink, thus rebuking my lamentable forgetfulness of an excellent travelling requisite; and I know from his talk that he makes more use of the telephone when in Bombay than I have ever cared to do when in Europe. And yet he believes in astrology! I puzzle over the incongruous elements which compose his character.

"Let us understand each other. You fully accept the theory that every man's career and every worldly event is controlled by stars whose distance from our planet is so great that it beggars imagination?"

"Yes, I do," he answers quietly.

I shrug my shoulders, not knowing what to say.

He assumes an apologetic air.

"My dear sir, why not go and try him for yourself? You say in your country, 'The proof of the pudding is in the eating.' Find out what Sudhei Babu can discover about you. I have no use for the cheap charlatans myself, but I believe in that man's genuineness."

"H'm. I am sceptical about those who make a business of foretelling. Still, I shall take you at your word. Will you take me to this astrologer?"

"Certainly. Come and have tiffin[1] with me to-morrow and then we shall visit him."

We continue to float by broad palaces and old temples and little shrines bespattered with yellow flowers. I look indifferently at the broad stone steps crowded with bathing pilgrims and reflect that, though science rightly flatters itself with having put a check to superstition, I have yet to learn that a scientific attitude should put a check to investigation. If my companion can produce some evidential facts for the marked feeling of fatalism which he shares in common with most of his countrymen, I shall study them with an open mind.

§

The next day my amiable acquaintance brings me to a narrow, archaic street which runs through a heap of flat-topped houses. We stop before a rambling, old, stone-built structure. He leads the way through a dark, low-roofed passage and then we climb several stone steps, which are no wider than a man's body. We pass through a narrow room and find ourselves on the veranda of a spacious inner courtyard, around which the house has been built.

[1] Light afternoon tea.

A chained dog sights us and furiously barks a challenge. An array of large pots, each holding some tropical flowerless plant, spreads along the veranda. I follow my companion into a dark, frowning room and nearly fall over some broken flagstones at the threshold. As I stoop, I notice that loose earth lies sprinkled in the room as freely as it is sprinkled on the veranda floor. Does the astrologer find relief from his starry studies in plant-growing, I wonder ?

The other man shouts for the astrologer, whose name is echoed back to us by the ancient walls. We wait for two or three minutes and assist the dog, by further calls for the astrologer, to punctuate the silence of this seemingly deserted building. I begin to think that we have come on a fruitless errand, when the sound of someone stirring descends from an upper floor. Soon after I hear shuffling steps approach our room.

The figure of a slight man, carrying a candle in one hand and jangling a bunch of keys in the other, appears on the threshold. There follows a brief conversation in the semi-gloom and the astrologer unlocks another door, through which we all pass. He draws aside two heavy curtains and opens the shutters which cover tall balcony windows.

The astrologer's face is suddenly illuminated by the light which falls through the opened windows. I see a man who seems more like a figure from the ghost world than one of flesh and blood. Never before have I seen anyone so " sicklied o'er with the pale cast of thought." His death-like countenance, incredibly lean body and unearthly slow movements combine to produce a weird effect. The whites of his eyes are so pronounced as to heighten this impression, their whiteness offering a strong contrast to the jet-black pupils.

He takes his seat at a large table, whose surface is littered with papers. I discover that he speaks tolerably good English, yet it is only after some persuasion that I can induce him to carry on a direct conversation without the aid of a third party as interpreter.

" Please understand that I come as an enquirer, not as a believer," I begin.

He nods his thin head.

" Yes, I shall cast your horoscope and then you must tell me if you are satisfied."

" What is your fee ? "

" I have no fixed charge. Some people of good position pay me sixty rupees ; others pay me twenty rupees. I leave the amount to you."

I proceed to make it clear to him that, before we bother about the future, I want to test his knowledge of the past. He agrees.

For a while he busies himself with calculations over my birth date. After ten minutes he stoops to the floor behind his chair and searches among a disorderly pile of yellowed papers and palm-leaf manuscripts. Finally he draws out a little bundle of oblong, time-stained slips. He sketches a queer diagram on a sheet of paper and says :

" This is a chart of the heavens at the time you were born. And these Sanskrit texts explain the meaning of every part of the chart. Now, I shall tell you what the stars declare."

He scrutinizes the diagram with minute care, refers to one of the slips, and speaks again, in that low, emotionless voice which befits his personality so well.

" You are a writer from the West ? Am I correct ? "

I nod in agreement.

He tells me thereafter about my youth and describes, in quick succession, a few happenings of the earlier years of my life. In all, he gives me seven important points about my past. Five of them are broadly correct, but the other two are utterly wrong. Thus I am able to check up on the value or worthlessness of his powers. The honesty of the man is transparent. I am already convinced that he is incapable of deliberate deception. A 75 per cent success in an initial test is startling enough to show that Hindu astrology calls for investigation, but it also indicates that the latter is no precise, infallible science.

Once again Sudhei Babu burrows among his scattered papers and then describes my character with a fair degree of accuracy. After that he pictures the mental capacities which have brought me to follow a profession congenial to them. Here again, when he lifts his intellectual head and asks, " Have I read correctly ? " I cannot dispute his words.

He shuffles his papers, silently studies the diagram, and begins to speak of the future.

" The world will become your home. You shall travel far and wide, yet always you will carry a pen and do your writing work." And in this strain he discourses of what is yet to be. But I can run no investigating rule over his prophecies, so I am content to leave them where I find them—written in the stars ![1]

[1] One of his predictions, which I had instantaneously and sceptically dismissed as a ridiculous impossibility, has now received ample confirmation. But a second event has failed to mature at the date he gave for it. The others still wait for time's comment.

With his last words he again asks if I am satisfied. His fairly correct description of my past forty years on this amazing planet ; his almost completely successful effort to show me my mental self—these things silence the criticisms which I have come prepared to utter.

I want to ask myself, " Is this man merely drawing a bow at a venture ? Is he doing nothing more than a bit of smart guess-work ? " but I must candidly confess that his prognostications impress me. Yet time alone can tell whether there is any worth in them or not.

Is my Western attitude toward the dark question of fate to tumble about me like a house of thin cards ? What can I say about the matter ? I move over to the window and stand there, staring out at the opposite house and jingling the silver rupees in my pocket. Finally I return to my seat and question the astrologer.

" Why should it seem impossible to you that such distant stars can influence the lives of men ? " he rejoins softly. " Do not the tides respond to the distant moon in their ebb and flow ? Does not the body of a woman undergo a change every lunar month ? Does not the absence of the sun make men more liable to depressed moods ? "

" Quite so. But that is a far cry from asserting the claims of astrology. Why should Jupiter or Mars care two annas whether I meet with shipwreck or not ? "

He looks at me with an unruffled face.

" It is better that you regard the planets as being only symbols which stand in the sky ; it is not they which really influence us, but our own past," he replies. " You will never understand the reasonable nature of astrology unless you accept the doctrine that man is born again and again, and that his fate follows him with every birth. If he escapes the results of his evil actions in one birth, they will punish him in his next ; and if he does not receive a due reward for his good actions in one lifetime, he will surely receive it in the next. Without this doctrine of the continued return of man's soul to this earth until such time as it becomes perfect, the changing fortunes of different persons would seem the result of mere chance or blind luck. How can that be allowed by a just Deity ? No—it is our belief that when a man dies, his character, desires, thoughts and will continue to exist until they enter a body of flesh once more and come among us in the form of a new-born baby. The good or evil actions committed in the former birth will be suitably rewarded or punished in the present or even future births. This is how we explain fate. When I said that you would be shipwrecked one day and in grave danger of drowning, that is the fit destiny which God, in His hidden justice, has portioned out to you because of something wrong which you did in a former birth. It is not the planets which force you into shipwreck, but the inescapable results of your former actions. The planets and their positions only act as a record of this destiny; why they should do so I cannot say. No man's brain could ever have invented astrology; it came to us from long ago, when it was revealed for man's benefit by the great seers of ancient times."

As I listen to this plausible pronouncement, I hardly know what comment to make. He would bind one's soul and fortune to the stake of fate, but no healthy Westerner will let himself be despoiled of the prized possession of free will. What inhabitant of the energetic Occident can wax enthusiastic over this belief that it is destiny, and not choice, which directs him to take his steps? I gaze in bewilderment at this lean dreamer, this sallow wanderer through remote signs of the zodiac. "Do you know," I tell him, "that in some parts of the South the astrologers rank next to the priests, and that nothing of any magnitude can be done without previously consulting them? We Europeans would laugh at such a position, for we do not look kindly upon predictive methods. We like to think that we are free individuals and not the hapless victims of an inexorable destiny."

The astrologer shrugs his shoulders.

"In one of our old books, the *Hitopadesa*, it is declared: 'No one is capable of opposing the predestinations of fate, which are written on the foreheads of men.'" He lets his words sink in. Then he continues:

"What can you do? We must bear with the fruit of our actions."

But I am dubious about this statement and express my feelings.

The prophet of personal fortunes rises from his chair. I take the hint and prepare to leave him. He murmurs musingly:

"All is in the power of God. Nothing can escape Him. Who of us is really free? Whither can we go where God is not?"

At the door he adds hesitatingly:

"If you wish to come again we may talk further on these matters."

I thank him and accept the invitation.

" Very well. I shall expect you to-morrow, after the sun has gone down, about the hour of six."

§

Next day I return with the dusk to the astrologer's house. I have no intention of accepting all that he tells me, but neither have I formed any plans for rejection. I come to listen, possibly to learn, though the latter rests on how far his statements can be verified by experiment. And at this time I am ready enough to make experiments, but only if sufficiently strong reasons can be given for them. Yet Sudhei Babu's reading of my horoscope has stirred me to the perception that Hindu astrology is not superstitious nonsense, and that it may well warrant a deeper investigation. That thought represents the limit of my present attitude.

We sit facing each other at his large writing-table. A paraffin lamp throws a dim light upon the scene. Millions of other Indian homes are being lit to-night in the same way.

" I have fourteen rooms in this house," the astrologer tells me. " They are filled with ancient manuscripts, which are mostly written in Sanskrit. That explains why I need such a large house, although I live alone. Come and see my collection."

He removes the hanging lamp and leads the way into another room. Open boxes are ranged around the walls. I peer inside one of them and find it full of books and papers. Even the floor of the room is hidden under a multitude of papers, bundles of palm-leaf manuscripts and books whose covers are discoloured with age. I take a small bundle in my hand ; each leaf is covered with incomprehensible, faded characters. We go from room to room and find the same scene everywhere. The astrologer's library appears to be in a state of hopeless disorder, but he assures me that he is familiar with the whereabouts of every book and paper. It seems to me that his house has gathered the wisdom of Hindustan. Surely much of the strange lores of India is contained in the almost undecipherable pages of these ancient rolls of manuscript and in these Sanskrit books ?

We return to our chairs and the other man informs me :

"Nearly all my money has been spent in buying those manuscripts and books. Many of them are very rare and cost me large sums. So it is that I am very poor to-day."

"What subjects do they deal with?"

"They deal with human life and divine mysteries, while many are concerned with astrology."

"Then you are also a philosopher?"

His thin mouth relaxes into a half-smile.

"A man who is not a good philosopher will make a poor astrologer."

"If you will pardon me for saying so, I hope you do not over-study all those books. I was shocked at your pallor when I first met you."

"That is not surprising," he replies calmly. "I have not eaten for six days."

I express my concern.

"It is not a question of money. The woman who comes every day to cook for me is away ill. She has been away for six days."

"Then why not call in another woman?"

He shakes his head firmly.

"No. My food must not be cooked by a lower caste woman. I would rather not eat for a month than permit that to happen. I must wait till my servant's health is restored. But I expect her to return in a day or two."

I peer at him intently and notice that he wears the sacred thread of "The Sons of Brahma." The triple cord of woven linen which nestles under his chin is placed around the neck of every Brahmin baby and is never to be removed till death. So he is a Brahmin.

"Why trouble yourself with a superstitious caste restriction," I urge. "Surely your health is more important than that?"

"It is not superstition. Everyone gives out a magnetic influence which is quite real, even though the instruments of your Western science have not yet discovered it. The cook who prepares food throws her influence into it, unconsciously of course. A cook of low character will thus taint the food with bad magnetism, which passes into the person who eats the food."

"What a strange theory!"

"But it is true."

I change the subject.

"How long have you been an astrologer?"

" For nineteen years. I took up the profession after my marriage."

" Ah, I understand."

" No, I am not a widower. Shall I explain? When I was a youth of thirteen I prayed often to God for knowledge, and so was led to various people who taught me and to different books. I became so fascinated by study that I would sit up reading all day and far into the night. My parents arranged a marriage for me. A few days after we were married, my wife got angry with me and said: 'I have married a human book!' On the eighth day she ran away with the man who used to drive our carriage!"

Sudhei Babu pauses. I cannot help smiling at his wife's caustic comment, though her speedy elopement must have created a sensation in conservative India. But the ways of women are tortuous and beyond the compass of a man's mind.

" After a while I recovered from the shock," he continues, " and forgot her. All my emotions were blotted out. I went deeper than ever into the study of astrology and the divine mysteries. It is then that I took up my greatest study, the book of Brahma Chinta."

" Perhaps you will tell me what that book is concerned with?"

" The title can be translated as *Divine Meditation*, or as *The Quest of Brahma*, or even as *God-Knowledge*. The entire work contains several thousand pages, but the part I study is only a section. It took me nearly twenty years to collect even that, because it exists only in scattered parts here and there. I have slowly obtained these different parts through agents in the various provinces of India. There are twelve chief divisions among its subjects, and many subdivisions. The chief topics are philosophy, astrology, Yoga, life after death, and other deep matters."

" Do you know if there is any English translation of the book?"

He shakes his head.

" I have never heard of one. Few, even, are the Hindus who know of the existence of the book. Hitherto, it has been jealously guarded and kept secret. It came originally from Tibet, where it is looked upon as very sacred and only chosen students are allowed to study it."

" When was it written?"

" It was composed thousands of years ago by the sage Bhrigu, who lived so long ago that I cannot give you the date.

It teaches a method of Yoga which is quite different from all others which exist in India. You are interested in Yoga, are you not ?"

"How do you know that ?"

For answer, Sudhei Babu quietly produces the chart which he has constructed around my birth-date, and moves his pencil among the strange glyphs which represent planetary configurations and zodiacal signs.

"Your horoscope surprises me. It is out of the ordinary for a European, and not even a common one for an Indian. It shows that you will have a great tendency to study Yoga and that you will enjoy the favour of sages who will help you to delve deeply into the subject. Yet you will not limit yourself to Yoga alone, but become versed in other mystic philosophies."

He pauses and looks at me straight in the eyes. I receive the subtle impression that he is about to make a statement which will be tantamount to a revelation of his inner life.

"There are two kinds of sages: those who selfishly keep their knowledge to themselves, and those who, after obtaining enlightenment, share it freely with others who are seeking for it. Your horoscope shows that you are almost at the gate of illumination and therefore my words will not fall on deaf ears. I am ready to impart my knowledge to you!"

I am taken aback at this strange turn of affairs. I first come to Sudhei Babu to check up on the claims of Indian astrology; I come again to listen to his further defence of its basic postulate. And now he unexpectedly offers to become my teacher in Yoga!

"If you will practise the methods of Brahma Chinta you will need no teacher," he continues. "Your own soul will become your teacher."

I suddenly realize my mistake and wonder whether he has read my thoughts.

"You take me by surprise!" is all I can say.

"I have already instructed a few persons in this knowledge but I never regard myself as their master—only as their brother or friend. So I do not undertake to become your teacher in the ordinary sense. The spirit of the sage Bhrigu will simply use this body and mind of mine to *communicate* his teachings to you."

"I do not understand how you can combine the profession of astrology with the teaching of a Yoga system?"

His thin hands spread themselves upon the table.

"The explanation is this. I live in the world and serve it

through my work, which happens to be astrology. Secondly, I refuse to be looked upon as a teacher of Yoga, because in our Brahma Chinta the only teacher acknowledged is God. He is the only preceptor we acknowledge. He, as the universal soul, is in us, and will teach us. Look on me as a brother, if you wish, but do not look on me as a spiritual preceptor. Those who have a teacher are too apt to lean on him and to depend on him instead of their own soul."

"And yet you depend on astrology for guidance," I retort quickly, "instead of your own soul."

"You are not right. I never look at my own horoscope now —in fact, I tore it up many years ago."

I express astonishment at this statement. He replies :

"I have found the light and do not need astrology to guide me, but those who still walk in darkness find it helpful. I have placed my life entirely in the Lord's hands. I carry that act to its proper conclusion by giving up all care about future or past. Whatever the Lord sends, that I accept as His will. I have given my whole self—body, mind, actions and feelings—to the will of the Almighty."

"Suppose you are threatened with death by a murderous ruffian, would you do nothing and accept that as God's will ? "

"When any danger arises I know that I have only to pray and instantly to receive His protection. Prayer is necessary but fear is not. I pray frequently and the Lord has marvellously protected me. Yet I have been through great troubles. Through all of them I was conscious of His help and I trust Him fully under every event. One day you, too, will disregard the future and become indifferent to it."

"There will have to be a remarkable change in me before that happens," I observe drily.

"That change will surely come."

"Are you certain ? "

"Yes, you cannot escape your destiny. This spiritual rebirth is an event which comes from God, whether one looks for it or not."

"You say strange things, Sudhei Babu."

The idea of Deity is the unknown factor which enters into so many of my conversations in this land. The Hindus are essentially religious and I am often tantalized by the familiar way in which they introduce mention of God. Is it possible for them to appreciate the view-point of a doubting Westerner, who has surrendered simple faith for complex reason ? I realize that it will be unavailing and suit no practical purpose to throw up this question of Deity into argument with the astrologer. I have no taste for partaking of any theological diet which he will probably place before me, so I turn the subject back to less controversial ground.

"Let us talk of other matters, for God and I have never met."

He looks at me fixedly, his peculiar black and white eyes searching my soul.

"The chart of your horoscope cannot be wrongly drawn or I might keep back my knowledge from an unready mind. But the stars move without fault; what you are unable to grasp to-day will linger in your thoughts for a time and then return with double force. I tell you again that I am ready to impart the way of Brahma Chinta to you."

"And I am ready to learn it."

§

Evening after evening I visit the old stone house of the astrologer and receive my lessons in Brahma Chinta. The pale lamplight throws flickering patterns upon his narrow face as he initiates me into the arcana of this primitive Tibetan Yoga system.[1] At no time does he adopt the attitude of spiritual superiority or egoistic tutorship. He is humility personified and usually prefaces his instruction with the phrase, "In this teaching of Brahma Chinta it is said——"

"What is the supreme object, the final goal of this Yoga of Brahma Chinta?" I ask him one evening.

"We seek the condition of sacred trance, for in that condition man obtains perfect proof that he is a soul. Then it is that he frees his mind from his surroundings; objects fade away and the outside world seems to disappear. He discovers the soul as a living, real being within himself; its bliss, peace and power overwhelm him. All he needs is a single experience of this kind

[1] I do not care to commit the details of this system to print, nor would Western readers derive any benefit even if I did so. Its essence is a series of meditations which aim at creating what the tutor described as "the vacuum mind!" There are six different paths of practice to be studied, and there are ten stages of attainment upon the principal path. It is neither right nor necessary for the average European to take up the practice of a method which is fit only for jungle retreats or mountain monasteries, and which might even prove dangerous. Insanity lies around the corner for Western amateurs who dabble in such practices.

to obtain the proof that there is a divine and undying life in himself; never again can he forget it."

A shred of doubt prompts my enquiry:

"Are you sure that all this is not a deep form of auto-suggestion?"

A ghost of a smile curls around his lips.

"When a mother gives birth to a child, is it possible that she can doubt, even for a single moment, what is happening? And when she comes to look back on that experience, could she ever think that it was only an auto-suggestion? And when she watches her child grow up beside her year after year, can she hesitate at any time and disbelieve in its existence? In the same way, the labour of spiritual rebirth comes as such a tremendous event in one's life that it cannot be forgotten; it changes everything for one. When one enters into the sacred trance, a kind of vacuum is created within the mind; God—or, as you do not seem to care for that word, the soul, the higher power, shall I say, enters and fills that vacuum. When that happens, it is impossible to avoid becomng filled with intense happiness. One also feels a great love for the whole of creation. The body will appear to an observer to be not only in a trance, but apparently dead, for all breathing stops when the deepest point is attained."

"Is that not dangerous?"

"No. The trance is attained in complete solitude or a friend may be permitted to watch over one. I frequently enter into the sacred trance and can always emerge from it whenever I wish I usually stay in it for two or three hours, and fix the time of its ending beforehand. It is a wonderful experience because what you see as the universe I see again within myself! That is why I say that all you need to learn can be learnt from your own soul. After I have communicated the complete Yoga of Brahma Chinta to you, no master will be necessary; you will need no outside guidance."

"You have never had a teacher yourself?"

"None. I have never looked for one since I discovered the secrets of Brahma Chinta. Nevertheless, some great masters have come to me from time to time. This has happened when I have entered the sacred trance and become conscious in the inner world. These great sages have appeared before me in their psychic forms and placed their hands on my head in blessing. Therefore I say again, trust the guidance of your own soul and teachers will come unbidden to you in the inner world."

For the next two minutes there is a brooding silence. The other man seems to be caught up in a cloud of thoughts. Then, very quietly, very humbly, this strange tutor says:

"Once, during the sacred trance, I saw Jesus."

"You mystify me!" I exclaim.

But he does not hasten to explain. Instead, he suddenly rolls the whites of his eyes upwards in a most alarming manner. There is another minute of intense silence, and only when he brings his eyes back to their normal appearance am I reassured.

When he addresses me again a faintly enigmatical smile hovers once more around his lips.

"Such is the greatness of this sacred trance that death cannot catch a man while he is in it. There are some Yogis on the Tibetan side of the Himalayas who have practised to perfection this path of Brahma Chinta. Because it pleases them to do so they have secluded themselves in mountain caves, where they have entered the profoundest degree of the sacred trance. In that condition, the pulse stops, the heart no longer beats and the blood does not flow through the unmoving body. Anyone finding them would think that they are dead. Do not imagine that they have gone into a kind of sleep, because they are as fully conscious as you or I. They have entered the inner world, where they live higher lives. Their minds have become released from the limits set by the body and they discover the whole universe within themselves. One day they will come out of their trance, but then they will be many hundreds of years old!"

So once again I hear this incredible tradition of perennial human life. Apparently it will follow my feet wherever I go under this Eastern sun. But shall I ever track down one of these legendary immortals and behold him face to face? And will the West ever discover and accept, as a scientific and psychological contribution, this ancient magic cradled in the bleak climate of Tibet? Who knows?

§

My last lesson in the fantastic doctrines of the Yoga of Brahma Chinta comes to an end.

I persuade the sedentary astrologer to venture out of his house, which he rarely leaves, and give his limbs a little exercise. We wander through narrow alleys, in an effort to avoid the packed bazaars which bar our way to the river. With all its ancient squalor and unhygienic overcrowding, Benares nevertheless presents a variety of colourful sights to the man who wanders its streets afoot.

It is afternoon and my companion carries an open, flat parasol on his shoulder so as to keep off the sun's rays. His frail figure and weary languid movements do not conduce to quick progress, and I change our route in order to shorten our journey.

We pass into the Street of the Brass Workers. The air rings with the hammers of bearded craftsmen, and their products, shining brazen vessels, gleam in the sunlight. Here, too, are multitudes of little brass images—earthly representations of the chief gods in the Hindu Pantheon.

An old man crouches in the shade by the roadside in another street. He looks up at me with feeble eyes and pathetic face. His fear removed, he begs for alms.

We drift through the Street of the Merchants of Grain, where little wooden platforms exhibit piles of red and golden grains. The shopkeepers sit on folded legs or squat on haunch and heel beside their goods. They throw a few glances at the odd couple that passes by, and then resume their patient waiting for customers.

Odours mingle indiscriminately in the other streets. As we approach the river, we walk right into a region which seems to be a hunting ground for those who seek alms. Lean beggars drag themselves along the dusty road. One of them comes near to me and looks inquiringly into my eyes. He possesses a face of unspeakable melancholy. My heart is moved embarrassingly.

Farther on I nearly stumble over a fleshless old woman, whose body is a bunch of hanging skin and protruding bones. She, too, glances into my eyes. There is no reproach, only dull acceptance. I bring out my purse. Immediately she becomes an animated creature once again. She extends a skinny arm and takes the proffered coins.

I tremble at my own good fortune in having plenty of food, good clothes, proper shelter and other desirable things. When I think of the haunting eyes of those unfortunate wretches, I feel guilty. By what right do I enjoy the possession of so many rupees, so many annas, when those poor beggars own nothing more than rags? Suppose, by some accident of birth or fluke of fate, I had been born in the place of one of them? I play for a while with this ghastly thought, but horror eventually causes me to send it into oblivion.

What is the meaning of this mystery of chance, which, by the mere fortune of birth, puts one man in dirt-stained rags upon this road and another in silken robes in yonder river-side palace? Life is truly a dark enigma; I cannot comprehend it.

"Let us sit down here," says the astrologer, when we reach the Ganges. We sit in the shade and look down the river upon the stretch of broad stone steps, rambling terraces and jutting platforms. Little groups of pilgrims are constantly coming and going.

The shapely forms of two slender minarets soar gracefully into the pearly sky to a height of nearly three hundred feet. They mark the charming Mosque of Aurungzeeb, that Muhammedan anachronism in this most Hindu of Hindu cities.

But the astrologer has noted my sad preoccupation with beggars, for he turns his sallow face towards me and says:

"India is a poor country." His voice is somewhat apologetic. "Its people have been sunk in inertia. The English race possesses some fine points and I believe that God brought them to our country for its benefit. Before they came life was unsafe; law and justice were often set aside. It is my hope that the English will not leave India; we need their help, but it should be given in friendship now, and not by force. However, the destiny of both nations must fulfil itself."

"Ah, your fatalism returns again!"

He ignores my comment and falls into silence. At length he asks:

"How can the two peoples avoid God's will? Day is ever followed by night, and night is ever followed by day. So is it with the history of nations. Great changes brood over the world. India has been sunk in sloth and inertia, but she will change until she becomes filled with desires and ambitions, which ever precede activity. Europe burns with practical activities, but the strength of its materialism will pass away and it will turn its face towards higher ideals. It will seek out the inner things. And the same will happen to America."

I listen in silence.

"For this reason the philosophic and spiritual teachings of our land will travel towards the West like a wave of the ocean," he continues gravely. "Scholars have already translated some of our Sanskrit manuscripts and sacred books into Western languages, but many texts are hidden away in cave libraries in out of the way parts of India, Nepal and Tibet. Those, too, must eventually be made known to the world. The time will come before long when the ancient philosophies and inner knowledge of India shall unite with the practical sciences of the West. The secrecy of past times must give way to the needs of this century. I am glad that all this will happen."

I stare into the greenish water of the Ganges. The river is so strangely tranquil that it hardly seems to flow. Its surface shimmers in the sunlight.

He addresses me yet again :

" The destiny of each race of people must be realized, just as the destiny of every person must be fulfilled. The Lord is omnipotent. Men and nations cannot escape from their self-earned fate, but they may be protected throughout their troubles and even saved from great dangers."

" And how does one obtain such protection ? "

" By prayer, by keeping a child-like nature when one turns towards the Almighty, and by remembering Him not on one's lips, but in one's heart, especially before one begins any action. In happy days try to enjoy them as a blessing of God, and in troubles try to think that it is very much like a medicine to heal your inner disease. Fear Him not, as He is all merciful."

" You do not believe that God is remote from this world, then ? "

" No. God is a Spirit which is hidden in people and throughout this universe. If you see any beauty in Nature, a beautiful landscape, for instance, do not worship it for its own sake, but remember that it is beautiful because of the Deity present in it. See the Divinity in objects and people, and do not be so captivated by the outer forms that you forget the inner Spirit which gives them life."

" You mingle your doctrines of fate, religion and astrology in a peculiar manner, Sudhei Babu."

He gazes solemnly at me.

" Why so ? These doctrines are not of my creation. They have descended to us from the most distant ages of the past. The tremendous power of destiny, the worship of our Creator and the lore of planetary influences were known to the earliest peoples. They were not such savages as you Westerners imagine. But have I not prophesied ? The West will rediscover before this century closes how real are these invisible forces which enter into the lives of all men."

" It will be extremely hard for the West to give up its inborn notion that a man's will is free to make or mar his own life."

" Whatever happens is by His will and what seems like free will really works by His power. The Almighty returns to men the good or evil fruits of their thoughts and deeds in earlier bodies. It is best to accept His will, but one will not tremble under sorrows if one looks to Him for the strength to endure them."

"Let us hope that you are right, for the sake of those unfortunate beggars whom we have just encountered."

"That is the only answer I can make," he rejoins shortly. "If you would follow the path into your own soul, the way of Brahma Chinta which I have shown you, these problems would clear themselves."

I realize that he has now conducted me to the limits of his argumentative possibilities and that I must find my own way henceforth.

One of my coat pockets hides a fateful telegram, that bids me whisk myself into a train out of Benares. In another pocket there reposes a folding kodak. I ask the astrologer to pose for his photograph. He politely declines.

I press him more insistently.

"But why?" he remonstrates. "My ugly face and shabby clothes?"

"Please! Your photograph will remind me of you in later years when I may be in distant lands."

"The best reminder," he replies gently, "will be holy thoughts and unselfish deeds."

I yield to his objection reluctantly, and the camera disappears again into my pocket.

When he rises to return at last and I begin to follow him, I discover, close by, a seated figure, who has taken shelter from the terrific sun under a huge, round, bamboo umbrella. His face is fixed in rapt meditation and I perceive by the ochre colour of his robe that he is a holy man belonging to a superior order.

We go a little way and find a cow—possibly a member of the sacred variety which abounds in Benares—sleeping in that strange posture familiar to its kind. It lies across our track with legs doubled back under its abdomen.

We reach the shop of a money-changer, where I hail a carriage and then our ways part.

§

I indulge in an orgy of travelling during the next few days. I spend my nights in wayside rest houses put up by a paternal government for travelling officials and other persons who have to journey into the interior.

One of these rest houses possesses no amenities worth

mentioning, but I discover that it has a plentiful population of ants. After two hours' slow torture and vain efforts to repel their attacks, I decide to leave the bed and spend the night in a chair.

Time trickles by unpleasantly until my thoughts let go of their surroundings and fasten themselves upon the fatalistic philosophy of the Benares astrologer.

Simultaneously I remember the wretched beggars who dragged their hungry bodies along the road. Life does not let them live and does not let them die. The wealthy Marwari money-lender may pass them in his ornate, comfortably-sprung carriage, but they accept him, as they accept their misery, with a complete submission to the will of God. In this land of a burning sky, even the pitiful leper seems content with his lot. Such is the narcotic fatalism which creeps into the bones of so many Indians!

I realize how vain it is for the Occidental partisan of free will to argue with the Oriental advocate of an all-powerful destiny. To the latter there is but one side to the problem, the side which unquestioningly accepts the dogma that there is no problem! Fate rules his roost and there is nothing more to be said.

What self-reliant Westerner likes to hear that we are but marionettes which dangle from the strings of fate, and which move up and down or from right to left at the bidding of an unseen hand? I remember that remarkable outburst of Napoleon before his army's brilliant dash across the Alps:

"Impossible? There is no such word in my dictionary!"

But I have studied and re-studied the fascinating records of Napoleon's entire life, and memory brings back to me strange lines which he wrote down at St. Helena, where his colossal brain raced again and again over the past.

"I was always a fatalist. What is written in the heavens is written. . . . My star grew dim; I felt the reins slip from my hands and yet I could do nothing."

The man who held such paradoxical, contradictory beliefs could not have solved the mystery and one doubts whether anyone has ever completely solved it. It may be that ever since the brain of man commenced to function, this ancient problem has been discussed by people all the way from the North Pole to the South. The cocksure, as usual, have settled it to their satisfaction. The philosophical still enter up the account of pros and cons but hesitate to strike a balance.

I have not forgotten the astrologer's surprisingly correct

interpretation of my horoscope. At odd moments I have mused over it, until I wonder whether some of this Oriental fatalistic foolishness has crept into my head. Whenever I have remembered how this man of modest assumptions read my past, how he recalled the fluttering phenomena of bygone events back to temporary existence, I hesitate and feel tempted to collect material for a fat treatise upon this hoary problem of fate and free will. But I know that it will be a useless task to let my pen play with the thought of destiny and that I may probably finish up in the same abysmal darkness with which I begin. For the problems of astrology will need to be brought in and my task will become complicated beyond my power. Yet such are the gigantic strides of modern invention, that the day when we shall take Cook's tours to the distant planets may not be far off! It will then be possible to discover whether the starry frame possesses any real significance in our lives. Meanwhile, one may test the powers of an astrologer or two, bearing in mind Sudhei Babu's warning about their fallibility and about the fragmentary nature of that portion of astrology which has been revealed to the world.

And yet, even assuming and admitting that in some strange fourth-dimensional manner the future already exists, is it desirable to learn those secrets of personal destiny which are curtained from one's eyes?

On this questioning note, my musings come to a dead end and sleep overtakes me.

A few days later I am in a town several hundred miles away from Benares, when the news comes of startling riots in the latter city. It is the unpleasant story of Hindu-Moslem strife, which usually begins in a petty way, but is used by ruffians who want a pseudo-religious pretext for their looting, maiming and murdering.

A reign of terror rules the city for several days. That lamentable period brings the usual tale of broken heads, tortured bodies and indiscriminate slaying. I feel concerned for the astrologer's safety, but it is impossible to get into touch with him. The postmen are too scared to venture into the streets and no private letter or telegram can be delivered.

I am compelled to wait until King Mob is dethroned in Benares, and then desptach one of the first wires which penetrate the unhappy city. Back comes a simple letter of thanks in which the astrologer ascribes his safety to "the protection of the Almighty." And upon the reverse side of the paper he has inscribed ten rules of practice of the Yoga of Brahma Chinta!

CHAPTER XIII

THE GARDEN OF THE LORD

OUT of the scurrying of my feet hither and thither over the face of North India, two tracks converge upon a unique, little-known colony, which is housed in a town that bears the poetical name of Dayalbagh, the Garden of the Lord.

One of the tracks starts in Lucknow, where I have the good offices of Sunderlal Nigam as guide, philosopher and friend during my stay in that picturesque city. We roam the city together and talk philosophy as we roam. He is, I suppose, not more than twenty-one or twenty-two, but, like many of his Indian brothers, he has matured early.

We wander through the old Moghul palaces and muse upon the inexorable fate which has overtaken the vanished kings. I fall in love anew with the glorious Indo-Persian architecture, whose graceful curves and delicate colourings reveal the refined taste of its creators. How shall I ever forget these bright days when I idle among the orange trees of the royal pleasure-gardens which grace Lucknow?

We explore colourful edifices where once the seductive favourites of the old kings of Oudh flaunted their olive-skinned beauty upon marble balconies and in golden baths. Now these palaces are empty of royal flesh and hold only memories.

I return again and again to a beautiful mosque which stands near the quaintly named Monkey Bridge. Its exterior is white throughout and gleams in the sunlight like a fairy palace. The shapely minarets seem to rise in perpetual prayer to bright heaven. Peeping inside, I see a crowd of worshippers prostrating themselves upon the ground and rhythmically invoking Allah. The scene receives accentuated charm from the brightly coloured little rugs upon which the devout perform their prostrations. None can doubt the fervour of these followers of the Prophet, for their religion seems a living force to them.

Amid all these excursions and peregrinations I become gradually impressed by certain characteristics belonging to my young guide. His shrewd remarks, his exceptional intellectuality and his matter-of-fact attitude towards mundane affairs, are somehow blent with the depth and mysticism of a student of Yoga. It is only after repeated meetings and ardent discussions, during which I become aware that he is sounding and probing my own beliefs and ideas, that he reveals himself to be a member of a semi-secret fraternity called the Radha Soamis.

§

I pick up the second track which leads me to Dayalbagh from Mallik, another member of the same brotherhood. He comes within my orbit at another place and time. As Indians go, he is a fine, fair-skinned, stalwart fellow. For centuries his people have had as neighbours, wild frontier tribes, who keep covetous eyes on their neighbours' possessions. But the wise British Government is taming these restless fire-eaters, not by recourse to the old methods of endless fighting, but by taking them into its service and pay.

Mallik is superintending some of the fierce tribesmen who have submitted to the more pacific and useful occupations of making roads across hill and desert, constructing bridges, and building defence forts and barracks. Many of these wild-looking persons carry their rifles—more perhaps from old habit than from present need. They are at work all along this stretch of the North-West Frontier, making new routes for traders and new defences for soldiers.

Mallik works hard and well near Dera Ismail Khan, that frontier outpost of Empire. His character harmoniously couples a sturdy self-reliance and intense practicality with nobility of character and profound thought. I am impressed by the careful balance of his qualities.

After a strong initial reticence which is in accord with all the ancient traditions of Yoga, he reluctantly yields to my enquiries and admits that he has a master whom he periodically visits, whenever his service leaves permit him to do so. His master, whose name is Sahabji Maharaj, is head of the Radha Soamis. And I learn for the second time that his master has conceived the astonishing and interesting notion of combining a Yoga discipline with a daily life based on Western ways and ideas.

§

The friendly efforts of these two men, Nigam and Mallik, bear fruit at last. I am to be the guest of His Holiness Sahabji Maharaj, who is uncrowned king of the Radha Soamis' own town of Dayalbagh.

I motor the few, dusty miles of road from Agra to the colony.

Dayalbagh—the Garden of the Lord! If my early impression is correct, the founder is striving to keep the town true to its beautiful name.

I am taken to a building which houses the master's private office. The waiting-room is furnished in an attractive European style. From my restful easy chair I can appreciate the nicely painted walls and the refined simplicity of the furniture.

Here is Westernization with a vengeance! I have encountered Yogis in bare, drab bungalows, in lonely mountain caves and in gloomy, thatched huts on river banks, but never have I expected to find one of the tribe housed in such a modern environment. What manner of man is the leader of this unusual fraternity, I wonder?

I am not left long in doubt, for the door slowly opens and he himself walks in. His figure is of medium height. His head is wrapped in a spotless white turban; his features are refined, though not typically Indian; with a slightly paler skin he might have passed for a quiet American. A pair of large spectacles cover his eyes and a short moustache adorns his upper lip. He wears the high-necked many-buttoned long coat which is the Indian tailor's adaptation of our Western style.

His bearing, as he approaches, is modest and gentle. He welcomes me with courtly dignity.

Our greeting over, I wait till he has settled down in his chair and then venture to compliment him on the artistic decorations of the room.

A row of brilliant teeth gleams across his mouth as he smiles his reply:

"God is not only love but beauty. As man begins to express the Spirit within him, he should express more beauty—not only in self but in surroundings and environments."

His English is noticeably well spoken. The voice is quick and confident.

There is a little period of silence and then he speaks again:

" But there is another decoration, upon a room's walls and furnishings, which is invisible. Yet it is very important. Do you know that these things carry the influence of people's thoughts and feelings ? Every room, every chair even, gives out the unseen influence of the person who has constantly used it. You may not see this atmosphere but it is nevertheless there, and all who enter within its range are unconsciously affected by it—to varying degrees."

" Do you mean that there are electrical or magnetic radiations around objects which reflect human characters ? "

" Quite so. Thoughts are real things on their own plane and they attach themselves, for shorter or longer periods, to whatever we consistently use."

" That is an interesting theory."

" It is more than a theory ; it is a fact ! Man possesses a subtler body than the physical, and in this subtle body there exist centres of activity which correspond to the physical organs of sense-activity. Through these centres he can discern invisible forces for, when they are energized, they bestow psychic and spiritual sight."

A brief pause follows and then he asks my impressions of India's condition. I frankly criticize his country's neglect of modern ways of living, its slowness in picking up all those pleasant comforts, handy conveniences and mechanical inventions which improve man's brief sojourn in this world, its inattention to the demands of sensible hygiene and proper sanitation, and its excessive devotion to stupid social customs and cruel practices, which are supposedly based on religious practices. I tell him freely that priestly preoccupations seem to have kept India's energies in a cul-de-sac with deplorable results. I instance some of the irrational things which I have seen done in the name of religion, but which merely succeed in proving how men can neglect or misuse the gift of intelligence which their God has bestowed upon them. My outspoken observations draw a definite assent from the lips of Sahabji Maharaj.

" You have hit on the very points which form part of my programme of reform," he remarks, gazing at me reminiscently.

" On the whole, it seems that many Indians expect God to do for them what they are perfectly capable of doing for themselves."

" Exactly. We Hindus talk glibly of religion in order to cover up a lot of things which have nothing to do with religion. The trouble is that for the first fifty years or so a religion is pure and vital. Later it degenerates into a mere philosophy; its followers become talkers—not religiously-living men. Finally it descends, for its last and longest phase, into the arms of hypocritical priests. In the end, hypocrisy becomes accepted as religion."

I gasp at such straightforward admissions.

"What is the use of wrangling about heaven and hell, about God and so forth? Humanity finds itself on the physical plane and it ought not to neglect the matters which pertain to this plane. Let us try to make our life here more beautiful and happier," he concludes.

"That is why I have sought you out. Your disciples seem such fine men, straining to be as practical and up-to-date as any European, making no parade of religion but living good lives, and withal they keep to their Yoga practices with faithful regularity."

Sahabji smiles in acknowledgment.

"I am glad you have observed that," he replies quickly. "By setting up these activities at Dayalbagh I am attempting to show the world the same thing—that a man can be perfectly spiritual without running away to caves, and that he can reach the highest attainments in Yoga while carrying on with worldly avocations."

"If you can succeed in that effort, the world may think a lot more of Indian teachings than it does now."

"We are going to succeed," comes the confident answer. "Let me tell you a story. When I first came here to begin the colony, one of my chief desires was to have plenty of trees about the place. But outsiders told me that it was impossible to grow trees in this barren, sandy soil. The Jumna is not far off and this site is one of its old tracks—an ancient river bed, in short. There were no experts among us and we had to learn by frequent experiment and constant failure which kind of tree could live in such unpromising soil. Almost all the trees planted during the first year—and there were over a thousand of them—died off. However, one tree thrived. We noted it and kept up our endeavours. Now there are nine thousand healthy trees growing in Dayalbagh. I tell you this because it is symbolical of the attitude with which we are facing our problems. We found barren ground here; it seemed so worthless that no one else would buy it. Look how it has been transformed!"

"Then it is your aim to build an Arcadia near Agra?"

He laughs.

I tell him of my desire to see the town.

"Certainly! I shall arrange it for you at once. See Dayalbagh first and then we can talk about its why and wherefore. You will understand my ideas better when you can see them in practice."

He rings a business-like bell. A few minutes later I am walking on a tour of inspection along half-finished streets and among bright-looking factory buildings. My guide is Captain Sharma, who was formerly in the Indian Army Medical Service, but who is now devoting all his services to the constructive effort which is being made here by his master. A quick reading of his character conveys the impression of another successful combination of Western striving with sincere spirituality.

A luxuriant avenue provides the entrance to Dayalbagh, which is a clean little town. All the streets are bordered by shady trees. Some beautiful flower gardens adorn the central place. I am told that they represent repeated efforts to conquer dry desert, which does not take kindly to horticultural activity.

A mulberry tree which was planted by Sahabji Maharaj in 1915, when he began to build his colony, stands as a symbol of his appreciation of an artistic background.

The industrial quarter's chief feature is a group of workshops which are called "Model Industries." They are sensibly designed, light, airy, clean and spacious.

§

My first steps take me into the footwear factory. Busy driving-belts hum continuously from an overhead spindle and set a long line of machines in operation. The dusky mechanics work with deft hands amid the din, and seem as expert at their task as the operators I have seen in huge English factories at Northampton. The workshop manager tells me that he had learnt his technique in Europe, whither he had gone to study twentiety-century methods of leather-goods manufacture.

Boots, shoes, sandals, handbags and belts pass noisily through all the processes of mechanical manufacture. The men at the machines had begun as raw novices and were taught and trained to their work by the manager.

Some of the goods produced find a local outlet in Dayalbagh and in Agra, while the rest goes to more distant cities. Shops are being opened in the latter places, the sales organization being based on the multiple store idea.

I pass into the next building, which proves to be a textile factory. The products are mercerized cloths and silks, which are made in a limited range of patterns.

In another building I find an up-to-date engineering machine-shop, a smithy and a moulding shop, where a monster sledge-hammer sounds the active inspiration of the place with each of its power-operated thuds. Scientific instruments, laboratory apparatus, balances and weights are being made in a nearby workshop, and made well enough to have won the patronage of the United Provinces Government. I watch the delicate operations of gold, nickel and brass electro-plating.

The other departments of "Model Industries" are busily producing electric fans, gramophones, knives and furniture. One of the mechanics has invented a special type of sound-box and this, too, will be manufactured in the near future.

I am surprised to discover a fountain-pen workshop and learn that it is the first one to come into existence in India. A long series of experiments has been necessary before the first pen could be marketed. One thing has baffled these industrial pioneers: how to put the iridium tip on gold nibs. They hope to discover the secret one day but meanwhile the nibs are sent to a European firm to undergo the process of tipping.

A complete printing equipment at the Dayalbagh Press looks after the town's print needs, both in the business and literary fields. I inspect samples of its output in three languages—Hindu, Urdu and English. A small weekly newspaper, the *Prem Pracharak*, is also run off the machines and posted to many Radha Soamists living in distant parts of the country.

In every building I find workers who are not merely satisfied but positively enthusiastic. A trade union would be an utter anomaly in this place. Everyone does his job, whether it be high or low, as though it were a real pleasure and not a task.

The town possesses its own electrical generating installation, which provides the power for all the machinery in factories and for the ventilating ceiling fans in larger houses. In addition, every house is electrically illuminated at communal expense, thus avoiding the necessity of costly meters.

The agricultural section contains a small but modern farm, which is still in an early stage of development. A steam tractor and a steam plough are amongst the mechanical equipment. The chief products are fresh vegetables and cow fodder.

Perhaps the most efficiently organized section is the dairy farm. Nowhere else in India have I seen its like. It constitutes a model dairy fit for exhibition purposes. Every head of cattle is a picked specimen which provides a significant and favourable contrast to the animals one need not go further than Agra to see. Scrupulous cleanliness is observed in the stalls and I am told that the scientific methods pursued have resulted in a substantially higher yield of milk than that obtained in the average Indian dairy. A pasteurizing and refrigerating plant has enabled those inhabitants of Dayalbagh and Agra who appreciate good, germ-free milk to obtain it for the first time. Another imported appliance is an electrical butter-making machine. All the credit for this section goes to a son of Sahabji Maharaj. That energetic and efficient young man informs me that he travelled to the chief dairying centres of England, Holland, Denmark and the United States in order to learn the most up-to-date methods used in his work.

The supply of water for the farms, as well as for the rest of the town, proved a difficult problem in the colony's early days. An irrigation canal was dug and a waterworks installation erected, but expanding demand forced Sahabji Maharaj to seek additional sources of supply. He enlisted the help of Government engineers, who bored a deep tube-well with successful results.

The colony possesses its own banking institution, a strongly built structure with iron-grilled windows bearing the words: "Radha Soami General and Assurance Bank, Limited." The bank has an authorized capital of twenty lakhs[1] of rupees, and not only transacts private banking business but controls the town's finances.

The Radha Soami Educational Institute stands in the centre of Dayalbagh; it is fitly placed for it is the finest building in the colony. Its two hundred feet of red brickwork look well to a Western eye. The windows are shaped into Gothic arches and surrounded by white marble. Flowering gardens front the edifice.

This modern High School has several hundred students and is managed by a Principal and thirty-two qualified teachers. The latter are idealists who are young, enthusiastic and filled with a desire to serve both their pupils and their master, Sahabji Maharaj. A high standard of general education is maintained. No formal religious teaching is given but an effort is made to develop noble character. In addition, Sahabji Maharaj visits the boys from time to time and every Sunday delivers a spiritual talk to the assembled school.

[1] A lakh is the equivalent of 100,000.

The boys are encouraged to practise sports ; hockey, football, cricket and tennis are their favourites. A library with seven thousand books and a curious little museum complete the institute.

Another magnificent building houses the Girls' College, which is conducted on similar lines. It represents a determined effort by Sahabji Maharaj to break down, within his own sphere of influence, the unenviable illiteracy which was forced on Indian women until recently.

The Technical College is the youngest of the educational institutions. It provides courses in mechanical, electrical and automobile engineering, and trains mechanicians and foremen for manufacturing industries. Special machines and benches have been placed in the " Model Industries " section for the use of college students, so that class-room instruction goes hand in hand with practical experience under factory conditions.

There are several attractive hostels for the hundreds of pupils who attend the three colleges. Each hostel is light, airy and modern.

The residential part of the town is under the supervision of the Dayalbagh Building Department, which provides the plans and erects all houses. Each street possesses its own pleasant harmony of architecture, and it is evident that artistic unity is one of the ideals of these town-planners. Ugly erections and defective, shoddy buildings are barred, because a prospective tenant is free to choose his style of house only from the Department's own plans. Four sizes of residence have been standardized at graded and fixed prices. The buyer pays actual cost plus a very small percentage.

The colony maintains a bright little hospital and a maternity home. It has fixed its aim at being self-contained in every way, so that I am hardly surprised when I learn that the uniformed policeman who brings his hand to a smart salute is also a member of the Radha Soami fraternity. Yet his presence raises a piquant note of enquiry in my mind, for I expect that the level of morality in Dayalbagh is so high as to render crime conspicuous by its absence. He is here to protect the place from undesirable intruders.

§

When Sahabji Maharaj is able to spare me a little time again from the pressure of his heavy duties, I pay my meed of tribute to his praiseworthy achievement and then tell him of my astonishment at finding such a progressive town in unprogressive India.

" But," I ask, " how do you finance it ? You have surely spent a great sum in capital outlay ? "

" You will probably have an opportunity later of seeing the money come in," he returns. " The members of the Radha Soami fraternity are themselves financing the colony. There is no compulsion on them to do this, nor are subscriptions required from them, but they regard it as a religious duty to give what they can to help Dayalbagh grow. But although we have had to depend on these contributions during the initial stages, my aim is to make it completely self-supporting. I shall not rest until we approach the stage of complete independence."

" You have wealthy supporters, then ? "

" Not at all. The rich Radha Soamis can be counted on the fingers of one hand. Our members are all in modest or moderate circumstances. The progress we have made has called for self-sacrifice on the part of many. Thanks to the grace of the Supreme Father, we have been able to find and spend many lakhs of rupees so far. The colony's future is assured, for its income will grow as our fraternity expands ; therefore, we shall never be out of funds."

" How many members have you ? "

" Our membership is over 110,000 but, of course, only a few thousands have settled here. The Radha Soami fraternity is nearly seventy years old but its greatest growth has been made during the last twenty years. And this progress has occurred, mind you, without any public propaganda because we are a semi-secret organization. If we cared to come out into the public eye and propagate our teachings openly, we could increase our membership tenfold. Our members are spread all over India already, but they look to Dayalbagh as their headquarters and visit us as often as they can. They are organized into local groups which meet every Sunday at precisely the same hour when we hold a special meeting at Dayalbagh."

Sahabji pauses to wipe his spectacles.

" Just consider. When we began building this colony we possessed no more than five thousand rupees, which had been presented for the purpose. Our first plot of ground was no larger than four acres ; now, Dayalbagh covers thousands of acres. Does it not seem that we are indeed growing ? "

" How large do you intend to make Dayalbagh ? "

" I expect to settle about ten to twelve thousand people here and then we shall stop. A town of twelve thousand people, if it is properly laid out, is large enough. I do not want to copy the monstrous towns of your Western countries ; they are overcrowded and therefore breed many undesirable qualities. I want to build a garden city where people can work and live happily, where they can have plenty of space and air. It will take a few years more to finish Dayalbagh's growth and then it will be a model community. Incidentally, when I first read Plato's *Republic* I was pleasantly surprised to find in that book many of the ideas I am trying to express here. When Dayalbagh is complete I want it to act as a prototype for the creation of similar communities all over India, or at least one in each province. I shall offer it as my solution of many problems."

" You want India to turn her energies into industrial development ? "

" Most certainly. That is her crying need. But—I would not like to see India lose herself completely in it, as you in the West have done," he laughs back. " Yes, India must build up an industrial civilization to rid herself of the poverty which grinds the masses, but she must build it up on a system which will avoid the fight between capital and labour that would otherwise accompany it."

" How do you propose to do that ? "

" By aiming at personal well-being through general well-being, and not at the expense of the community. We work on a co-operative principle and everyone sets the success of Dayalbagh as being higher than personal success. There are pioneers working here for salaries much lower than those they could obtain elsewhere ; I refer to trained and educated men, not to illiterate labourers, of course, who do this voluntarily and gladly. This principle works well here only because we are inspired by a spiritual purpose, which is also the motive power behind all our other efforts. Some men, who are in a position to do so, are even giving their services freely. This will show you what a fine spirit and enthusiasm our people have. But when Dayalbagh is fully developed and completely self-supporting, I hope such sacrifices will be unnecessary. Anyway, it is the ideal of making spiritual progress more quickly which has brought these people here, for that is the fundamental aim of our fraternity. If you were to come here and join our colony, you might be worth a thousand rupees a month, but you might have to take only one-third that amount because we cannot afford to pay high salaries. Then, gradually, you might build a house, acquire a wife and beget children. But if, in this process, you begin to think only of the material side of your career and to lose sight of the spiritual ideal for which you really joined us, then to that extent you begin to fail. Despite all these material activities you see here, we try never to lose sight of the central purpose for which our fraternity was founded."

"I see."

"Now we are not socialists in your Western sense, but it is a fact that the industries, the farms and colleges are owned by the community. Moreover, this ownership extends to land and houses. You may build a house here but it is yours only whilst you tenant it. Beyond these limits, everyone is perfectly free to possess and accumulate whatever money and property he has and wherever he has it. This, of course, completely divides us from the tyrannies of socialism. All our communal properties and all the money offerings voluntarily made by members are regarded as trusts to be administered in a religious spirit. Everything is subordinated to our spiritual ideal. This administration is supervised by a body of forty-five members, representative of the various provinces in India, which meets twice a year to scrutinize accounts and consider budgets. The ordinary work and general control is in the hands of an executive committee of eleven members."

"You said before that you would offer Dayalbagh as a solution of many problems. I do not see how you can offer it as a solution of the economic problem, which is, perhaps, the chief one to-day."

Sahabji Maharaj smiles confidently.

"Even India may have something useful to contribute on that point," he rejoins. "Let me tell you about a plan which we have lately put into operation in order to quicken our rate of growth during the next few years. This plan, to my mind, embodies economic and social principles of radical importance. We have established an inheritance fund which invites offerings from those of our members who are able to subscribe one thousand rupees and upwards. Every such subscriber then receives an annuity of not less than 5 per cent from our administrative committee. At his death, the same annuity will be paid to his wife, child or whoever else he has previously named. The second person has the same right to name his or her successor to the annuity. But with the death of the third generation, all payment ceases. Should the original subscriber find himself in difficult circumstances or urgent need, then part or even all of his sum may be repaid him. Thus, lakhs of rupees will, in course of time, pour into the coffers of our committee through the inheritance fund, yet the purses of our members will not be laid under heavy toll. Whatever contribution they make, they will be sure of a moderate income in return."[1]

"I take it that you are trying to find a clear place between the evils of capitalism and the fancies of socialism. Anyway, I am sure you will deserve every bit of your success and I hope it comes quickly."

It becomes clear to me that Dayalbagh possesses assured resources for a successful future in the ever-growing inheritance fund, in the constant stream of voluntary donations and in those industries which have reached a profit-making stage.

"Several well-known leaders in India are watching our experiment and waiting to see its result," says the white-turbaned head of the Radha Soamis. "Some have visited Dayalbagh and even critics who oppose our ideas have come here. You see, the Indian people are among the weakest and poorest in the world, and its leaders offer conflicting panaceas. Gandhi came here once and engaged me in a long conversation. He wanted me to join his political campaign, but I refused. We have nothing to do with politics here. We believe in concentrating on the practical means of regeneration. Although I do not concern myself with Gandhi's political plans, I scout his economic ideas as being visionary and unpractical."

"He wants India to throw all machinery into the sea."

Sahabji shakes his head.

"India cannot go back to the past; she must go forward and develop the best points of a material civilization, if she is to become more prosperous. My countrymen had better take a lesson from America and Japan. The hand spinner and the hand weaver can no longer stand the onslaught of modern rationalized methods."

And as Sahabji Maharaj expounds his ideas I catch the picture of an alert American mind encased in a brown Hindu body, so efficient and business-like is his manner, so precise is the expression of his thoughts. My rational temperament is

[1] European economists have long been familiar with an almost identical scheme evolved by Professor Rignano, of Italy, who proposed to modify the law of inheritance in such a way as to cause the least opposition and entail the least sacrifice.

attracted by his air of common sense, balance and sanity—qualities not very common in this sub-continent.

I realize anew the curious paradox which his character presents. Master of over one hundred thousand people, who practise a mysterious form of Yoga; prime organizer of the multifarious and materialistic activities which seethe around me in Dayalbagh; taken all in all, I write him down as a brilliant and breath-taking man. Nowhere in India, nowhere in the entire world, may I expect to meet his like again.

His voice breaks into my thoughts.

"You have seen two aspects of our life here in Dayalbagh, but our activities are threefold. Man's own nature is threefold—spirit, mind and body. Therefore we have the workshops and farms for physical work, the colleges for mental growth, and lastly there are the group meetings for spiritual activities. Thus we aim at harmonious and all-round growth for each individual. But we place the greatest emphasis on the spiritual side and every member of our fraternity endeavours to carry out his individual Yoga practices regularly, wherever he may be."

"May I join one of your group meetings?"

"With pleasure. We shall welcome you at every gathering."

§

Dayalbagh's activities begin at six o'clock in the morning with the first group meeting. Dawn swiftly rubs away the darkness of night; sweet chirrups mingle with the funereal cries of crows; and all the birds begin their matutinal homage to the sun. I follow my guide to a gigantic canvas structure, which is supported by wooden posts.

A huge crowd of people presses around the entrance, where each person removes his sandals or shoes and hands them to waiting attendants. I follow the requirements of custom and then enter the great tented hall.

A raised platform stands in the centre and His Holiness Sahabji Maharaj sits there in a chair. Hundreds of his followers squat in circling ranks around him, so that the entire floor is carpeted with human bodies. All eyes are turned upon the master, all tongues are still in silent reverence.

I make my way to a place beneath the platform and then squeeze myself into the narrow space. Soon, two men stand up at the rear of the hall and their voices break out into a slow chant. The words are Hindi and the rhythm is extremely agreeable to one's ears. This continues for some fifteen minutes, by which time the strange, sacred words have lulled one into a peaceful mood. And then the voices diminish in volume until they die down altogether.

I look around. Every person in the vast tent is quiet, motionless, sunk in meditation or prayer. I look at the modest, plainly dressed figure on the platform, from whose lips no single word has yet come. His face is graver than usual ; his alert, active manner has disappeared ; and a serene contemplation seems to engage his mind. What thoughts cross and criss-cross under his white turban, I wonder ? What responsibility lies upon his shoulders, for all these people regard him as their sacred link with a higher life !

The utter silence lasts for another half-hour. Not a cough, not even a stir ! Have all these contemplative Orientals withdrawn their minds into a world barred to the sceptical Westerner ? Who knows ? But it is a striking prelude to the forceful activities which will soon make the town hum.

We recover our footgear and quietly disperse homewards.

During the morning hours I enter into conversation with many Radha Soamists, both residents and visiting members. Several of them speak good English. There are turbaned men from the North-West, pig-tailed Tamils from the South, active little Bengalees from the East and bearded figures from the Central Provinces. I am impressed by their air of self-respect and by the shrewd practicality which counterpoises their spiritual aspirations. If their desires soar into the empyrean, their feet still walk firmly on the solid earth. Here, I reflect, is a type of citizen of whom any town might be proud. I like them instinctively and admire them immensely, for they possess that rare quality—character !

A smaller meeting takes place during the afternoon. It is a brief, informal affair intended for the benefit of visiting members. Individual problems are discussed, questions answered and some matters of general concern are dealt with. Sahabji Maharaj reveals an uncommon resourcefulness in the way he disposes of everything which comes up. He adopts a chatty, witty tone, is never at a loss for an answer to the subtlest query, and delivers quick, confident opinions upon the most varied spiritual and material problems. His entire attitude betokens an unusual and successful reconciliation of complete self-confidence with quiet humility. He shows that he possesses an engaging sense of humour, which crops up again and again in merry remarks.

The evening brings another group meeting. Every workshop, store and farm in the colony has closed its activities for the day and a vast gathering once more fills the giant tent. Sahabji Maharaj occupies his platform chair again. I watch a file of his followers approach his seat and voluntarily place contributions for the funds of the board of management at his feet. Two committee members collect and record all these contributions.

The chief event which follows is a lengthy address by the master. His thousands of followers listen to the well-spoken Hindi with absorbed attention, for he has a good oratorical style. He seems to speak from the heart in a picturesque manner which is pregnant with deep feeling. He is so animated by a fiery vigour and ardent enthusiasm that the inspiring effect upon his hearers becomes almost palpable.

§

Each day the same unvarying programme is followed. The evening meeting is the longest, for it lasts nearly two hours. It says much for the power of Sahabji Maharaj's mentality that he can keep up this programme without difficulty and with his usual dynamic power. No one knows beforehand what the subject of his evening address will be. I question him upon the point and he replies :

" When I sit down in the chair I am quite unaware of the subject. Even after I have begun, I do not know what my next sentence will be or even how I will finish. I trust myself unreservedly to the Supreme Father. He tells me instantly whatever I need to know. I take my orders from Him internally. I am actually in His hands."

The words of his first address haunt me for some days. Its theme of surrendering to a master piques my mind until I broach it eventually to Sahabji. We sit on a carpeted piece of ground in the centre of Dayalbagh—it is something like a village green—and develop a friendly discussion.

He reiterates his point and adds :

" The master is absolutely necessary. There is no such thing as self-reliance in the spiritual sphere."

" But did you find one necessary ? " I ask boldly.

" Without a doubt. I spent fourteen years searching for a true master before I found him."

" Fourteen years! A fifth of your life! Was it worth while ? "

" The time spent in search of a true master is never wasted, even if it is twenty years," he replies, quick as a flash. " Before I became a believer I was as sceptical as you are. And then I grew desperate in trying to discover a teacher who could open the way to spiritual illumination. I was young and simply crazy to find the truth. I asked the trees, the grass, and the sky to enlighten me if truth existed. I sobbed my heart out like a child, with head bent low, begging for light. Finally I could stand the strain no longer. One day I resolved to give up eating and starve to death, unless and until the divine power saw fit to grant me some illumination. I could no longer work even. The next night I had a vivid dream, wherein a master appeared to me and revealed himself as such. I asked for his address. His answer was : ' Allahabad! You will know my full address later.' The next day I spoke to a friend who belonged to that town and told him of my dream. He went away and returned with a group photograph and asked me if I could indentify the master's face in the group. I at once pointed to it. My friend then explained that he belonged to a semi-secret society in Allahabad and that the figure I indicated was the master. I quickly got into touch with him and became a disciple."

" How interesting! "

" Even if you take up Yoga exercises alone and depend on your own powers, the day your true prayer is heard will be the day when you will be led to meet a master. There is no escape. You must have a guide. A sincere, fully determined seeker will eventually be brought to his real master."

" How is one to recognize him ? " I murmur questioningly.

Sahabji's face relaxes and an amused expression flickers across his eyes for a moment.

" The master knows beforehand who is to come to him and he will draw them magnetically to him. His power meets their destiny and the result is inescapable."

A little company of variegated figures has gathered around us and is rapidly increasing. Soon, Sahabji Maharaj will have not one hearer, but two or three score.

" I have been trying to form a clear understanding of your Radha Soami doctrines," I tell him, " but they are hard nuts. One of your disciples has loaned me some writings on the subject by an earlier master of your fraternity, His Holiness

Brahm Sankar Misra, with the result that my brain is working overtime."

Sahabji laughs.

"If you want to understand the truths of Radha Soami teachings, you must perform our Yoga practices. We regard the daily performance of these practices as being far more important than theoretical understanding of our doctrines. I am sorry that I cannot explain the detailed methods of meditation we employ, because they are only imparted under a vow of secrecy to those who apply to join us and are accepted. But the basis of them is 'Sound-Yoga,' or 'listening for the internal sound,' as we usually call it."

"The writings I am studying say that sound is the force which called the universe into being."

"From a material standpoint you understand it correctly, but rather it is that a current of sound was the first activity of the Supreme Being at the beginning of creation. The universe is not the result of blind forces. Now this divine sound is known to our fraternity and can be phonetically transcribed. It is our belief that sounds bear the impress of their source, of the power which created them. Therefore, when one of our members listens internally and expectantly for the divine sound, with controlled body, mind and will, he will become lifted up towards the bliss and wisdom of the Supreme Being as soon as he hears the divine sound."

"Is it not possible to imagine that the sound of the blood beating through one's arteries is the divine sound? What other sound can one hear internally?"

"Ah, we do not mean any material sound, but a spiritual one. The force which appears as sound on our material plane is only a reflection of that subtler force whose workings evolved the universe. Just as your scientists have reduced matter to electricity, so we may trace the force which we hear on the material plane as sound to a higher vibration that escapes our physical ears because it exists on the spiritual plane. A sound carries the influence of the region whence it emanates and so, if you concentrate your attention inwardly in a certain way, you may one day hear the mystic words which sounded forth at the first upheaval in the primeval chaos and which form the true name of the Creator. The echoes of those words reverberate back into man's spiritual nature; to catch those echoes, by means of our secret Yoga practice, and to trace them up to their origin is literally to be carried up to paradise. The man who faithfully carries out our Radha Soami practices which are intended to enable him to hear the mystic sound, will forget himself in utter ecstasy when at last it impinges itself upon his inner ear."

"Your teachings are startlingly novel."

"To the West, but not to India! Kabir taught the Sound-Yoga in Benares as far back as the fifteenth century."

"One hardly knows what to say about them."

"Why the difficulty? You will readily admit that one form of sound—music—can throw a man into emotional ecstasy. Then how much more will the heavenly internal music affect him?"

"Agreed!—if one could prove that the internal music really does exist."

Sahabji shrugs his shoulders.

"I might present you with several arguments to convince your reason, but I fancy you are looking for something more than that. How can I prove the existence of super-physical states by mere reasoning? It is natural for the unprepared brain to perceive nothing beyond this physical world. If you want the best proof—first-hand experience—of these spiritual truths, then you must persistently follow up a course of Yoga practices. I assure you that the human body is really capable of higher functions than those we commonly know; that the innermost parts of our brain centres are associated with subtle worlds of being; that, after proper training, these centres can be energized until we become aware of these subtler worlds; and that the most important centre of all enables us to obtain divine consciousness of the highest order."

"Are you referring to the brain centres known to anatomists?"

"Partly. They are merely the physical organs through which the subtler centres work; the real activity takes place in the latter. The most important of these centres is the pineal gland, which, as you know, is situated in the region between the eyebrows. It is the seat of the spirit-entity in man. Shoot a man through that spot and death is certain and instantaneous. The spirit-currents which flow through the auditory, optic, olfactory and other nerves converge in that gland."

"Our medical men are still puzzled about the chief functions of the pineal gland," I comment.

"And well they might be, considering that it is the focus of the individual spirit-entity which gives life and vitality to man's mind and body. It is when this spirit-entity recedes from the pineal gland that the conditions of dream, deep sleep or trance supervene, and when it finally leaves the gland the body falls dead. Since the human body is an epitome of the entire universe, inasmuch as all the elements employed in the evolution of creation are represented in it on a miniature scale, and since it contains links with all the subtler spheres, it is quite possible for the spirit-entity in us to reach the highest spiritual world. When it leaves the pineal gland and passes upwards, its passage through the grey matter of the brain brings it into contact with the region of universal mind, and its passage through the white matter exalts its consciousness to lofty spiritual realities. But to attain this spiritual consciousness all the activities of the bodily senses have to be brought to a standstill, otherwise it is not possible to shut off external stimuli. Therefore the essence of our Yoga practices is a complete concentration which turns the current of attention inwards, away from one's environment, until a profound degree of internal contemplation is attained."

I look away, trying to digest this suavely-spoken flow of subtle, recondite ideas. A goodly-sized gathering around us is taking a keen interest in the talk. The tranquil assurance which underlies their master's words attracts me, but . . .

" You say that the only way to verify these statements is to practise your Sound-Yoga exercises. But you keep those exercises secret," I complain.

" Whoever applies for admission to our fraternity and is accepted, will have our methods of spiritual practice communicated verbally to him."

" Can you not give me some personal experience first, some convincing proof at first hand ? What you say may be perfectly true—indeed, my heart wants to believe it."

" You must join us first."

" I am sorry. That I cannot do. I am built in such a way that it is difficult to give belief before proof."

Sahabji spreads out his hands in a helpless gesture.

" What can I do then ? I am in the hands of the Supreme Father."

§

Day after day I attend all the group meetings as regularly as the members of the society themselves ; I meditate silently in their midst and listen to their master's addresses ; I question them freely and study such portions of the Radha Soami teachings concerning the universe and man as are made available to me.

Late one afternoon I wander with a disciple about one mile or so away from Dayalbagh to where the jungle begins. Then we turn our feet towards the Jumna and eventually sit down on the banks of that wide river. From the steep and sandy height we watch the slow-moving water wind its placid way through the plain which stretches to Agra. Now and then a great vulture flaps its way over our heads towards its home.

The Jumna ! Somewhere along these banks Krishna moved victoriously among the milkmaids, charming them with his wondrous lute and his love-making. To-day he is probably one of the most worshipped gods in the Hindu pantheon.

" Up till recent years," murmurs my companion, " this place was the abode of wild animals and at night they roamed over the very site on which Dayalbagh has been built. And now they avoid the place."

We sit silently for a couple of minutes and then he says :

" You are the first European to sit in our group meetings, though you will certainly not be the last. We appreciate the understanding and sympathy you have shown. Why don't you join our society ? "

" Because I have no faith in faith. Because I realize that it is fatally easy to believe in what you want to believe."

He draws his knees up and rests his chin upon them.

" The contact that you are having with our master will benefit you in any case. I shall not press you to join. We do not attempt to make converts and our members are not allowed to preach."

" How did you learn of the existence of the society ? "

" Very simply. My father has been a member for many years. He does not live at Dayalbagh, but visits it from time to time. He brought me with him on some of those visits, but never, on any occasion, did he attempt to induce me to join. About two years ago I began to puzzle over things and went about questioning various friends as to their beliefs. I questioned my father, too, and what he told me drew me to the Radha Soami teachings. I was accepted as a member of the fraternity and time has confirmed my faith. I was fortunate, perhaps, because others have come to us only after a lifetime spent in perplexity."

"If I could settle my doubts as easily and as quickly as you settled yours. . . . ?" I respond vacantly.

Once again we both revert to silence. The dark blue Jumna water draws my gaze and I slip insensibly into a profound reverie.

All the conscious and unconscious thinking of these Indians is coloured by faith, by the necessity of owning allegiance to some sort of a religion, creed or sacred script. Every kind of faith from the most degraded to the most dignified is represented in India.

Once I stumbled across a little temple on the Ganges. Its pillars were covered with carved reliefs depicting men and women engaged in sexual embrace, and its walls were frescoed with erotic scenes which might horrify a Western clergyman. There is room for this kind of thing in Indian religion, and it may well be that the religious recognition of sex is a better thing than its relegation to the gutter, but then—there is also room for faiths embodying the loftiest and purest conceptions possible to man. Such is India!

But nowhere in this land have I come across such an amazing cult as the Radha Soamis. It is undeniably unique. What brain other than Sahabji Maharaj's could have conceived this paradoxical combination of Yoga, the oldest learning in the world, with the high-pressure, mechanized civilization of an up-to-date European or American city?

Is Dayalbagh likely to loom forth in Indian history out of all proportion to its present apparent unimportance? If India is a crossword puzzle to which no one seems to have yet found the correct solution, that is not to say that the coming years shall not provide an answer.

Sahabji had laughed at Gandhi's preaching of medievalism, and the town of Ahmedabad, where Gandhi's own headquarters lie, still echoes back this laughter. From the Sabarmati River one can count half a hundred tall factory chimneys, which smoke defiance at the little cluster of white, wooden bungalows where the gospel of peasant handicrafts finds its inspiration.

The forceful impact of Western ways has begun to disintegrate India's traditional methods of carrying on the necessary business of living. The first Europeans who appeared off the sea coast of India brought not only bales of goods, but also ideas. When Vasco da Gama landed his rough-bearded sailors in the quiet harbour of Calicut, there began that process of Westernization which is moving at such a quick rate to-day.

The industrialization of India has begun in a tentative and timid fashion, but it has begun. Europe has faced in turn the Renaissance of intellect, the religious reformation and the industrial revolution, and she has left these things behind. India has awakened and finds them lying in her stride. These are now her problems. Will she blindly imitate the Europeans or will she work out her own—and perhaps better—way of solving them? Will Sahabji Maharaj's unique contribution focus her attention one day?

If I am certain of anything I am certain of this: India will be thrown into a melting-pot of unparalleled character before long. Thousands of years of a society tied up in worn-out traditions, imprisoned in hide-bound religious conventions, will vanish within two or three decades at most. It will seem a miracle, but it will happen.

Sahabji Maharaj has evidently grasped this situation clearly enough. He realizes that we live in a new epoch; the old order of things is being destroyed everywhere, and in India as in other countries. Are Asiatic lethargy and Western practicality to remain twin incompatibilities? He thinks not. Why should not the Yogi put on a worldling's clothing? And so he gives forth the fiat that the Yogi must come out of his habitual seclusion and mingle with the noisy assemblages where men command machines. He thinks it is time for the Yogi to descend into the factory, the office and the school and attempt to spiritualize them—not by preaching and propaganda, but by inspired action. The way of hustling everyday activity can and must be made the way of heaven. A spiritually based way of living like Yoga, which stands too aloof from workaday men, may come to be regarded by them as a deceptive form of self-important stupidity.

If Yoga is to remain the hobby of a few hermits, the modern world will have no use for it and the last traces of the dying science will disappear from existence. If it is to serve only as the delectation of some lean anchorites, we who push pens or ploughs, move amid the grease and grime of engine-rooms, who have to endure the hubbub of stock exchanges and the busy barter of shops, we shall roughly turn our heads away. And the attitude of the modern West will shortly be the attitude of modern India.

Sahabji Maharaj has shrewdly foreseen the inevitable trend of things and has made a striking effort to save the ancient science of Yoga for modern use. This inspiring and strenuous man will certainly leave his mark upon his native land. He has realized that his country has lain in lethargy long enough. He sees clearly why the West, throbbing with manufacture and trade and its agriculture modernized, lives a wealthier life. He sees also that the culture of Yoga remains one of the valuable inheritances which India has received from her ancient sages, but that the few masters who keep this culture alive in lonely places are a fading remnant of their class; when they die, the real secrets of Yoga will die with them. And so he has come down from the rarefied air of those peaks of thought to our own times, to the energetic strivings of the twentieth century, and is endeavouring to relate the two.

Is his effort too fantastic? On the contrary, it is highly admirable. We live in days when Muhammed's tomb in Arabia is illumined by electric light, when the camel is being pushed off the desert sands of Morocco by luxuriously fitted motor cars. What then of India? This vast country, startled from the sleep of many hundred years by the impact of a completely opposite culture, must go on opening its heavy-lidded eyes. The English have done more than turn sandy deserts into fertile fields; than build canals and dams to assist agriculture and regulate the floods of great rivers; than fling an impenetrable barrier of highly efficient soldiers across the North-West Frontier to keep peace and property secure; than bring in a healthy breeze of sane, rational ideas.

Out of the grey North and distant West came the white men. Fate placed India at their feet and the country became theirs with but a few efforts.

Why?

Perhaps the world, incubating over Asiatic wisdom and Western science, will one day hatch out a civilization that will shame antiquity, deride modernity and amaze posterity.

The trail of my meditation comes to an end. I raise my head and address a questioning word to my companion. I do not think he hears me. He continues to stare across the river, which reflects the last red light of sunset. It is the twilight hour. I watch the great orb make its rapid disappearance from the sky. The stillness is indescribable; all nature, dumb at the lovely sight, seems to have come to momentary rest. My heart drinks in the superb peace. Once more I glance at the other man. His figure is now wrapped in the shroud of fast-gathering dusk.

So we sit in the dead silence for a few more minutes until the sun slips suddenly into black night.

My companion rises and quietly leads me through the

shadows back to Dayalbagh. Our walk terminates under a canopy of thousands of starry points of light.

§

Sahabji Maharaj decides to leave Dayalbagh and go down to a place in the Central Provinces for a well-earned rest. I take the event as our destined time of farewell and plan a move in the same direction. We shall travel together as far as Timarni and then our ways will diverge.

About one hour after midnight we descend on Agra Station. A score of close disciples accompany their master and so the size of our party is quite noticeable. Someone procures a chair for Sahabji, and while he sits in the midst of his devoted followers I pace the half-lit platform.

During the day I have reviewed my stay at Dayalbagh and realize with regret that no memorable inner experience has occurred, no soul-upheaving vision of life's secret meaning has been vouchsafed to me. I had hoped that some illuminating Yogic expansion of consciousness might pierce my mental gloom for an hour or two, so that I could then follow up the track of Yoga with sight and not with faith. But no, the benediction is not for me. Perhaps I am not worthy of it ; maybe I demand far too much ; I do not know.

From time to time I glance at the seated figure. Sahabji Maharaj possesses a magnetic personality which fascinates me. He is a curious mixture of American alertness and practicality, British predilection for correct conduct and Indian devoutness and contemplativeness. He is a type which is rare in the modern world. Over one hundred thousand men and women have entrusted the guidance of their inner lives to this man, yet he sits there in quiet modesty and humility, this unassuming master of the Radha Soamis.

At last our train roars into the station and a giant headlight throws an uncanny illumination upon the scene through which the rails pass. Sahabji enters his reserved compartment and the rest of us sort ourselves into other carriages. I stretch myself out for a few hours' sleep and know nothing more until I awake in the morning with an incredibly dry throat.

At every halt which the train makes during the next few hours, followers of Sahabji who live in the vicinity or even many miles away crowd around his compartment window. They have been notified of his journey in advance and eagerly seize the opportunity of obtaining this brief contact, for it is said in India that even a minute's contact with a master will produce important spiritual and material results.

I seek and obtain Sahabji's permission to spend my last three hours with him in his own compartment. We fall into a long talk about world conditions, about the nations of the West, about India's future and about the future of his own cult. At the end he tells me in his pleasant, suave manner :

" Let me assure you that I have no consciousness of India being my own country. I am cosmopolitan in outlook and look on all men as my brothers."

Such amazing frankness delights me. It is so with all his conversations. He always goes straight to the point ; he shoots every sentence at a definite target, and he has the full courage of his convictions. To converse with him, to commune with his mind, is a welcome experience. Always he comes out with some unexpected phrase, some new view-point on things.

The train now moves across country at an angle which brings an intolerable sun through the window and into my eyes. The torrid heat bakes one's flesh, the merciless rays weary one's mind. I pull up the wooden sun-blind, that peculiar structure which is so curiously like a Venetian blind, and switch on the electric fan, thus gaining a slight relief from the midday heat. Sahabji Maharaj notices my discomfort and draws some oranges out of a travelling bag. He puts them on the small table and asks me to share them with him.

" They will cool your throat," he observes.

As his knife slowly parts the coloured peel, he remarks musingly :

" You are right in being so careful about taking anyone as your master. Scepticism is a useful attitude before you decide on him, but afterwards you must have full faith. Don't rest until you find your spiritual preceptor. He is absolutely essential."

Before long there is a grinding sound and someone noisily shouts :

" Timarni ! "

Sahabji Maharaj rises to depart. Something awakens in me before his disciples can come and capture him. It breaks my reserve, ignores my Western pride, crushes my anti-religious temperament and speaks through my lips.

" Your Holiness, may I have your blessing ? "

He turns with a friendly smile, beams pleasantly through his glasses, and cordially pats my shoulder.

" You have that already ! " he assures me in farewell.

I return to my compartment and the train moves rapidly away. Dun-coloured fields flash by the window. Little groups of drowsy-eyed cattle munch contentedly on the sparse herbage. My eyes register them only half-consciously, for my mind is carrying away a picture of a notable man, whom I greatly like and profoundly admire. For he is at once an inspired dreamer, a serenely-minded Yogi, a practical man of the world and a polished gentleman !

CHAPTER XIV

AT THE PARSEE MESSIAH'S HEADQUARTERS

THE trail from Agra to Nasik is a long one, but I shall make no more mention of it than this short paragraph, so that the record of my wanderings may come to its allotted end.

The wheel of time turns its inevitable course and so carries me around India on its spokes. Once again I am to see Meher Baba, the Parsee holy man and self-styled " new messiah."

It is with no keen desire that I return to him. The cold serpents of doubt have firmly coiled themselves around my mind, and a strong inner feeling tells me that my proposed stay near him will be a waste of time, and that Meher Baba, though a good man and one living an ascetic life, is unfortunatly suffering from colossal delusions about his own greatness. Incidentally, I have taken the trouble to investigate during my travels the few so-called miracles of healing which he is alleged to have performed. One is a case of appendicitis, and the sufferer's simple faith in Meher is said to have completely cured him. But strict enquiry shows that the doctor who has attended this man could discover nothing worse than severe indigestion ! In another case a nice old gentleman, who has been reported cured overnight of a whole catalogue of ailments, seems to have had little more than a swollen ankle ! In short, the marvellous healing power of their master has been grossly exaggerated by his disciples, whose exuberant fervour is understandable enough in a country where fable often runs faster than fact.

I do not believe that the Parsee messiah can keep the extraordinary promises of wonderful experiences which he has made me ; but because I have agreed to spend a month near him, I think my pledge is not to be lightly broken. So, against every instinct and all judgment, I take train for Nasik, that he may not accuse me of never having given him the chance to prove his alleged powers.

§

Meher has set up his headquarters in some modern houses on the extreme outskirts of the town. A retinue of forty disciples wander aimlessly about the place.

" What are you thinking about ? " is one of his first questions to me when we meet. I feel tired and travel-worn ; he has probably mistaken my haggard appearance for the pallor of profound meditation, but no matter, my reply is instantly forthcoming.

" I am thinking of the dozen or more messiahs whom I have discovered in India since I have been here."

Meher Baba does not seem surprised.

" Yes," he rejoins with fingers moving slickly across his alphabet board, " I also have heard of some of them."

" How do you explain it ? " I ask innocently.

His forehead contracts into wrinkles, but his mouth smiles in a superior sort of way.

" If they are honest, then they are mistaken. If they are dishonest, then they are deceiving others. There are holy men who make good progress and then develop spiritual ' swelled-head.' Such a sad state of affairs usually arrives when they have no proper master to advise and guide them. There is a point which is midway along the mystical path and which is most difficult to cross ; it often happens that the person whose devotions have brought him to this point foolishly believes that he has reached the highest goal. It takes little more for him to imagine himself a messiah ! "

" An excellent and logical explanation. But unfortunately I have heard very much the same thing from the other men who claim to be messiahs. Each asserts that he is perfect ; each allots imperfection to his rivals ! "

" Do not worry about it. All these people are unconsciously helping to do my work. I know who I am. When the time comes for me to fulfil my mission, the world will also know who I am."

It is not possible to argue rationally in such an atmosphere, so I let the matter drop. Meher Baba indulges in some pleasant platitudes and then dismisses me.

I settle down to live in a bungalow which is two or three minutes' walk from his headquarters. I resolve ruthlessly to thrust my feelings aside and keep a perfectly open mind to the events of the coming four weeks. There shall be no mental hostility to Meher, no inner attitude of scepticism, but rather a mood of expectant waiting.

Each day I associate closely with the disciples : I see their manner of existence, study their psychological make-up and probe into the history of their spiritual relationship to Meher. Each day the Parsee messiah gives me a little of his time. We talk about many things and he answers many questions, but not once does he make any reference to the strange promises which he gave me at Ahmednagar. I resolve to make no attempt to jog his memory and so the matter seemingly falls into abeyance.

One result of the constant rain of questions which I let fall upon him and his disciples—partly out of my journalistic instinct of curiosity and partly out of a sincere desire to find enough facts, either to buttress my intuitions of the futility of my visit or to dispose of them altogether—is that he places at my disposal a set of secret diaries which have been kept by his command for several years. They contain a connected history of the chief events concerning the messiah and his group of followers, and a record of every important teaching, message and prophecy which he has verbally given out. These books cover nearly two thousand pages of closely written manuscript, which is mostly composed in English.

The diaries have clearly been compiled in a spirit of blind faith, but I find them to be a valuable searchlight upon Meher's character and powers. The very honesty of these pages, despite their devoutness, in recording matters which might seem trivial to an outsider excellently serves my purpose, for I view these matters as psychological straws that show which way Meher's mind is moving. The two disciples who have kept these diaries are young men with only a fragmentary experience of life beyond their extremely limited circle, but their very naïvete and complete trust in their master have caused them to place on record things which are really uncomplimentary to him.

Why have they recorded that Meher struck one of his most intimate disciples a stinging blow on the ears during a train journey to Muttra, a blow so severe that the unfortunate follower had to seek medical attention ? Why have they recorded the lame excuse of their master, this man who preaches a gospel of divine love, that when a messiah pretends to show anger towards one of his devotees, the sins of the latter which are awaiting punishment are thereby heavily reduced ? Why have they recorded the comical incident of the disciple who was "lost" at Arangaon for whom Meher sent out a search party which returned after several hours without its quarry. He turned up of his own accord ultimately and explained that having suffered with insomnia for several nights, he had unexpectedly fallen asleep in a disused building which stood close to Meher's own abode! The master, who claims to have been taken into the council of the gods and to know the future of all mankind, did not know that his "lost" disciple was in the next field!

I find enough matter, therefore, to feed the doubts which live repressed existences in my own mind. I find also that Meher Baba is a fallible authority, a man subject to constantly changing moods, and an egotist who demands complete enslavement on the part of his brain-stupefied followers. And lastly, I find in these pages that he is a prophet whose predictions are seldom verified. At our first meeting near Ahmednagar he prophesied a coming world-war, but refused to say when it is going to happen, although he was careful to impress me with the claim that he knows the date. Now, in these diaries, I discover that he has made the same prophesy to his intimate disciples, and that he has made it not once but several times. On each occasion he has had to give a different date for that calamitous event because, as each date arrives, no war arrives. One year, when things look ominous in Asia, he has placed the outbreak in the East; another year, when things look dark in Europe, and when he has forgotten his earlier failure, he has placed it in the West, and so on. His caution in hesitating to give me a date at Ahmednagar now becomes comprehensible. I tax one of the more intelligent disciples with this series of unfulfilled predictions and he candidly admits that most of his master's prophecies are generally wrong. "I doubt whether the war will ever take place as an ordinary war, but it will probably happen as an economic war!" he concludes naïvely.

Though I turn the last page of these astonishing diaries with a smile, I candidly confess to myself that I have read lofty and soul-elevating discourses in them, and that Meher Baba possesses religious genius. Whatever success he may have will arise from that last quality. But I do not forget one of his own sayings, recorded somewhere in these pages, that "Ability in advising others about virtue is no proof of saintliness, nor is it a mark of wisdom."

§

It is better to pass over the rest of my stay in prudent silence If I am living in the company of a world deliverer and redeemer of mankind, there is little to make me aware of my good fortune. This, perhaps, is because I am more interested in tangible facts than mythical legends. I shall not enter into the tale of childish actions and unfulfilled predictions, blind obedience to irrational orders on the part of disciples, and messianic advice which only increases the troubles of those who follow it.

Meher Baba seems to be avoiding contacts with me as my stay draws to its close, or it may be my fancy. When I do see him, he is always in a tremendous hurry, and rushes away a few minutes after. Each day I become conscious of my false position, and it is possible that Meher himself knows the discomfort which increasingly troubles me.

I wait for the wonderful experiences he has promised me, though I never expect them to arrive. My expectations are completely fulfilled! Nothing unusual happens nor do I see anything unusual happening to the other men. I make no effort to put Meher under a stringent interrogatory, merely because I realize the futility of such a proceeding. However, with the passing of the month I announce my impending departure and then tax Meher Baba with his failure to redeem his words. For answer he lightly transfers the date of his promised marvels to a couple of months later, and then dismisses the matter! I may be mistaken, but I fancy that an inward nervousness is affecting him, a peculiar impatience with my presence, a condition which I sense rather than see with my eyes. Yet I make no attempt to argue with him, for I see that it is useless to pit my straightforward direct question in unequal combat with his elusive Oriental mind.

Even at the last moment of parting, when I bid an amicable adieu and polite farewell for ever to Meher Baba, he talks as though there can be no question but that he *is* the world teacher for whom many are waiting. He even asserts that when he is ready to go to the West one day and spread his work there, he will send for me and I shall have to travel with him! [1]

Such is the result of my foolish attempt to take this man at his word. What can one say of *soi-disant* " divine teachers "

[1] He went to the West in due course, but his prediction as regards myself proved utterly fallacious.

who promise an ecstasy of the spirit, but give instead an exasperation of the mind ?

§

Is it possible to find any acceptable explanation of Meher Baba's strange career and curious conduct ? A superficial estimate of the man may easily dismiss him as a rogue or as a charlatan. This has been done, but does not explain several things in his life and is manifestly unjust. I prefer to accept the opinion of old Judge Khandalawalla, of Bombay, who has known Meher Baba since the latter was a boy, and who told me that the Parsee messiah was simply an honest but mistaken man. This explanation is good as far as it goes, but for me it does not go far enough.

A little analysis of Meher Baba's character will make my theory more comprehensible. I have already mentioned that, at our first meeting near Ahmednagar, I was impressed by the peace and gentleness of his attitude. But observation during my stay at Nasik revealed, through everyday incidents, that this was the calmness of a weak character and the gentleness of a frail physique. I discovered that he is really an irresolute man, influenced by others and by circumstances. His small pointed chin is eloquent on this point. Moreover, sudden unaccountable impulses mark his conduct. He is obviously a highly emotional man. His passion for the theatrical, his childish but Oriental fondness for spectacular demonstrations also evidence the fact that he loves to dramatize himself. He seems to live more for an audience than for himself. And although he claims to have appeared on the stage of life in a serious part, those who see only an element of comedy in his acting are not wholly to blame !

My own theory is that the old Muhammedan woman faqueer, Hazrat Babajan, did really create an upheaval in Meher Baba's character that upset his equilibrium, in fact, so completely as to precipitate him into a condition which neither he nor those around him understand. My own experience with the remarkable lady, brief though it was, convinces me that she possessed some strange power sufficient to startle the most hide-bound rationalist. I do not know why Hazrat Babajan should have suddenly intervened in Meher Baba's career, swept him off at a tangent and started him on a course whose outcome—whether merely farcical or really momentous—we have yet to witness. But I do know that she was quite capable of doing to him something which, metaphorically speaking, took the earth from under his feet.

The kiss which she gave him was nothing in itself, but became important as the symbolic conveyance of her psychic inner grace. The peculiar cerebral condition which he developed as a result is significant in view of his later history. "My mind received a great shock which caused it violent vibrations for some time," he told me once in reference to this event. He was clearly quite unprepared for it. He had gone through no training and no discipline to fit himself for what might be tantamount to a Yogic initiation. "When I was a friend of Baba in his youth," said his disciple Abdullah, "I never found him interested in religion or philosophy. He was always keener on sports, games and fun. He played a principal part in our school debates and activities. His sudden departure into spiritual matters took us by surprise."

I believe that the youthful Meher became quite unbalanced as a result of this unexpected experience. This was obvious enough when he fell into a condition of semi-idiocy and behaved like a human robot, but it is not so obvious now that he has recovered sanity. I do not believe that he has returned to normality as a human being. To some people, a sudden overdose of religion, Yogic trance, or mystic ecstasy is as unbalancing as a sudden overdose of certain drugs. In short, I believe that Meher Baba has not yet recovered from the first intoxication of his exalted mood, and a lack of balance still exists as a result of the tremendous derangement which occurred to his mental faculties at such an early age. On no other hypothesis can I account for the extraordinary behaviour which he manifests from time to time.

He shows, on the one hand, all the qualities of a mystic—love, gentleness, religious intuition, and so on, but on the other hand he shows signs of the mental disease of paranoia. He exaggerates everything which pertains to his own self. This condition is also found among religious enthusiasts who experience sudden but temporary states of ecstasy. They emerge with the awareness that something colossal has happened to them. It is only another step for them to make unwarranted claims to spiritual greatness, and so they begin to found new cults or to set up queer societies with themselves at the head. The deification of self, the belief that they are messiahs destined to save all mankind, is the final step taken by the audacious few.

In India I find that there are men who want the exalted consciousness which Yoga promises its votaries, but are unwilling to pay the price in training and discipline which it demands. So they take drugs, such as opium and hasheesh, and thus obtain a colourable imitation of that transcendental consciousness. I have watched the behaviour of these drug addicts and discovered that one quality (or vice) is common to all of them. They exaggerate tremendously the small or great phenomena of their lives, and will tell you outright lies in the firm belief that they are telling you the truth! Hence the development of paranoia, which is an exaggeration of self-consciousness to the point of complete delusion.

The drug addict may notice a woman glance carelessly at him. At once he weaves a whole romance with her in his mind. His world revolves entirely around his own glorified self. He will make such fantastic assertions about his own wonderful powers that one wonders whether he is in full possession of his faculties. And his actions spring out of sudden, inexplicable impulses.

Some of the unbalanced qualities which mark the characters and lives of such unfortunate persons, also mark the character and life of Meher Baba, but with this qualification—he never descends into the evil depths it is possible for them to fall into, because the origin of his abnormality is not drugs, but a spiritual and benign experience. To borrow a phrase from Nietzsche, the Parsee messiah is "human, all-too-human."

Much ado is made in regard to the time when he will break his silence. One wonders whether he will ever dare to do so, but it needs no great discernment to see that his voice, if at long last it comes forth, will fall futile upon the world's ears. Words cannot work miracles. His rash prophecies may or may not be realized; what matters is that the prophet himself has proved unreliable: his promises are not kept, his predictions are not realized, and his conduct is both egotistic and erratic. He fails to illustrate in himself the high message which he proposes to convey—to others. The message of such a man must necessarily fall on deaf and unheeding ears.

What of his ardent followers? Will Time come with cold hands and undeceive them? That is unlikely. The story of Meher Baba is a typical story of Indian credulity and provides a handy illustration of the strength of this defect in Indian character. India suffers from the defects of an illiterate and over-religious race, untrained in those scientific modes of thought which demand the divorce of emotion from reason, history from hearsay, and fact from imagination. It is easy enough to gather a flock of enthusiastic followers, whether from sincere aspirants, foolish and inexperienced persons, or those who deem it wise to attach themselves and their fortunes to stars of greater magnitude than themselves.

I have neither the space nor the patience to point them out, but it is a fact that Meher Baba has committed blunders at every step of his career. So have I. But he claims to be a divinely inspired messiah, whereas I am only too painfully aware of my limitations as an ordinary mortal. My point is that his followers will never admit that Meher Baba can commit blunders. Always they naïvely assume that some mysterious esoteric purpose lies behind everything he says or does. They are content to follow blindly, as indeed they must, for reason soon rebels at what they have to swallow. My own experience with him only tended to confirm and deepen that cynicism which has taken the allegiance of so much of my life, and to strengthen that radical scepticism which hid the inner sensitivity that guided my wanderings around this subcontinent.

All over the East there have been recurring hints of a coming event which is to prove the greatest thing history has given us for many hundred years. The prophecy of a Coming rears its head among the brown faces of India, the stocky people of Tibet, the almond-eyed masses of China, and the old greybeards of Africa. To the vivid and devout Oriental imagination, the hour is ripe and our restless time bears outward portent of the near approach of this event. What more natural than for Meher Baba to regard his sudden psychological change as an indication of his own messianic destiny? What more natural than his fondly cherished belief that one day he will announce himself to an awe stricken world? What more natural than for his own obedient flock to take it upon themselves to spread the news of their messiah's advent? Nevertheless one is compelled to condemn the theatrical methods which he has used. No great religious teacher worthy the name has ever used them, or is ever likely to break the spiritual etiquette of thousands of centuries. I have a shrewd suspicion as to what form the future vagaries of this spectacular "saint" will take. But time will reveal them for the world's entertainment better than the present writer.

And as this long reflection draws to an end, I realize that I need not deny that many high and sublime sayings have been communicated through the lithe fingers of Meher Baba. But, when he descends from his religious inspirations, as descend he must, and stoops to talk of his own personal greatness and personal fortunes, it is time to put on one's shoes again. For the future leader of mankind is then likely to become its misleader ![1]

[1] Meher Baba has since appeared in the West and a Western cult has started to gather around him. He still promises wonderful things, which will happen when he breaks his silence. He has several times visited England, has acquired a following in France, Spain and Turkey, and has been twice to Persia. He made a theatrical journey across the continent of America with a mixed retinue of men and women. When he arrived in Hollywood, he was given a royal reception. Mary Pickford entertained him in her home, Tallulah Bankhead became interested in him, while a thousand leading people were presented to him at Hollywood's largest hotel. A large tract of land was acquired in the United States to establish his Western headquarters. Meanwhile dumbness still lies upon his lips, the while he flits impulsively from country to country on brief visits. At last he has been brought into the glare of notoriety.

CHAPTER XV

A STRANGE ENCOUNTER

I WANDER about Western India for the second time in a leisurely and indeterminate manner. Tired of travelling in dusty railway trains and seatless bullock-carts, I take to an old, but sturdy touring car with a Hindu who plays the threefold part of companion, chauffeur and servant.

We move on through several changes of scenery, while the miles speed away under our tyres. In the forest areas the chauffeur stops at nightfall, if unable to reach a village in time, and halts till dawn breaks. Throughout the night he keeps a large fire burning, feeding it with twigs and bushes. He assures me that the flames will keep wild beasts from approaching us. Leopards and panthers haunt the forests, but such is the fear which a simple fire seems to inspire in them that they keep at a respectful distance. Not so the jackals. Among the hills we hear their lugubrious barking quite close to us at times. And during the daytime we meet on occasions with vultures soaring out of their eyries into the brassy sky.

Late one afternoon, while we are motoring along a road which is thickly covered with dust, we overtake a queer couple sitting by the wayside. One is a middle-aged holy man, crouching on his hams and apparently contemplating his navel under the thin shade of some scanty-leaved bushes ; the other is his youthful attendant, probably a disciple. The older man's hands are joined, his eyes are half-shut in meditation, and he sits perfectly unmoved as we pass. We do not succeed in winning so much as a glance from him, although his youthful devotee stares in a dull way at our car. Something in the man's face attracts me and decides me to stop a little way off. My Hindu companion goes back to question them and I watch him nervously approach the couple. At length he gets into a lengthy conversation with the young man.

When he returns he informs me, amongst a multitude of trivial details, that the couple are indeed master and disciple, that the older man's name is Chandi Das, and that according to the youngster's tribute, he is a Yogi gifted with exceptional faculties. They are wandering from village to village and have already covered a great distance, partly on foot and partly by train, since they left their native Bengal nearly two years ago.

I offer them a lift which they immediately accept, the older man with benign grace and the younger one with impulsive gratitude. And so, half an hour later, the car deposits a strangely mixed crew in the next village, where we resolve to spend the night.

No other soul has been in sight on the route except, when nearing the village, a boy tending a small herd of scraggy cows. The afternoon is drawing to its end as we stand beside the village well and drink some refreshing though dubiously coloured liquid. The forty or fifty huts and cottages which make up the village's single straggling street, with their unevenly thatched grass roofs, low irregular mud walls and rough bamboo uprights, depress me a little with their squalid appearance. A few inhabitants squat in the shade before their unattractive dwellings. A grey, sad woman with half-hidden shrivelled breasts approaches the well, stares at us, fills her brass pitcher with water, and sets out for home again.

My Hindu companion collects the things for making tea and goes off in search of the village headman's house. The Yogi and his faithful attendant-disciple squat in the dust and rest. The former knows no English, and I have already discovered in the car that the latter possesses a smattering of the language, though hardly adequate enough to carry on a proper conversation. After a few attempts I found it more profitable to wait until we could all settle down in the evening for the interview I am determined to secure, when I can call on the services of my Hindu interpreter.

Meanwhile a little group of men, women and children has collected around us. These inhabitants of the interior seldom come into contact with Europeans. I have often found it an interesting experience to talk to some of them, if only for the unsophisticated and innocent view-point of life which such talks disclose. The children are shy at first, but I win them by distributing a few annas. They regard my alarm watch with incredulous wonder and naïve delight, as I set the dial and let the little peals ring forth for their benefit.

A woman approaches the Yogi, prostrates herself before him in the open street, touches his feet and then puts her fingers to her own forehead.

My Hindu servant returns with the headman and with the announcement that tea is ready. He is a college graduate, but is quite content to act as bearer, chauffeur and interpreter, for he is seeking to fathom my Western experience and lives in the constant hope that one day I will take him to Europe. I treat him as a companion and with that friendliness which I feel his good intelligence and character deserve.

Meanwhile someone has captured the Yogi and his disciple and taken them off to a hut for hospitality. Certainly these village folk are kindlier than their brethren of the towns.

As we walk down to the headman's house, I watch the west reddenning behind the distant hills as an orange sun flickers out its life. We halt at a superior-looking cottage, and inside I take the opportunity of thanking the headman.

" The honour of your visit overwhelms me," he replies simply.

We rest awhile after the tea. The shadows of a brief twilight now lie across the fields and I can hear the cattle being driven into the village for the night. Later my servant goes out to visit the Yogi and succeeds in preparing the way for me. He leads me to the door of one of the humbler huts.

I enter the square, low-roofed room and my feet tread an earthen floor. Hardly any furniture is to be seen, though a few clay pots lie around the rude hearth. A bamboo pole stuck into the wall acts as a kind of wardrobe, for clothes and rags hang upon it. One corner is graced with a brass water-jug. I think how bare the place looks in the pale light of the primitive lamp. Such are the cheerless comforts of a poorer peasant's home.

The Yogi's disciple greets me with his broken English, but his master is not visible. The latter has been called to the side of an ailing mother for his blessing. I wait for his return.

At length there is a sound outside in the street and then a tall figure appears on the threshold. He enters the room gravely. Seeing me, he makes a gesture of acknowledgment and murmurs some words. My bearer whispers the translation:

" Greetings, sahib. May the gods protect you ! "

He refuses my offer of a cotton blanket to squat on and drops to the floor, where he crosses his legs. We confront each other, and I take the opportunity to study him more closely. The man before me is probably fifty years of age, though the short rugged beard on his chin gives him an older appearance. His hair hangs down in tangled strands to his neck ; his mouth is serious and always unsmiling. But what struck me most when we first met strikes me anew at this moment—the strange glitter of his coal-black eyes, their lustrous brilliance. I know that such unearthly eyes will continue to haunt me for days.

"You have travelled far?" he asks quietly.

I nod assent.

"What do you think of the Master Mahasaya?" he demands suddenly.

I am startled. How has he come to know that I have been to his native Bengal and visited Mahasaya in Calcutta? I gaze at him for a while in bewilderment and then recall myself to his question.

"He is a man who has won my heart," I reply. "But why do you ask?"

He ignores my counter-question. There is an embarrassing silence. I try to keep up the conversation by saying:

"I am looking forward to seeing him again when I revisit Calcutta. Does he know you? Shall I carry your greetings?"

The Yogi shakes his head firmly.

"You will never see Mahasaya again. Even now Yama, the god of death, is calling to his spirit."

Another pause. And then I tell him:

"I am interested in the lives and thoughts of Yogis. Will you not tell me how you came to be one and what wisdom you have gained?"

Chandi Das does not encourage my attempt to interview him.

"The past is but a heap of ashes," he answers. "Do not ask me to poke my finger in the ashes and pick out dead experiences. I live neither in the past nor the future. In the depths of the human spirit, these things are no more real than shadows. That also is the wisdom I have learnt."

This is disconcerting. His stiff hieratic attitude upsets my composure.

"But we who live in the world of time must take account of them," I object.

"Time?" he queries. "Are you sure there is such a thing?"

I fear that our talk is becoming fantastic. Does this man really possess the wonderful gifts which his disciple claims on his behalf? Aloud I say:

"If time did not exist, then the past and the future would both be here now. But experience tells us to the contrary."

"So? What you mean is that *your* experience, the world's experience, tells you that!"

"Surely, you do not suggest that you have a different experience of the matter?"

"There is truth in your talk," comes the strange answer.

"Am I to understand that the future shows itself to you?"

"I live in the eternal," replies Chandi Das. "I never seek to discover the events that coming years will pass over my head."

"But you can for others?"

"If I wish—yes!"

I am determined to get the thing clear in my mind.

"Then you can give them an understanding of events which are yet to happen?"

"Only in part. The lives of men do not move so smoothly that every detail is ordained for them."

"Then will you reveal that part of my future which you can discover?"

"Wherefore do you seek to know these things?"

I hesitate.

"God has not dropped a veil over what is to come without fit cause," continues the other man almost sternly.

What can I say? And then an inspiration comes.

"Grave problems vex my mind. In the hope of finding some light upon them I have come to your land. Perhaps in what you can tell me there may be guidance for my feet, or perhaps I shall know whether I have come on a fruitless errand."

The Yogi turns his shining black eyes upon me. In the silence which ensues I am impressed once more by the grave dignity of this man. He seems so profound, so pontifically wise as he sits there with folded legs and interlocked feet, as to transcend his mean surroundings in this poor hut of a remote jungle village.

I notice, for the first time, a lizard watching us from the upper part of a wall. Its bead-like eyes never leave us, and its grotesquely wide mouth is so fantastic that I almost believe it is grinning wickedly at me.

At last Chandi Das finds his voice.

"I am not adorned with the polished jewels of learning, but if you will listen to what I have to say, then your journey will not be fruitless. Go back to the same place where you started your Indian journey and, before a new moon will have risen, you shall have your desire satisfied."

"Do you mean that I should return to Bombay?"

"You speak rightly."

I am puzzled. What can that hybrid half-Western city hold for me?

"But I have never found anything there to help me on my quest," I protest.

Chandi Das looks at me coolly.

"There is your path. Follow it as quickly as your heels can carry you. Lose no time, but hasten back to Bombay to-morrow."

"Is that all you can tell me?"

"There is more, but I have not troubled to perceive it."

He reverts to silence. His eyes become as expressionless as still water. A while later he speaks:

"You will leave India and return to the Western lands before the next equinox. A grievous illness will fall upon your body almost as soon as you leave our soil. The spirit will struggle in the wracked body, but not yet is its hour of escape. And then the hidden work of destiny will come to light, for it will send you back to Aryavarta (India) so that in all you visit us thrice. A sage awaits you even now and for his sake, since you are tied to him by ancient threads, you will come back to dwell among us."[1]

His voice stops and a faint tremor passes across his eyelids. When, later, he looks directly at me, he adds:

"You have heard. There is nothing more to say."

The rest of our talk is desultory and unimportant. Chandi Das refuses to enter into further discussion about himself, so that I am left wondering how to receive his strange words, although I feel that there is more behind them.

There is an amusing moment when, in the course of a brief conversation with his youthful disciple, the latter asks me earnestly:

"Do you not see such things among the Yogis of England?"

I try to restrain a smile.

"There are no Yogis in that country," I answer.

Everyone else has sat still and silent throughout the evening, but when the Yogi signifies that the interview is over, the owner of the hut, a peasant probably, approaches us and asks if we will share his humble meal with him. I tell him that we have brought some food in the car and that we will go over to the headman's house to cook it, since the headman had promised to accommodate us in a room of his house for the night. But the peasant replies that he will not have it said that he has forgotten how to be hospitable. I tell him that I have eaten well to-day and beg him not to trouble. However, he is firm and insistent, so, rather than disappoint him, I accept.

[1] Time has written its confirmation of the first half of this prediction.

"It ill becomes me to receive a guest and give him no food," he remarks, when he offers a dish of fried grain.

I look through the barred hole which serves as a window. The opal crescent of the moon thrusts a pale light through the hole as I reflect upon the superior character and kindliness which one finds so often in these simple, illiterate peasants. No college education, no business acumen can compensate for the degeneration of character which so often marks the folk of the towns.

And when I have taken farewell of Chandi Das and his disciple, the peasant lifts the cheap lantern which hangs from a narrow beam in the roof and accompanies us to the street. I reassure him, so he touches his forehead, smiles, and stands in the open doorway. I follow in the wake of my servant, each of us flashing a torch, towards our place of rest for the night. Sleep eludes me; for, mingling with my thoughts of the mysterious Yogi from Bengal are the eerie cries of jackals and the peculiar long howl of a pariah dog.

§

If I do not follow the counsel of Chandi Das to the strict letter, at least I turn the car's radiator towards Bombay and make a gradual return to that city. When I succeed in arriving there and installing myself in a hotel, I succeed also in falling ill.

Cooped up between four walls, tired in mind and sick in body, I begin to develop, for the first time, a pessimistic outlook. I begin to feel that I have had enough of India. I have covered many thousands of miles of travel in this country, and occasionally under dismal conditions. The India I have been seeking is not to be found in the European quarters, where wining, dining, dancing, bridge and whisky-and-sodas make up the pattern of an attractive picture. Sojourn in the Indian quarters of towns, whenever decently possible, has helped me in my quest, but has not improved my health, while sojourn in up-country districts and jungle villages, with unsuitable food and bad water, unsettled life and tropical sleeplessness, has proved itself dangerous. My body is now a weary burden flung on a bed of pain.

I wonder how much longer I can stave off a breakdown. I have grown heavy-eyed with lack of sleep. For months I have been unable to exorcise this wraith of insomnia which has relentlessly pursued me throughout this land. And the need to walk warily between the strange types of men with whom I have come into contact has played sad havoc with my nerves. The necessity of keeping a careful inner balance, of being critical and yet receptive at the same time, while penetrating the unfamiliar circles of India's secret hinterland, has imposed a prolonged strain upon me. I have had to learn how to pick my way between genuine sages and fools who mistake their egotistic fancies for divine knowledge, between true religious mystics and mere mystery-mongers, between pseudo holy men working black magic and true followers of the way of Yoga. And I have had to cram and concentrate my investigations into minimum time, for I cannot afford to spend years out of a life upon a single quest.

If my physical and mental condition is bad, my spiritual state is little better. I am disheartened by a sense of failure. True, I have met some men of remarkable attainments and fine character, as well as others who can do amazing things, but I have not settled down to any positive inward recognition that here is the spiritual superman of my quest, the master who appeals to my rationalistic make-up and to whom I can gladly attach myself. Enthusiastic disciples have vainly endeavoured to draw me into their own teachers' folds, but I can see that, just as youth takes its first adolescent adventure as the last measure of love, so these good folk have been so thrilled by their early experiences that they have not thought to seek any farther. Besides, I have no desire to become the depository of another man's doctrines; it is a living, first-hand, personal experience which I seek, a spiritual illumination entirely my own and not someone else's.

But, after all, I am only a humble and irresponsible scribe wandering in the East after abandoning his ambitions. Who am I to expect to be favoured with such a meeting? And so depression throws its heavy mantle around my heart.

When I am well enough to drag my body around, I sit at the hotel table with an Army captain as my neighbour. He unfolds a long story of a sick wife, a slow recovery, cancelled leave arrangements, and so on. He makes my own morbidity worse. When we have finished and are out on the veranda, he sticks a long cigar in his mouth and mutters:

"Some game—life, eh?"

"Yes—some!" I agree laconically.

Half an hour later I am in a taxi speeding along Hornby Road. We stop outside the tall, piazza-like façade of a shipping company's offices. I pay for my ticket with the consciousness that I have done the only possible thing in taking this sudden exit from India.

Despising the grimy hovels, dusty shops, ornate palaces and efficient-looking office blocks which are Bombay, I return to my hotel room in order to continue my unhappy ruminations.

Evening comes. The waiter sets a delicious curry on the table, but the dinner repels me. I take a couple of iced drinks and then taxi across the city. I get out and saunter slowly along a street until I find myself standing in front of one of the West's gifts to urban India—a great, gaudy-faced cinema theatre. I pause awhile before its brightly lit entrance and study its flaringly coloured posters.

Always fond of movies, they seem to offer to-night a welcome drink of the cup of Lethe. I do not imagine that I shall ever be completely forlorn while I can buy, for a rupee or its equivalent, a padded and plush-covered seat at a cinema in any city throughout the world.

Inside I settle down to watch the inevitable fragments of American life turned into tabloids and flung in shadows upon a white screen. Once again there reappears a foolish wife and faithless husband, both moving on a background of palatial apartments. I try hard to fix my attention on them, but somehow find myself becoming increasingly bored. To my surprise I discover that the old zest for cinema pictures has suddenly deserted me. The tales of human passion, tragedy and comedy have strangely lost their power to sadden my heart or move me to laughter.

Half-way through the show the screen figures flicker away into sheer unreality. My attention becomes quite abstracted and my thoughts fasten themselves once again upon my strange quest. I realize unexpectedly that I have become a pilgrim without a God, a wanderer from city to city and from village to village seeking a place where the mind may rest, but finding none. How I have gazed into the faces of many men, hoping to find the exotic lineaments of a spiritual superman who has cast the plumb-line of thought deeper than the men of my own land and time ; how I have looked into the dark flashing eyes of other peoples, hoping to find a pair that will echo back the mysterious answer which will satisfy me !

And then a peculiar tenseness arises in my brain and the atmosphere around me seems to be charged with potent electrical vibrations. I am aware that some profoundly dynamic psychic change is occurring within me. Suddenly a mental voice thrusts itself into the field of attention and forces me to listen, amazed, as it scornfully says to me :

" Life itself is nothing more than a cinema play unrolling its episodes from the cradle to the grave. Where now are the past scenes—can you hold them ? Where are those yet to come—can you grasp them ? Instead of trying to find the Real, the Enduring, the Eternal, you come here and waste time on what is even more deceptive than ordinary existence—a wholly imaginary story, an illusion within the great illusion."

Thereupon I lose the last shred of interest in the spinning film of human love and tragedy. To retain my seat any longer will be a farce. I rise and walk out of the theatre.

I wander slowly and aimlessly through the street under the brilliant moon which, in the East, seems so close to man's life. At a corner a beggar approaches me, and I gaze into his face as he utters his first unrecognizable sound. I recoil in horror, for he is disfigured by a terrible disease, which has left the skin of his face clinging in patches to the bone. But a profound pity for this fellow-victim of life replaces my first disgust and I thrust all my loose change into his outstretched hand.

I make my way to the seashore, to a lonelier part where one can remain untroubled by the motley crowds of varied races which throng the Back Bay promenade each night. Gazing at the stars, which form a beautiful canopy to this city, I realize that I have reached an unexpected crisis.

§

Within a few days my ship will head its way to Europe and slide through the greenish-blue waters of the Arabian Sea. Once on board I shall bid farewell to philosophy and toss my Oriental quest into the waters of oblivion. No longer shall I give all that I have to offer—time, thought, energy, money—upon the altar of a search for supposititious masters.

But the inescapable mental voice persists in troubling me again.

" Fool ! " it flings scornfully at me. " So this is to be the empty result of years of investigation and aspiration ! You are to tread the same road as other men, to forget all you have learnt, to drown your better feelings in hard egotism and sensuality ? But take care ! Your apprenticeship to life has been served with terrible masters ; unending thought has stripped the veneer off existence, ceaseless activity has lashed you with its whip, and spiritual loneliness has segregated your soul. Think you that you can escape the results of such an indenture ? Not so, for it has put invisible chains on your feet ! "

I see-saw from one mood to another, the while I stare at the thick star-clusters which overpower the Oriental sky. I seek to defend myself against the merciless psychic voice, pleading my helplessness in the face of failure.

The voice answers :

" Are you *sure* none of the men you met here in India can be the Master you seek ? "

A long gallery of faces passes before my mind's eye. Quick-tempered Northern faces, placid Southern ones, nervous emotional Eastern faces and strong silent Mahratti faces from the West : friendly faces, foolish faces, wise faces, dangerous faces, evil faces and inscrutable ones.

A single face disentangles itself out of the procession and persistently hovers before me, its eyes quietly gazing into mine. It is the calm, Sphinx-like countenance of the Maharishee, the sage who has spent his life on the Hill of the Holy Beacon in the South. I have never forgotten him ; indeed, a tender thought of the Maharishee has arisen for a brief life again and again, but the abrupt character of my experiences, the whirling panorama of faces and events and the sudden changes which came during my quest have deeply overlaid the impressions of my short period with him.

Yet I realize now that he has passed through my life like a star, which moves across the dark void with its lonely light and then is gone. And I have to admit, in answer to my inner questioner, that he is the one man who has impressed me more than any other person I have ever met, whether in the East or West. But he had seemed so aloof, so remote from a European mentality, and so indifferent whether I became his pupil or not.

The silent voice now grips me with its intensity.

" How can you be sure that he was indifferent ? You did not stay long, but hurried away."

" Yes," I confess, feebly. " I had to carry out my self-imposed programme. What else could I do ? "

" There is one thing you can do now. Go back to him."

" How can I force myself upon him ? "

" Your personal feelings are of less importance than success in this search. Go back to the Maharishee."

" He is at the other end of India and I am too ill to start my wanderings again."

" What does that matter ? If you want a Master you must pay the price."

" I doubt whether I want one now, for I feel too tired to want anything. Anyway, I have booked a steamer berth and must sail in three days ; it is too late to alter things."

The voice almost sneers at me.

" Too late, eh ? What has happened to your sense of values ? You admit that the Maharishee is the most wonderful man you ever met, but you are quite willing to run away from him before you have hardly tried to know him. Return to him."

I remain sullen and obstinate. The brain answers " Yes," but the blood says " No ! "

Once more the voice urges me :

" Change your plans again. You *must* go back to the Maharishee."

Thereupon something surges up from the inner depths of my being and demands immediate assent to the command of that inexplicable voice. It overwhelms me and so forcibly does it master my reason-born objections and the protests of my enfeebled body that I become as a babe in its hands. Through all this sudden overpowering urgency which asks my instant return to the Maharishee, I see his summoning irresistible eyes in a most vivid manner.

I cease all further argument with the inner voice, because I know that I am now helpless in its hands. I shall travel at once to the Maharishee and, if he accepts me, entrust myself to his tutelage. I shall hitch my wagon to his shining star. The die is cast. Something has conquered me, though I do not understand what it is.

I return to the hotel, mop my brow and sip a cup of lukewarm tea. As I drink it I realize that I am a changed man. I am conscious that my dark burden of wretchedness and doubt is falling from my shoulders.

Next morning I come down to breakfast aware that I am smiling for the first time since I came back to Bombay. The tall bearded Sikh servant, resplendent in white jacket, golden cummerbund and white trousers, smiles back in response as he stands with folded arms behind my chair. Then he says :

" A letter for you, sir."

I look at the cover. It has been twice readdressed and has followed me from place to place. As I take my seat I slit it open.

To my delight and surprise I discover that it has been written in the hermitage at the foot of the Hill of the Holy

Beacon. Its writer, once a prominent public man and Member of the Madras Legislative Council, has withdrawn from worldly affairs following a tragic domestic bereavement and become a disciple of the Maharishee, whom he visits on occasions. I had met him and we were engaged in a desultory correspondence.

The letter is full of encouraging thoughts and suggests that I shall be welcome if I care to revisit the hermitage. When I finish reading it one sentence flames out in memory so as to obliterate the others.

"You have had the good fortune to meet a real Master," it runs.

I treat the letter as an omen favourable to my new-born decision to return to the Maharishee. A ride down to the shipping offices follows breakfast, and I leave the intimation that I am not sailing.

It is not long before I bid adieu to Bombay and carry out my new plan. I cross hundreds of miles of flat colourless Deccan tableland, with long stretches where solitary bamboo trees alone rear their leafy heads to vary the scene. The train cannot roll through the scanty grass and occasional trees of this Indian prairie fast enough for me. As it flies joltingly along the rails, I feel that I am speeding towards a great occasion—spiritual enlightenment and the most mysterious personality I have ever encountered. For as I look out of the screened compartment window, my slumbering hopes of discovering a Rishee, a spiritual superman, awaken once more.

When, on the second day, we have covered over a thousand miles and have begun to enter the placid Southern landscape, broken by a few red hills, I feel strangely happy. And when we leave the torrid plains behind, I find the dank, steamy heat of Madras City positively welcome, for it means that I have broken the back of my journey.

After leaving the South Mahratta Company's terminus, I have to cross the scattered town in order to change on to the South Indian Railway. Finding that I have a few hours to spare before the train starts, I use the time to make some necessary purchases and to have a hurried chat with the Indian author who introduced me to His Holiness Shri Shankara, the spiritual head of South India.

He greets me warmly, and when I inform him that I am on the way to the Maharishee, the writer exclaims:

"I am not surprised! That is what I expected."

I am taken aback, but ask him:

" Why do you say that ? "

He smiles.

" My friend, do you not remember how we parted from His Holiness in the town of Chingleput ? Did you not notice that he whispered something to me in the ante-room just before we left ? "

" Yes, now that you remind me, I certainly do remember it."

The author's thin, refined face still keeps its smile.

" This is what His Holiness told me. 'Your friend will travel all round India. He will visit many Yogis and listen to many teachers. But, in the end, he will have to return to the Maharishee. For him, the Maharishee alone is the right Master.' "

These words, coming as they do on the eve of my return, deeply impress me. They reveal the prophetic power of Shri Shankara ; more, they offer a kind of confirmation that I am taking the right course.

How strange are the wanderings which my stars have imposed upon me.

CHAPTER XVI

IN A JUNGLE HERMITAGE

THERE are moments unforgettable which mark themselves in golden figures upon the calendar of our years. Such a moment comes to me now, as I walk into the hall of the Maharishee.

He sits as usual upon the magnificent tiger-skin which covers the centre of his divan. The joss-sticks burn slowly away on a little table near him, spreading the penetrating fragrance of incense around the hall. Not to-day is he remote from men and wrapped up in some trance-like spiritual absorption, as on that strange occasion when I first visited him. His eyes are clearly open to this world and glance at me comprehendingly as I bow, and his mouth is stretched in a kindly smile of welcome.

Squatting at a respectful distance from their master are a few disciples; otherwise the long hall is bare. One of them pulls the punkah-fan, which flaps lazily through the heavy air.

In my heart I know that I come as one seeking to take up the position of a disciple, and that there will be no rest for my mind until I hear the Maharishee's decision. It is true that I live in a great hope of being accepted, for that which sent me scurrying out of Bombay to this place came as an absolute command, a decisive and authoritative injunction from a supernormal region. In a few words I dispose of the preliminary explanations, and then put my request briefly and bluntly to the Maharishee.

He continues to smile at me, but says nothing.

I repeat my question with some emphasis.

There is another protracted pause, but at length he answers me, disdaining to call for the services of an interpreter and expressing himself directly in English.

"What is all this talk of masters and disciples? All these differences exist only from the disciple's standpoint. To the one who has realized the true self there is neither master nor disciple. Such a one regards all people with equal eye."

I am slightly conscious of an initial rebuff, and though I press my request in other ways the Maharishee refuses to yield on the point. But in the end he does say :

"You must find the master within you, within your own spiritual self. You must regard his body in the same way that he himself regards it ; the body is not his true self."

It begins to voice itself in my thoughts that the Maharishee is not to be drawn into giving me a direct affirmative response, and that the answer I seek must be found in some other way, doubtless in the subtle, obscure manner at which he hints. So I let the matter drop and our talk then turns to the outward and material side of my visit.

I spend the afternoon making some arrangements for a protracted stay.

§

The ensuing weeks absorb me into a strange, unwonted life. My days are spent in the hall of the Maharishee, where I slowly pick up the unrelated fragments of his wisdom and the faint clues to the answer I seek ; my nights continue as heretofore in torturing sleeplessness, with my body stretched out on a blanket laid on the hard earthen floor of a hastily built hut.

This humble abode stands about three hundred feet away from the hermitage. Its thick walls are composed of thinly plastered earth, but the roof is solidly tiled to withstand the monsoon rains. The ground around it is virgin bush, somewhat thickly overgrown, being in fact the fringe of the jungle which stretches away to the west. The rugged landscape reveals Nature in all her own wild uncultivated grandeur. Cactus hedges are scattered numerously and irregularly around, the spines of these prickly plants looking like coarse needles. Beyond them the jungle drops a curtain of scrub bush and stunted trees upon the land. To the north rises the gaunt figure of the mountain, a mass of metallic-tinted rocks and brown soil. To the south lies a long pool, whose placid water has attracted me to the spot, and whose banks are bordered with clumps of trees holding families of grey and brown monkeys.

Each day is a duplicate of the one before. I rise early in the mornings and watch the jungle dawn turn from grey to green and then to gold. Next comes a plunge into the water and a swift swim up and down the pool, making as much noise as I possibly can so as to scare away lurking snakes. Then, dressing, shaving, and the only luxury I can secure in this place—three cups of deliciously refreshing tea.

"Master, the pot of tea-water is ready," says Rajoo, my hired boy. From an initial total ignorance of the English language, he has acquired that much, and more, under my occasional tuition. As a servant he is a gem, for he will scour up and down the little township with optimistic determination in quest of the strange articles and foods for which his Western employer speculatively sends him, or he will hover outside the Maharishee's hall in discreet silence during meditation hours should he happen to come along for orders at such times. But as a cook he is unable to comprehend Western taste, which seems a queer distorted thing to him. After a few painful experiments I myself take charge of the more serious culinary arrangements, reducing my labour by reducing my solid meals to a single one each day. Tea, taken thrice daily, becomes both my solitary earthly joy and the mainstay of my energy. Rajoo stands in the sunshine and watches with wonderment my addiction to the glorious brown brew. His body shines in the hard yellow light like polished ebony, for he is a true son of the black Dravidians, the primal inhabitants of India.

After breakfast comes my quiet lazy stroll to the hermitage, a halt for a couple of minutes beside the sweet rose bushes in the compound garden, which is fenced in by bamboo posts, or a rest under the drooping fronds of palm trees whose heads are heavy with coconuts. It is a beautiful experience to wander around the hermitage garden before the sun has waxed in power and to see and smell the variegated flowers.

And then I enter the hall, bow before the Maharishee, and quietly sit down on folded legs. I may read or write for a while, or engage in conversation with one or two of the other men, or tackle the Maharishee on some point, or plunge into meditation for an hour along the lines which the sage has indicated, although evening usually constitutes the time specially assigned to meditation in the hall. But whatever I am doing I never fail to become gradually aware of the mysterious atmosphere of the place, of the benign radiations which steadily percolate into my brain. I enjoy an ineffable tranquillity merely by sitting for a while in the neighbourhood of the

Maharishee. By careful observation and frequent analysis I arrive in time at the complete certitude that a reciprocal inter-influence arises whenever our presences neighbour each other. The thing is most subtle. But it is quite unmistakable.

At eleven I return to the hut for the midday meal and a rest and then go back to the hall to repeat my programme of the morning. I vary my meditations and conversations sometimes by roaming the countryside or descending on the little township to make further explorations of the colossal temple.

From time to time the Maharishee unexpectedly visits me at the hut after finishing his own lunch. I seize the opportunity to plague him with further questions, which he patiently answers in terse epigrammatic phrases, clipped so short as rarely to constitute complete sentences. But once, when I propound some fresh problem, he makes no answer. Instead, he gazes out towards the jungle-covered hills which stretch to the horizon and remains motionless. Many minutes pass, but still his eyes are fixed, his presence remote. I am quite unable to discern whether his attention is being given to some invisible psychic being in the distance or whether it is being turned on some inward preoccupation. At first I wonder whether he has heard me, but in the tense silence which ensues, and which I feel unable or unwilling to break, a force greater than my rationalistic mind commences to awe me until it ends by overwhelming me.

The realization forces itself through my wonderment that all my questions are moves in an endless game, the play of thoughts which possess no limit to their extent ; that somewhere within me there is a well of certitude which can provide me with all the waters of truth I require ; and that it will be better to cease my questioning and attempt to realize the tremendous potencies of my own spiritual nature. So I remain silent and wait.

For almost half an hour the Maharishee's eyes continue to stare straight in front of him in a fixed, unmoving gaze. He appears to have forgotten me, but I am perfectly aware that the sublime realization which has suddenly fallen upon me is nothing else than a spreading ripple of telepathic radiation from this mysterious and imperturbable man.

On another visit he finds me in a pessimistic mood. He tells me of the glorious goal which waits for the man who takes to the way he has shown.

" But, Maharishee, this path is full of difficulties and I am so conscious of my own weaknesses," I plead.

" That is the surest way to handicap oneself," he answers

unmoved, " this burdening of one's mind with the fear of failure and the thought of one's failings."

" Yet if it is true——? " I persist.

" It is not true. The greatest error of a man is to think that he is weak by nature, evil by nature. Every man is divine and strong in his real nature. What are weak and evil are his habits, his desires and thoughts, but not himself."

His words come as an invigorating tonic. They refresh and inspire me. From another man's lips, from some lesser and feebler soul, I would refuse to accept them at such worth and would persist in refuting them. But an inward monitor assures me that the sage speaks out of the depths of a great and authentic spiritual experience, and not as some theorizing philosopher mounted on the thin stilts of speculation.

Another time, when we are discussing the West, I make the retort :

" It is easy for you to attain and keep spiritual serenity in this jungle retreat, where there is nothing to disturb or distract you."

" When the goal is reached, when you know the Knower, there is no difference between living in a house in London and living in the solitude of a jungle," comes the calm rejoinder.

And once I criticize the Indians for their neglect of material development. To my surprise the Maharishee frankly admits the accusation.

" It is true. We are a backward race. But we are a people with few wants. Our society needs improving, but we are contented with much fewer things than your people. So to be backward is not to mean that we are less happy."

§

How has the Maharishee arrived at the strange power and stranger outlook which he possesses ? Bit by bit, from his own reluctant lips and from those of his disciples, I piece together a fragmentary pattern of his life story.

He was born in 1879 in a village about thirty miles distant from Madura, which is a noted South Indian town possessing one of the largest temples in the country. His father followed some avocation connected with law and came of good Brahmin stock. His father appears to have been an extremely charitable man who fed and clothed many poor persons. The boy eventually passed to Madura to carry on his education, and it was here that he picked up the rudiments of English from some American missionaries who were conducting a school.

At first young Ramana was fond of play and sport. He wrestled, boxed and swam dangerous rivers. He betrayed no special interest in religious or philosophical concerns. The only exceptional thing in his life at the time was a tendency to somnambulism or sleep-walking, and to a condition of sleep so profound that the most disturbing interruptions could not awaken him. His schoolmates eventually discovered this and took advantage of it to sport with him. During the daytime they were afraid of his quick punch, but at night they would come into his bedroom, take him into the playground, beat his body and box his ears, and then lead him back to bed. He was quite unconscious of these experiences and had no remembrance of them in the mornings.

The psychologist who has correctly understood the nature of sleep will find in this account of the boy's abnormal depth of attention, sufficient indication of the mystical nature which he possessed.

One day a relative came to Madura and, in answer to Ramana's question, mentioned that he had just returned from a pilgrimage to the temple of Arunachala. The name stirred some slumbering depths in the boy's mind, thrilling him with peculiar expectations which he could not understand. He enquired as to the whereabouts of this temple and ever after found himself haunted by thoughts of it. It seemed to be of paramount importance to him, yet he could not even explain to himself why Arunachala should mean anything more to him than the dozens of other great temples which are scattered over India.

He continued his studies at the mission school without showing any special aptitude for them, although he always evinced a fair degree of intelligence in his work. But when he was seventeen, destiny, with swift and sudden stroke, got into action and thrust its hands through the even tenor of his days.

He suddenly left the school and completely abandoned all his studies. He gave no notice to his teachers or to his relatives, and told no one before the event actually occurred. What was the reason of this unpromising change, which cast a cloud upon his future worldly prospects?

The reason was satisfying enough to himself, though it might have seemed mind-perplexing to others. For life, which in the ultimate is the teacher of men, set the young student on another course than that which his school-teachers had assigned him. And the change came in a curious way about six weeks before he dropped his studies and disappeared from Madura for ever.

He was sitting alone one day in his room when a sudden and inexplicable fear of death took hold of him. He became acutely aware that he was going to die, although outwardly he was in good health. The thing was a psychological phenomenon, because there was no apparent reason why he should die. Yet he became obsessed with this notion and immediately began to prepare for the coming event.

He stretched his body prone upon the floor, fixed his limbs in the rigidity of a corpse, closed his eyes and mouth, and finally held his breath. " Well, then," said I to myself, " this body is dead. It will be carried stiff to the burning ground and then reduced to ashes. But with the death of the body, am *I* dead ? Is the body *I* ? This body is now silent and stiff. But I continue to feel the full force of my self apart from its condition."

Those are the words which the Maharishee used in describing the weird experience through which he passed. What happened next is difficult to understand though easy to describe. He seemed to fall into a profound conscious trance wherein he became merged into the very source of selfhood, the very essence of being. He understood quite clearly that the body was a thing apart and that the *I* remained untouched by death. The true self was very real, but it was so deep down in man's nature that hitherto he had ignored it.

Ramana emerged from this amazing experience an utterly changed youth. He lost most of his interest in studies, sports, friends, and so on, because his chief interest was now centred in the sublime consciousness of the true self which he had found so unexpectedly. Fear of death vanished as mysteriously as it came. He enjoyed an inward serenity and a spiritual strength which have never since left him. Formerly he had been quick to retaliate at the other boys when they had chaffed him or attempted to take liberties, but now he put up with everything quite meekly. He suffered unjust acts with indifference and bore himself among others with complete humility. He gave up old habits and tried to be alone as much as possible, for then he would sink into meditation and surrender himself to the absorbing current of divine consciousness which constantly drew his attention inwards.

These profound changes in his character were, of course, noticed by others. One day his elder brother came into the room when the boy was supposed to be doing his homework and found him sunk in meditation with closed eyes. The school books and papers had been tossed across the room in disgust. The brother was so annoyed at this neglect of studies that he jeered at him with sharp words :

" What business has a fellow like you here ? If you want to behave like a Yogi, why are you studying for a career ? "

Young Ramana was deeply stung by these words. He immediately realized their truth and silently decided to act upon them. His father was dead and he knew that his uncle and other brothers would take care of his mother. Truly he had no business there. And back into his mind there flashed the name which had haunted him for nearly a year, the name whose very syllables fascinated him, the name of the temple of Arunachala. Thither would he go, although why he should select that place he was quite unable to say. But an impelling urgency arose within him and formed the decision for him of its own accord. It was entirely unpremeditated.

" I was literally charmed here," said the Maharishee to me. " The same force which drew you to this place from Bombay, drew me to it from Madura."

And so young Ramana, feeling this inner pull within his heart, left friends, family, school and studies, and took the road which eventually brought him to Arunachala and to a still profounder spiritual attainment. He left behind a brief farewell letter, which is still preserved in the hermitage. Its flourishing Tamil characters read as follows :

" I have, in search of my Father and in obedience to His command, started from here. This is only embarking on a virtuous enterprise. Therefore none need grieve over this affair. To trace this out, no money need be spent."

With three rupees in his pocket and an utter ignorance of the world, he set out on the journey into the interior of the South. The amazing incidents which marked that journey prove conclusively that some mysterious power was protecting and guiding him. When at last he arrived at his destination, he was utterly destitute and among total strangers. But the emotion of total renunciation was burning strong within him. Such was the youth's scorn for all earthly possessions, at the time, that he flung his robe aside and took up his meditative posture in the temple precinct quite nude. A priest observed this and remonstrated with him, but to no purpose. Other shocked priests came along, and, after vehement efforts, forced a concession from the youth. He consented to wear a semi-loincloth, and that is all he has ever worn to this day.

For six months he occupied various spots in the precinct, never going anywhere else. He lived on some rice which was brought him once a day by a priest who was struck by the precocious behaviour of the youth. For Ramana spent the entire day plunged in mystical trances and spiritual ecstasies so profound that he was entirely oblivious of the world around him. When some rough Moslem youths flung mud at him and ran away, he was quite unaware of the fact until some hours later. He felt no resentment against them in his heart.

The stream of pilgrims who descended on the temple made it difficult for him to obtain the seclusion he desired, so he left the place and moved to a quiet shrine set in the fields some distance from the village. Here he continued to stay for a year and a half. He was satisfied with the food brought by the few people who visited this shrine.

Throughout this time he spoke to no one ; indeed, he never opened his lips to talk until three years passed since his arrival in the district. This was not because he had taken a vow of silence, but because his inner monitor urged him to concentrate all his energy and attention upon his spiritual life. When his mystic goal was attained the inhibition was no longer necessary and he began to talk again, though the Maharishee has remained an extremely taciturn man.

He kept his identity a complete secret, but, by a chain of coincidences, his mother discovered his whereabouts two years after his disappearance. She set out for the place with her eldest son and tearfully pleaded with him to return home. The lad refused to budge. When tears failed to persuade him she began to upbraid him for his indifference. Eventually he wrote down a reply on a piece of paper to the effect that a higher power controls the fate of men and that whatever she did could not change his destiny. He concluded by advising her to accept the situation and to cease moaning about it. And so she had to yield to his obstinacy.

When, through this incident, people began to intrude on his seclusion in order to stare at the youthful Yogi, he left the place and climbed up the Hill of the Holy Beacon and made his residence in a large cavern, where he lived for several years. There are quite a few other caves on this hill and each one shelters holy men or Yogis. But the cave which sheltered young Ramana was noteworthy because it also contained the tomb of a great Yogi of the past.

Cremation is the usual custom of the Hindus in disposing of their dead, but it is often prohibited in the case of a Yogi who is believed to have made the highest attainment, because it is also believed that the vital breath or unseen life-current remains in his body for thousands of years and renders the flesh exempt from corruption. In such a case the Yogi's body is bathed and anointed and then placed in a tomb in a sitting posture with crossed legs, as though he were still plunged in meditation. The entrance to the tomb is sealed with a heavy stone and then cemented over. Usually the mausoleum becomes a place of pilgrimage. There exists still another reason why great Yogis are buried and not cremated, and that is because of the belief that their bodies do not need to be purified by fire since they were purified during their lifetimes.

It is interesting to consider that caves have always been a favourite residence of Yogis and holy men. The ancients consecrated them to the gods; Zoroaster, the founder of the Parsee faith, practised his meditations in a cave, while Muhammed received his religious experiences in a cave also. The Indian Yogis have very good reasons for preferring caves or subterranean retreats when better places are not available. For here they can find shelter from the vicissitudes of weather and from the rapid changes of temperature which divide days from nights in the tropics. There is less light and noise to disturb their meditations. And breathing the confined atmosphere of a cave causes the appetite to diminish markedly, thus conducing to a minimum of bodily cares.

Still another reason which may have attracted Ramana to this particular cave on the Hill of the Holy Beacon was the beauty of its outlook. One can stand on a projecting spur adjoining the cave and see the little township stretched out flat in the distant plain, with the giant temple rising as its centre-piece. Far beyond the plain stands a long line of hills which frontier a charming panorama of Nature.

Anyway, Ramana lived in this somewhat gloomy cavern for several years, engaged in his mysterious meditations and plunged in profound trances. He was not a Yogi in the orthodox sense, for he had never studied any system of Yoga and he had never practised under any teacher. The inner path which he followed was simply a track leading to self-knowledge; it was laid down by what he conceived to be the divine monitor within him.

In 1905 plague appeared in the locality. The dread visitant was probably carried into the district by some pilgrim to the temple of Arunachala. It devastated the population so fiercely that almost everyone left the little township and fled in terror to safer villages or towns. So quiet did the deserted place become that tigers and leopards came out of their lurking dens in the jungle and moved openly through the streets. But, though they must have roamed the hill-side many times, for it stood in their path to the township, though they must have passed and repassed the Maharishee's cave, he refused to leave, but remained as calm and unmoved as ever.

By this time the young hermit had involuntarily acquired a solitary disciple, who had become very much attached to him and persisted in staying by his side and attending to his needs. The man is now dead, but the legend has been handed down to other disciples that each night a large tiger came to the cave and licked Ramana's hands, and that the tiger was in return fondled by the hermit. It sat in front of him throughout the night and departed only at dawn.

There is a widespread notion throughout India that Yogis and faqueers who live in the jungles or on the mountains, exposed to danger from lions, tigers, snakes and other wild creatures, move unharmed and untouched if they have attained a sufficient degree of Yogic power. Another story about Ramaṇa told how he was once sitting in the afternoon outside the narrow entrance to his abode when a large cobra came swishing through the rocks and stopped in front of him. It raised its body and spread out its hood, but the hermit did not attempt to move. The two beings—man and beast—faced each other for some minutes, gaze meeting gaze. In the end the snake withdrew and left him unharmed, although it was within striking distance.

The austere lonely life of this strange young man closed its first phase with his firm and permanent establishment in the deepest point of his own spirit. Seclusion was no longer an imperative need, but he continued to live at the cave until the visit of an illustrious Brahmin pundit, Ganapati Shastri, proved another turning-point of his outer life, which was now to enter on a more social period. The pundit had recently come to stay near the temple for study and meditation. He heard by chance that there was a very young Yogi on the hill and out of curiosity he went in search of him. When he found Ramana, the latter was staring fixedly at the sun. It was not at all uncommon for the hermit to keep his eyes on the dazzling sun for some hours till it disappeared below the western horizon. The glaring light of the rays of an afternoon sun in India can hardly be appreciated by a European who has never experienced it. I remember once, when I had set out to climb the steep ascent of the hill at a wrong hour being caught without shelter by the full glare of the sun at midday on my return journey. I staggered and reeled about like a drunken man for quite a time. So the feat of young Ramana in enduring the merciless glare of the sun, with face uplifted and eyes unflinching, may therefore be better evaluated.

The pundit had studied all the chief books of Hindu wisdom for a dozen years and had undergone rigorous penances in an endeavour to reach some tangible spiritual benefit, but he was still afflicted by doubts and perplexities. He put a question to Ramana and after fifteen minutes received a reply which amazed him with its wisdom. He put further questions, involving his own philosophical and spiritual problems, and was still more astounded at the clearing-up of perplexities which had troubled him for years. As a result he prostrated himself before the young hermit and became a disciple. Shastri had his own group of followers in the town of Vellore and he went back later and told them that he had found a Maharishee (Great Sage or Seer), because the latter was undoubtedly a man of the highest spiritual realization whose teachings were so original that the pundit had found nothing exactly like them in any book he had read. From that time the title of Maharishee began to be applied to young Ramana by cultured people, although the common folk wanted to worship him as a divine being when his existence and character became better known to them. But the Maharishee strongly forbade every manifestation of such worship in his presence. Among themselves and in private talk with me, most of his devotees and people in the locality insist on calling him a god.

A small group of disciples attached themselves to the Maharishee in time. They built a wooden frame bungalow on a lower spur of the hill and persuaded him to live in it with them. In different years his mother had paid him short visits and became reconciled to his vocation. When death parted her from her eldest son and other relatives, she came to the Maharishee and begged him to let her live with him. He consented. She spent the six years of life which were left to her at his side, and finished up by becoming an ardent disciple of her own son. In return for the hospitality which was given her in the little hermitage, she acted as cook.

When the old lady died, her ashes were buried at the foot of the hill and some of the Maharishee's devotees built a small shrine over the place. Here, ever-burning sacred lamps glow in memory of this woman, who gave a great sage to mankind, and little heaps of scented jasmines and marigolds, snatched from their stalks, are thrown on a tiny altar in offering to her spirit.

The efflux of time spread the reputation of the Maharishee throughout the locality, so that pilgrims to the temple were often induced to go up the hill and see him before they returned home. Quite recently the Maharishee yielded to incessant requests and consented to grace the new and large hall which was built at the foot of the hill as a residence for him and his disciples.

The Maharishee has never asked for anything but food, and consistently refuses to handle money. Whatever else has come to him has been voluntarily pressed upon him by others. During those early years when he tried to live a solitary existence, when he built a wall of almost impenetrable silent reserve around himself whilst he was perfecting his spiritual powers, he did not disdain to leave his cave with a begging bowl in hand and wander to the village for some food whenever the pangs of hunger stirred his body. An old widow took pity on him and thenceforth regularly supplied him with food, eventually insisting on bringing it up to his cave. Thus his venture of faith in leaving his comfortable middle-class home was, in a measure, justified, at any rate to the extent that whatever powers there be have ensured his shelter and food. Many gifts have since been offered him, but as a rule he turns them away.

When a gang of dacoits broke into the hall one night not long ago and searched the place for money, they were unable to find more than a few rupees, which was in the care of the man who superintended the purchase of food. The robbers were so angry at this disappointment that they belaboured the Maharishee with stout clubs, severely marking his body. The sage not only bore their attack patiently, but requested them to take a meal before they departed. He actually offered them some food. He had no hate towards them in his heart. Pity for their spiritual ignorance was the sole emotion they aroused. He let them escape freely, but within a year they were caught while committing another crime elsewhere and received stiff sentences of penal servitude.

Not a few Western minds will inevitably consider that this life of the Maharishee's is a wasted one. But perhaps it may be good for us to have a few men who sit apart from our world of unending activity and survey it for us from afar. The onlooker may see more of the game and sometimes he gets a truer perspective. It may also be that a jungle sage, with self lying conquered at his feet, is not inferior to a worldly fool who is blown hither and thither by every circumstance.

§

Day after day brings its fresh indications of the greatness of this man. Among the strangely diversified company of human beings who pass through the hermitage, a pariah stumbles into the hall in some great agony of soul or circumstance and pours out his tribulation at the Maharishee's feet. The sage does not reply, for his silence and reserve are habitual ; one can easily count up the number of words he uses in a single day. Instead, he gazes quietly at the suffering man, whose cries gradually diminish until he leaves the hall two hours later a more serene and stronger man.

I am learning to see that this is the Maharishee's way of helping others, this unobtrusive, silent and steady outpouring of healing vibrations into troubled souls, this mysterious telepathic process for which science will one day be required to account.

A cultured Brahmin, college-bred, arrives with his questions. One can never be certain whether the sage will make a verbal response or not, for often he is eloquent enough without opening his lips. But to-day he is in a communicative mood and a few of his terse phrases, packed with profound meanings as they usually are, open many vistas of thought for the visitor.

A large group of visitors and devotees are in the hall when someone arrives with the news that a certain man, whose criminal reputation is a byword in the little township, is dead. Immediately there is some discussion about him and, as is the wont of human nature, various people engage in recalling some of his crimes and the more dastardly phases of his character. When the hubbub has subsided and the discussion appears to have ended, the Maharishee opens his mouth for the first time and quietly observes :

" Yes, but he kept himself very clean, for he bathed two or three times a day ! "

A peasant and his family have travelled over one hundred miles to pay silent homage to the sage. He is totally illiterate, knows little beyond his daily work, his religious rites and ancestral superstitions. He has heard from someone that there is a god in human form living at the foot of the Hill of the Holy Beacon. He sits on the floor quietly after having prostrated himself three times. He firmly believes that some blessing of spirit or fortune will come to him as a result of this journey. His wife moves gracefully to his side and drops to the floor. She is clothed in a purple robe which flows smoothly from head to ankles and is then tucked into her waist. Her sleek and smooth hair is glossy with scented oil. Her daughter accompanies her. She is a pretty girl whose ankle-rings click in consort as she steps into the hall. And she follows the charming custom of wearing a white flower behind her ear.

The little family stay for a few hours, hardly speaking, and gaze in reverence at the Maharishee. It is clear that his mere presence provides them with spiritual assurance, emotional felicity and, most paradoxical of all, renewed faith in their creed. For the sage treats all creeds alike, regards them all as significant and sincere expressions of a great experience, and honours Jesus no less than Krishna.

On my left squats an old man of seventy-five. A quid of betel is comfortably tucked in his cheek, a Sanskrit book lies between his hands, and his heavy-lidded eyes stare meditatively at the bold print. He is a Brahmin who was a station-master near Madras for many years. He retired from the railway service at sixty and soon after his wife died. He took the opportunity thus presented of realizing some long-deferred aspirations. For fourteen years he travelled about the country on pilgrimage to the sages and saints and Yogis, trying to find one whose teachings and personality were sufficiently appealing to him. He had circled India thrice, but no such master had been discoverable. He had set up a very individual standard apparently. When we met and compared notes he lamented his failure. His rugged honest face, carved by wrinkles into dark furrows, appealed to me. He was not an intellectual man, but simple and quite intuitive. Being considerably younger than he, I felt it incumbent on me to give the old man some good advice! His surprising response was a request to become his master! "Your master is not far off," I told him and conducted him straightaway to the Maharishee. It did not take long for him to agree with me and become an enthusiastic devotee of the sage.

Another man in the hall is bespectacled, silken-clad and prosperous-looking. He is a judge who has taken advantage of a law vacation to pay a visit to the Maharishee. He is a keen disciple and strong admirer and never fails to come at least once a year. This cultured, refined and highly educated gentleman squats democratically among a group of Tamils who are poor, naked to the waist and smeared with oil, so that their bodies glisten like varnished ebony. That which brings them together, destroys the insufferable snobbishness of caste, and produces unity, is that which caused Princes and Rajahs to come from afar in ancient times to consult the forest Rishees—the deep recognition that true wisdom is worth the sacrifice of superficial differences.

A young woman with a gaily attired child enters and prostrates herself in veneration before the sage. Some profound problems of life are being discussed, so she sits in silence, not venturing to take part in intellectual conversation. Learning is not regarded as an ornament for Hindu women and she knows little outside the purlieus of culinary and domestic matters. But she knows when she is in the presence of undeniable greatness.

With the descent of dusk comes the time for a general group meditation in the hall. Not infrequently the Maharishee will signal the time by entering, so gently as occasionally to be unnoticed, the trance-like abstraction wherein he locks his senses against the world outside. During these daily meditations in the potent neighbourhood of the sage, I have learnt how to carry my thoughts inward to an ever-deepening point. It is impossible to be in frequent contact with him without becoming lit up inwardly, as it were, mentally illumined by a sparkling ray from his spiritual orb. Again and again I become conscious that he is drawing my mind into his own atmosphere during these periods of quiet repose. And it is at such times that one begins to understand why the silences of this man are more significant than his utterances. His quiet unhurried poise veils a dynamic attainment, which can powerfully affect a person without the medium of audible speech or visible action. There are moments when I feel this power of his so greatly that I know he has only to issue the most disturbing command and I will readily obey it. But the Maharishee is the last person in the world to place his followers in the chains of servile obedience, and allows everyone the utmost freedom of action. In this respect he is quite refreshingly different from most of the teachers and Yogis I have met in India.

My meditations take the line he had indicated during my first visit, when he had tantalized me by the vagueness which seemed to surround many of his answers. I have begun to look into my own self.

Who am I?

Am I this body of flesh, blood and bone?

Am I the mind, the thoughts and the feelings which distinguish me from every other person ?

One has hitherto naturally and unquestioningly accepted the affirmative answers to these questions, but the Maharishee has warned me not to take them for granted. Yet he has refused to formulate any systematic teaching. The gist of his message is :

" Pursue the enquiry ' Who am I ? ' relentlessly. Analyse your entire personality. Try to find out where the I-thought begins. Go on with your meditations. Keep turning your attention within. One day the wheel of thought will slow down and an intuition will mysteriously arise. Follow that intuition, let your thinking stop, and it will eventually lead you to the goal."

I struggle daily with my thoughts and cut my way slowly into the inner recesses of mind. In the helpful proximity of the Maharishee, my meditations and self-soliloquies become increasingly less tiring and more effective. A strong expectancy and sense of being guided inspire my constantly repeated efforts. There are strange hours when I am clearly conscious of the unseen power of the sage being powerfully impacted on my mentality, with the result that I penetrate a little deeper still into the shrouded borderland of being which surrounds the human mind.

The close of every evening sees the emptying of the hall as the sage, his disciples and visitors, adjourn for supper to the dining-room. As I do not care for their food and will not trouble to prepare my own, I usually remain alone and await their return. However, there is one item of the hermitage diet which I find attractive and palatable, and that is curds. The Maharishee, having discovered my fondness for it, usually asks the cook to bring me a cupful of the drink each night.

About half an hour after their return, the inmates of the hermitage, together with those visitors who have remained, wrap themselves up in sheets or thin cotton blankets and retire to sleep on the tiled floor of the hall. The sage himself uses his divan as a bed. Before he finally covers himself with the white sheets, his faithful attendant thoroughly massages his limbs with oil.

I take up a glazed iron lantern when leaving the hall and set out on my lonely walk to the hut. Countless fireflies move amongst the flowers and plants and trees in the garden compound. Once, when I am two or three hours later than usual and midnight is approaching, I observe these strange insects put out their weird lights. Often they are just as numerous among the thick growths of bush and cactus through which I have later to pass. One has to be careful not to tread on scorpions or snakes in the dark. Sometimes the current of meditation has seized me so profoundly that I am unable and unwilling to stop it, so that I pay little heed to the narrow path of lighted ground upon which I walk. And so I retire to my modest hut, close the tightly fitting heavy door, and draw the shutters over glassless windows to keep out unwelcome animal intruders. My last glimpse is of a thicket of palm trees which stands on one side of my clearing in the bush, the silver moonlight coming in streams over their interlaced feathery tops.

CHAPTER XVII

TABLETS OF FORGOTTEN TRUTH

ONE afternoon I notice a new visitor walk with dignified step into the hall and take his seat quite close to the Maharishee's couch. He is extremely dark-skinned, but otherwise his face is highly refined. He makes no attempt to speak, but the Maharishee immediately gives him a welcoming smile.

The man's personality makes a powerful impression upon me. He looks like a graven Buddha. Extraordinary tranquillity is deeply charactered on his face. When our eyes meet eventually, he gazes for a long time at me until I turn away disquieted. Throughout the afternoon he does not utter a single word.

My next contact with him comes the following day and in a totally unexpected manner. I leave the hall and return to my hut to prepare tea, as the servant Rajoo has gone off to the township for some things. Unlocking the heavy door I am about to step on the threshold, when something moves across the floor and stops within a few inches of my feet. Its furtive gliding motion and the faint hissing which I fancy I can hear warn me almost before I see it that a snake is in the room. For the moment I am so struck with horror at my escape from the death which lurks underfoot, that I am at a complete loss what to do. The creature holds my fascinated gaze . . . and yet it terrifies me. My nerves are strung to their highest pitch of tension. Horror and loathing rise up in the depths of my heart, but my eyes remain staring at the handsome shapely head of the creature. The surprise encounter has quite overwhelmed me. The malevolent reptile continues to watch me in a cold-blooded way, its hood raised around its sinewy neck and its sinister eyes fixed upon mine.

At last I manage to recover my senses and draw back with a rush. I am about to go off for a heavy stick with which to break its spine, when the figure of yesterday's new visitor appears in the clearing. His noble face, with its habitual look of dignified reflection, slightly restores my calm. He approaches my hut, takes the situation in at a glance, and imperturbably begins to enter the room. I shout a warning to him, but he takes no notice. Once more I am distinctly unnerved. For, weaponless as he is, he holds both hands out towards the snake !

Its forked tongue moves about in its open mouth, but it does not attempt to attack him. Just then two men, attracted by the sound of my shout, come hurrying to the hut from the pool where they have been washing themselves. Before they reach us, the strange visitor stands quite close to the snake, which bends its head before him, and then he gently strokes its tail !

The fangs cease their sinister movement in the handsome, but venomous, head until the arrival of the other two men. Then the supple body of the snake begins to move with a quick writhing movement as it seems to recollect itself and, before four pairs of eyes, it slithers quickly out of the hut into the safe refuge of the jungle undergrowth.

" It is a young cobra," remarks one of the late arrivals, who is a leading merchant in the township, and who often comes to pay his respects to the sage or to have a chat with me.

I express my astonishment at the fearless way in which my first visitor handled the snake.

" Ah, that is Yogi Ramiah," replies the merchant when I ask for an explanation. " He is one of the most advanced disciples of the Maharishee. A remarkable man ! "

It is not possible to enter into conversation with the Yogi because I discover that part of the special discipline which he has imposed upon himself consists in keeping strict silence, and because he comes from a Telegu-speaking district. His acquaintance with English is as limited as mine with Telegu ; that is, almost nil. I learn also that he maintains an almost complete reserve and does not associate with the others in the place, as a rule ; that he stays in a small stone shelter which he has had constructed under the shadow of some huge boulders on the other side of the pool ; and that he has been a disciple of the Maharishee's for ten years.

The gap between us is bridged, however, soon after. I meet him at the pool, whither he has come with a brass pitcher for water. His darkly mysterious, but benignant, countenance again attracts me and, as I happen to have a camera in my pocket, I request him by means of gestures to pose for his photograph. He offers no objection, and even follows me to the hut after it is taken. There we encounter the ex-station-master, who is squatting outside my door and awaiting my arrival.

In the result I discover that the old man knows Telegu almost as well as he knows English and is quite agreeable to play the interpreter between us, with pencilled notes as a substitute for vocal speech. The Yogi is not very communicative and evidently dislikes being interviewed, but I manage to elicit a few more facts about him.

Ramiah is still on the right side of forty. He owns some landed property in the Nellore district, and although he has not formally renounced the world, he lets his family carry on the active control of his estates so that he can give more time to his Yoga interests. He has a group of his own disciples in Nellore, but once every year he leaves them to visit the Maharishee, with whom he stays for two or three months at a time.

He has made an extensive tour of South India in his younger days, when he sought actively for a master in Yoga. He has studied under different teachers and developed some exceptional faculties and powers. Breathing exercises and meditation practices come easily to him. He appears to have outstripped his teachers, because he obtained experiences which they could not explain satisfactorily to him. As a consequence he came at last to the Maharishee, who quickly provided him with the correct explanation and assisted his further course.

Yogi Ramiah tells me that he has come to stay for two months, bringing his own personal servant with him, and that he has been glad to find a Westerner taking an interest in the ancient wisdom of the East. I show him an illustrated English magazine and he makes a curious commentary upon one of the pictures.

" When your wise men in the West leave off trying to make engines run faster than those which they already have and begin to look into their own selves, your race may then find more real happiness. Can you say that your people become more contented each time they discover something that enables them to travel more quickly ? "

Before he leaves me I question him about the incident with the young cobra. He smilingly scribbles a reply :

" What have I to be afraid of ? I approached it without hatred and with love for all beings in my heart."

I fancy that there is more behind the Yogi's words than his somewhat sentimental explanation implies, but without further questioning I let him return to his lonely dwelling across the pool.

During the weeks which succeed my first meeting with Ramiah, I come to know him a little better. We meet frequently in the little clearing around my hut, or at the pool-side, or even outside his own dwelling. I find in his outlook something which is conformable to my own temperament, while his large dark eyes possess a tranquillity which is singularly attractive. We strike up a strange kind of silent friendship, which culminates one day when he gives me his blessing by stroking my head and then clasping each hand in his own. Aside from a few pencilled notes in Telegu which the old man translates for me, no word is spoken during the whole of our association. Yet I feel that something is being built up between Ramiah and me which can never be broken down. From time to time I accompany him on short walks through the jungle areas, and once or twice we toil up the rugged hillside amid great boulders, but wherever we go he is always a serene dignified figure whose noble carriage I cannot help but admire.

It is not long, however, before I receive another striking revelation of his extraordinary power. A letter has found its way to me, bringing extremely bad news. It means, so far as I can see, that my financial fuel will unexpectedly run so low soon that my stay in India must be cut short. I can, of course, enjoy the protracted hospitality of the Maharishee's hermitage which the disciples will doubtless offer, but such a position would go right against the grain of my nature. And in any case the matter is settled for me by certain obligations which I consider it my duty faithfully to meet, and which can now be met only through the resumption of activities in the West.

The news provides an excellent test of the mental and spiritual training which I have been undergoing, and so poor is my material that I emerge quite uncreditably. I feel badly shaken. I am unable to effect my usual inner contact with the Maharishee in the hall, and leave him abruptly after a short visit. For the rest of the day I wander about somewhat disconsolate, a silent rebel against the crushing power of fate, which can upset all one's plans by a single blow.

I turn into the hut and fling a weary body and wearier mind upon the blanket. Some kind of deep reverie must have supervened, for, a while later, I start with sudden shock at a gentle tap on the door. I bid the visitor enter. Very slowly the door opens and to my surprise Ramiah's figure enters the hut.

I rise hastily and then, when he squats down, do the same

facing him. He looks intently at me, a questioning expression in his eyes. I am alone with a man whose tongue I cannot speak and who cannot speak a word of English. Yet a queer feeling impels me to address him in my tongue which is so alien to him, in the almost fantastic expectation that he will catch my thoughts, though he fail to catch my words ! And so, in a few jerky phrases, I hint at the difficulties which have suddenly dropped out of the skies upon me, and supplement my speech with gestures of defeat and expressions of disgust.

Ramiah listens quietly. When I finish he nods his head gravely in sympathetic response. A little later he rises and, with signs and gestures, invites me to follow him outside. Our path lies through shaded jungle, but before long emerges in a large dusty open space, where we are exposed to the full glare of the afternoon sun. I continue to follow him for about half an hour, when I seek the shelter of a banyan tree which then lends its protecting shade to my overheated body. After a short rest we travel on for another half-hour, again crossing a patch of scrub jungle, and ultimately wander down to a great pool by a route with which Ramiah appears to be familiar. Our feet sink deeply into its soft, sandy bank as we walk up to a patch of water which is overgrown with coloured lotuses.

The Yogi selects the shade of an exceptionally low tree and seats himself beneath it. I drop to the sand and squat beside him. The tufted head of the palmyra is spread out above us like a green umbrella. We seem to be entirely alone in this quiet corner of our turning globe, for a bare deserted landscape stretches away for a couple of miles until it meets dense hilly jungle again.

Ramiah crosses his legs and folds his feet under him in his customary meditation posture. He beckons me with his finger to approach a trifle closer. Then his placid face turns to the front and his eyes gaze steadily across the water, and he quickly sinks into a condition of profound meditation.

The minutes which seem so slow creep past, but Ramiah remains quite motionless, with his face as tranquil as the surface of the pool beside which we squat, and with his body fitting into Nature's landscape like a tree unstirred by the slightest wind. A half-hour passes, yet he still sits under the palmyra, very strange and very quiet, wrapt in introspective silence. His face now seems transfigured by a profounder peace than usual, and his rigid eyes are fixed either in vacancy or on the distant hills—I do not know which.

It is not much longer before I become acutely susceptible to the silence of our lonely surroundings and to the amazing calm of my companion. Little by little, with an insidious but persistent gentleness, peace weaves itself into the texture of my soul. The mood of serene triumph over personal distresses, which I could not reach before, now comes to me more easily. In his own mysterious way the Yogi is helping me; I cannot doubt that. Barely a breath comes from his quiet form, so sunk is he in deepest contemplation. What is the secret of his sublime condition? What is the source of this beneficent radiation which emanates from him?

The heat is lessening with the approach of evening, and the baked sand begins to cool. A ray of vivid gold from the westering sun falls on the Yogi's face, turning his motionless body for the nonce into a haloed idol. I let go of him in thought that I may turn again to enjoy the increasing peace which is flowing in waves over my being. The changes and chances of mundane existence now take their fit proportions, as I begin to live in my own diviner depths. I perceive with startling clarity that a man can look serenely upon his tribulations, if only he can find the standpoint of his deeper self; that it is foolish to cling to the transient comfort of worldly hopes when the unchanging certainty of a diviner protection awaits his acceptance; *and that the reason why the wise Galilean told his disciples to take no thought for the morrow was because a higher power had taken thought for them.* I perceive, too, that once a man accepts this invitation to place his confidence in the prophetic element within his being, he may pass through the vicissitudes of human life in this world without fear and without faltering. And I feel that somewhere close at hand there is the fundamental value of life, in whose calm air no cares may exist. Thus the burden which lay so heavy on my mind vanishes with this change of spiritual atmosphere.

I reck little of time during this beautiful experience, and I do not know how one can satisfactorily explain the mystery of the divine within-ness and its independence of any temporal sense. Twilight falls upon the vivid scene. Somewhere in the dim recesses of memory I am aware that night comes in these tropic parts with surprising quickness, yet I feel no concern about the matter. It is enough that this wonderful man at my side is content to stay and lead me inwards to the sovereign good, serenity.

When at length he lightly touches my arm as a signal to rise, the darkness is complete. Hand in hand we wander into the night through this lonely and desolate region, making the homeward journey without light and without track, guided only by Yogi Ramiah's uncanny sense of location. At any other time this place would have filled me with unpleasant fears, for past experience of the jungle at night has left eerie memories; one felt that a world of unseen living forms was close at hand, with animals moving hither and thither. And for a moment or two there flashes across my mind's eye a picture of Jackie, the dog which often companions my walks in the district and my meals at the hut, with the two scars around his throat from cheetah-bites, and of his unfortunate brother who was captured by the same cheetah and never seen again. Perchance I, too, may see the glowing jade-green eyes of a prowling, hungry cheetah, or tread unwittingly in the darkness on a cobra lying coiled up on the ground, or even touch a king scorpion, that deadly, little white monster, with my sandalled foot. But, almost immediately afterwards, I feel ashamed of these thoughts in the Yogi's fearless presence and at once resign myself to his protective aura, which I somehow feel is enfolding me.

The strange chorus of nature which begins with the Indian dawn is now being rivalled by the stranger chorus which begins when the night is somewhat advanced. A jackal sounds repeatedly in the distance, and once there comes the ominous echo of a wild beast's snarl, and when we near the pool which divides our respective dwellings the croaks of frogs, lizards and bats come to our ears. . . .

In the morning I open my eyes on a sunny universe and my heart to its sunny message.

§

My pen would wander on into some account of the scenic life around me, and into further record of many talks with the Maharishee, but it is now time to draw this chronicle to a close.

I study him intently and gradually come to see in him the child of a remote Past, when the discovery of spiritual truth was reckoned of no less value than is the discovery of a gold mine to-day. It dawns upon me with increasing force that in this quiet and obscure corner of South India, I have been led to one of the last of India's spiritual supermen. The serene figure of this living sage brings the legendary figures of his country's ancient Rishees nearer to me. One senses that the most wonderful part of this man is withheld. His deepest soul, which one instinctively recognizes as being loaded with rich wisdom, eludes one. At times he still remains curiously aloof, and at other times the kindly benediction of his interior grace binds me to him with hoops of steel. I learn to submit to the enigma of his personality, and to accept him as I find him. But if, humanly speaking, he is well insulated against outside contacts, whoever discovers the requisite Ariadne's thread can walk the inner path leading to spiritual contact with him. And I like him greatly because he is so simple and modest, when an atmosphere of authentic greatness lies so palpably around him; because he makes no claims to occult powers and hierophantic knowledge to impress the mystery-loving nature of his countrymen; and because he is so totally without any traces of pretension that he strongly resists every effort to canonize him during his lifetime.

It seems to me that the presence of men like the Maharishee ensures the continuity down history of a divine message from regions not easily accessible to us all. It seems to me, further, that one must accept the fact that such a sage comes to reveal something to us, not to argue anything with us. At any rate, his teachings make a strong appeal to me for his personal attitude and practical method, when understood, are quite scientific in their way. He brings in no supernatural power and demands no blind religious faith. The sublime spirituality of the Maharishee's atmosphere and the rational self-questioning of his philosophy find but a faint echo in yonder temple. Even the word "God" is rarely on his lips. He avoids the dark and debatable waters of wizardry, in which so many promising voyages have ended in shipwreck. He simply puts forward a way of self-analysis, which can be practised irrespective of any ancient or modern theories and beliefs which one may hold, a way that will finally lead man to true self-understanding.

I follow this process of self-divestment in the effort to arrive at pure integral being. Again and again I am aware that the Maharishee's mind is imparting something to my own, though no words may be passing between us. The shadow of impending departure hangs over my efforts, yet I spin out my stay until bad health takes a renewed hand in the game and accelerates an irrevocable decision to go. Indeed, out of the deep inner urgency which drew me here, has come enough will power to overthrow the plaints of a tired sick body and a weary brain and to enable me to maintain residence in this hot static air. But Nature will not be defeated for long and before long a physical breakdown becomes threateningly imminent. Spiritually my life is nearing its peak, but—strange paradox!—physically it is slipping downwards to a point lower than it has hitherto touched. For a few hours before the arrival of the culminating experience of my contact with the Maharishee, I start to shiver violently and to perspire with abnormal profuseness—intimations of coming fever.

I return hastily from an exploration of some usually veiled sanctuaries of the great temple and enter the hall when the evening meditation period has run out half its life. I slip quietly to the floor and straightway assume my regular meditation posture. In a few seconds I compose myself and bring all wandering thoughts to a strong centre. An intense interiorization of consciousness comes with the closing of eyes.

The Maharishee's seated form floats in a vivid manner before my mind's eye. Following his frequently repeated instruction I endeavour to pierce through the mental picture into that which is formless, his real being and inner nature, his soul. To my surprise the effort meets with almost instantaneous success and the picture disappears again, leaving me with nothing more than a strongly felt sense of his intimate presence.

The mental questionings which have marked most of my earlier meditations have lately begun to cease. I have repeatedly interrogated my consciousness of physical, emotional and mental sensations in turn, but, dissatisfied in the quest of self, have eventually left them all. I have then applied the attention of consciousness to its own centre, striving to become aware of its place of origin. Now comes the supreme moment. In that concentration of stillness, the mind withdrawn into itself, one's familiar world begins to fade off into shadowy vagueness. One is apparently environed for a while by sheer nothingness, having arrived at a kind of mental blank wall. And one has to be as intense as possible to maintain one's fixed attention. But how hard to leave the lazy dalliance of our surface life and draw the mind inwards to a pin-point of concentration!

To-night I flash swiftly to this point, with barely a skirmish against the continuous sequence of thoughts which usually play the prelude to its arrival. Some new and powerful force comes into dynamic action within my inner world and bears me inwards with resistless speed. The first great battle is over, almost without a stroke, and a pleasurable, happy, easeful feeling succeeds its high tension.

In the next stage I stand apart from the intellect, conscious that it is thinking, but warned by an intuitive voice that it is merely an instrument. I watch these thoughts with a weird detachment. The power to think, which has hitherto been a matter for merely ordinary pride, now becomes a thing from which to escape, for I perceive with startling clarity that I have been its unconscious captive. There follows the sudden desire to stand outside the intellect and just *be*. I want to dive into a place deeper than thought. I want to know what it will feel like to deliver myself from the constant bondage of the brain, but to do so with all my attention awake and alert.

It is strange enough to be able to stand aside and watch the very action of the brain as though it were someone else's, and to see how thoughts take their rise and then die, but it is stranger still to realize intuitively that one is about to penetrate into the mysteries which hide the innermost recesses of man's soul. I feel like some Columbus about to land on an uncharted continent. A perfectly controlled and subdued anticipation quietly thrills me.

But how divorce oneself from the age-old tyranny of thoughts? I remember that the Maharishee has never suggested that I should attempt to force the stoppage of thinking. "Trace thought to its place of origin," is his reiterated counsel, "watch for the real self to reveal itself, and then your thoughts will die down of their own accord." So, feeling that I have found the birthplace of thinking, I let go of the powerfully positive attitude which has brought my attention to this point and surrender myself to complete passivity, yet still keeping as intently watchful as a snake of its prey.

This poised condition reigns until I discover the correctness of the sage's prophecy. The waves of thought naturally begin to diminish. The workings of logical rational sense drop towards zero point. The strangest sensation I have experienced till now grips me. Time seems to reel dizzily as the antennæ of my rapidly growing intuition begin to reach out into the unknown. The reports of my bodily senses are no longer heard, felt, remembered. I know that at any moment I shall be standing *outside* things, on the very edge of the world's secret. . . .

Finally it happens. Thought is extinguished like a snuffed candle. The intellect withdraws into its real ground, that is, consciousness working unhindered by thoughts. I perceive, what I have suspected for some time and what the Maharishee has confidently affirmed, that the mind takes its rise in a transcendental source. The brain has passed into a state of complete suspension, as it does in deep sleep, yet there is not the slightest loss of consciousness. I remain perfectly calm and fully aware of who I am and what is occurring. Yet my sense of awareness has been drawn out of the narrow confines of the separate personality; it has turned into something sublimely all-embracing. Self still exists, but it is a changed, radiant self. For something that is far superior to the unimportant personality which *was* I, some deeper, diviner being rises into consciousness and *becomes* me. With it arrives an amazing new sense of absolute freedom, for thought is like a loom-shuttle which is always going to and fro, and to be freed from its tyrannical motion is to step out of prison into the open air.

I find myself outside the rim of world consciousness. The planet which has so far harboured me, disappears. I am in the midst of an ocean of blazing light. The latter, I feel rather than think, is the primeval stuff out of which worlds are created, the first state of matter. It stretches away into untellable infinite space, incredibly *alive*.

I touch, as in a flash, the meaning of this mysterious universal drama which is being enacted in space, and then return to the primal point of my being. I, the new I, rest in the lap of holy bliss. I have drunk the Platonic Cup of Lethe, so that yesterday's bitter memories and to-morrow's anxious cares have disappeared completely. I have attained a divine liberty and an almost indescribable felicity. My arms embrace all creation with profound sympathy, for I understand in the deepest possible way that to know all is not merely to pardon all, but to love all. My heart is remoulded in rapture.

How shall I record these experiences through which I next pass, when they are too delicate for the touch of my pen? Yet the starry truths which I learn may be translated into the language of earth, and the effort will not be a vain one. So I seek, all too roughly, to bring back some memorials of the wonderful archaic world which stretches out, untracked and unpathed, behind the human mind.

§

¶ *Man is grandly related and a greater Being suckled him than his mother. In his wiser moments he may come to know this.*

¶ *Once, in the far days of his own past, man took an oath of lofty allegiance and walked, turbaned in divine grandeur, with the gods. If to-day the busy world calls to him with imperious demand and he gives himself up to it, there are those who have not forgotten his oath and he shall be reminded of it at the appropriate hour.*

¶ *There is That in man which belongs to an imperishable race. He neglects his true self almost completely, but his neglect can never affect or alter its shining greatness. He may forget it and entirely go to sleep in the senses, yet on the day when it stretches forth its hand and touches him, he shall remember who he is and recover his soul.*

¶ *Man does not put the true value upon himself because he has lost the divine sense. Therefore he runs after another man's opinion, when he could find complete certitude more surely in the spiritually authoritative centre of his own being. The Sphinx surveys no earthly landscape. Its unflinching gaze is always directed inwards, and the secret of its inscrutable smile is self-knowledge.*

¶ *He who looks within himself and perceives only discontent, frailty, darkness and fear, need not curl his lip in mocking doubt. Let him look deeper and longer, deeper and longer, until he presently becomes aware of faint tokens and breath-like indications which appear when the heart is still. Let him heed them well, for they will take life and grow into high thoughts that will cross the threshold of his mind like wandering angels, and these again shall become forerunners of a voice which will come later—the voice of a hidden, recondite and mysterious being who inhabits his centre, who is his own ancient self.*

¶ *The divine nature reveals itself anew in every human life, but if a man walk indifferently by, then the revelation is as seed on stony ground. No one is excluded from this divine consciousness ; it is man who excludes himself. Men make formal and pretentious enquiry into the mystery and meaning of life, when all the while each bird perched upon a green bough, each child holding its fond mother's hand, has solved the riddle and carries the answer in its face. That Life which brought you to birth, O Man! is nobler and greater than your farthest thought; believe in its beneficent intention towards you and obey its subtle injunctions whispered to your heart in half-felt intuitions.*

¶ *The man who thinks he may live as freely as his unconsidered desires prompt him and yet not carry the burden of an eventual reckoning, is binding his life to a hollow dream. Whoever sins against his fellows or against himself pronounces his own sentence thereby. He may hide his sins from the sight of others, but he cannot hide them from the all-recording eyes of the gods. Justice still rules the world with inexorable weight, though its operations are often unseen and though it is not always to be found in stone-built courts of law. Whoever escapes from paying the legal penalties of earth can never escape from paying the just penalties which the gods impose. Nemesis—remorseless and implacable—holds such a man in jeopardy every hour.*

¶ *Those who have been held under the bitter waters of sorrow, those who have moved through shadowed years in the mist of tears, will be somewhat readier to receive the truth which life is ever silently voicing. If they can perceive nothing else, they can perceive the tragical transience which attends the smiles of fortune. Those who refuse to be deluded by their brighter hours will not suffer so greatly from their darker ones. There is no life that is not made up of the warp of pleasure and the woof of suffering. Therefore no man can afford to walk with proud and pontifical air. He who does so takes his perambulation at a grave peril. For humility is the only befitting robe to wear in the presence of the unseen gods, who may remove in a few days what has been acquired during many years. The fate of all things moves in cycles and only the thoughtless observer can fail to note this fact. Even in the universe it may be seen that every perihelion is succeeded by an aphelion. So in the life and fortunes of man, the flood of prosperity may be succeeded by the ebb of privation, health may be a fickle guest, while love may come only to wander again. But when the night of protracted agony dies, the dawn of new-found wisdom glimmers. The last lesson of these things is that the eternal refuge in man, unnoticed and unsought as it may be, must become what it was once—his solace, or disappointment and suffering will periodically conspire to drive him in upon it. No man is so lucky that the gods permit him to avoid these two great tutors of the race.*

¶ *A man will feel safe, protected, secure, only when he discovers that the radiant wings of sublimity enfold him. While he persists in remaining unillumined his best inventions shall become his worst impediments, and everything that draws him closer to the material frame of things shall become another knot he must later untie. For he is inseparably allied to his ancient past, he stands always in the presence of his inner divinity and cannot shake it off. Let him, then, not remain unwitting of this fact but deliver himself, his worldly cares and secret burdens, into the beautiful care of his better self and it shall not fail him. Let him do this, if he would live with gracious peace and die with fearless dignity.*

¶ *He who has once seen his real self will never again hate another There is no sin greater than hatred, no sorrow worse than the legacy of lands splashed with blood which it inevitably bestows, no result more certain than that it will recoil on those who send it forth. Though none can hope to pass beyond their sight, the gods themselves stand unseen as silent witnesses of man's awful handiwork. A moaning world lies in woe all around them, yet sublime peace is close at hand for all ; weary men, tried by sorrow and torn by doubts, stumble and grope their way through the darkened streets of life, yet a great light beats down upon the paving-stones before them. Hate will pass from the world only when man learns to see the faces of his fellows, not merely by the ordinary light of day, but by the transfiguring light of their divine possibilities ; when he can regard them with the reverence they deserve as the faces of beings in whose hearts dwells an element akin to that Power which men name God.*

¶ *All that is truly grand in Nature and inspiringly beautiful in the arts speaks to man of himself. Where the priest has failed his people the illumined artist takes up his forgotten message and procures hints of the soul for them. Whoever can recall rare moments when beauty made him a dweller amid the eternities should, whenever the world tires him, turn memory into a spur and seek out the sanctuary within. Thither he should wander for a little peace, a flush of strength and a glimmer of light, confident that the moment he succeeds in touching his true selfhood he will draw infinite support and find perfect compensation. Scholars may burrow like moles among the growing piles of modern books and ancient manuscripts which line the walls of the house of learning, but they can learn no deeper secret than this, no higher truth than the supreme truth that man's very self is divine. The wistful hopes of man may wane as the years pass, but the hope of undying life, the hope of perfect love, and the hope of assured happiness, shall ultimately find a certain fulfilment ; for they constitute prophetic instincts of an ineluctable destiny which can in no way be avoided.*

¶ *The world looks to ancient prophets for its finest thoughts and cringes before dusty eras for its noblest ethics. But when a man receives the august revelation of his own starry nature, he is overwhelmed. All that is worthy in thought and feeling now comes unsought to his feet. Inside the cloistral quiet of his mind arise visions not less sacred than those of the Hebrew and Arab seers, who reminded their race of its divine source. By this same auroral light Buddha understood and brought news of Nirvana to men. And such is the all-embracing love which this understanding awakens, that Mary Magdalene wept out her soiled life at the feet of Jesus.*

¶ *No dust can ever settle on the grave grandeur of these ancient truths, though they have lain in time since the early days of our race. No people has ever existed but has also received intimations of this deeper life which is open to man. Whoever is ready to accept them must not only apprehend these truths with his intelligence, until they sparkle among his thoughts like stars among the asteroids, but must appropriate them with his heart until they inspire him to diviner action.*

§

I return to this mundane sphere impelled by a force which I cannot resist. By slow unhurried stages I become aware of my surroundings. I discover that I am still sitting in the hall of the Maharishee and that it is apparently deserted. My eyes catch sight of the hermitage clock and I realize that the inmates must be in the dining-room at their evening meal. And then I become aware of someone on my left. It is the seventy-five-year-old ex-stationmaster, who is squatting close beside me on the floor with his gaze turned benevolently on me.

" You have been in a spiritual trance for nearly two hours," he informs me. His face, seamed with years and lined with old cares, breaks into smiles as though he rejoices in my own happiness.[1]

I endeavour to make some reply, but discover to my astonishment that my power of speech has gone. Not for almost fifteen minutes do I recover it. Meanwhile the old man supplements the further statement :

" The Maharishee watched you closely all the time. I believe his thoughts guided you."

When the sage returns to the hall, those who follow him take up their positions for the short interval which precedes the final retirement for the night. He raises himself up on the divan and crosses his legs ; then, resting an elbow on the right thigh, he holds his chin within the upright hand, two fingers covering his cheek. Our eyes meet across the intervening space and he continues to look intently at me.

[1]The reader should not be misled into believing that such an experience remains continuous and permanent; it is only a temporary but valuable raising of consciousness which passes away. It is of the category which I have called "Moments of Illumination." The nature of such a glimpse is explained in the last chapter of my book *The Spiritual Crisis of Man*. To establish oneself on, and keep this high level it is essential in most cases to work on oneself and develop the right conditions within oneself. For the philosophical enlightenment see *The Hidden Teaching Beyond Yoga* and *The Wisdom of the Overself*.

And when the attendant lowers the wicks of the hall's lamps, following the customary nightly practice, I am struck once again by the strange lustre in the Maharishee's calm eyes. They glow like twin stars through the half-darkness. I remind myself that never have I met in any man eyes as remarkable as those of this last descendant of India's Rishees. In so far as the human eyes can mirror divine power, it is a fact that the sage's do that.

The heavily scented incense smoke rises in soft spirals the while I watch those eyes that never flicker. During the forty minutes which pass so strangely, I say nothing to him and he says nothing to me. What use are words ? We now understand each other better without them, for in this profound silence our minds approach a beautiful harmony, and in this optic telegraphy I receive a clear unuttered message. Now that I have caught a wonderful and memorable glimpse of the Maharishee's view-point on life, my own inner life has begun to mingle with his.

§

I fight the oncoming fever during the two days which follow and manage to keep it at bay.

The old man approaches my hut in the afternoon.

" Your stay among us draws to an end, my brother," he says regretfully. " But you will surely return to us one day ? "

" Most surely ! " I echo confidently.

When he leaves me I stand at the door and look up at the Hill of the Holy Beacon—Arunachala, the Sacred Red Mountain, as the people of the countryside prefer to call it. It has become the colourful background of all my existence ; always I have but to raise my eyes from whatever I am doing, whether eating, walking, talking or meditating, and there is its strange, flat-headed shape confronting me in the open or through a window. It is somehow inescapable in this place, but the strange spell it throws over me is more inescapable still. I begin to wonder whether this queer, solitary peak has enchanted me. There is a local tradition that it is entirely hollow and that in its interior dwell several great spiritual beings who are invisible to mortal gaze, but I disdain the story as a childish legend. And yet this lonely hill holds me in a powerful thrall, despite the fact that I have seen others infinitely more attractive. This rugged piece of Nature, with its red laterite boulders tumbled about in disorderly masses and glowing like dull fire in the sunlight, possesses a strong personality which emanates a palpable awe-creating influence.

With the fall of dusk I take my farewells of everyone except the Maharishee. I feel quietly content because my battle for spiritual certitude has been won, and because I have won it without sacrificing my dearly held rationalism for a blind credulity. Yet when the Maharishee comes to the courtyard with me a little later, my contentment suddenly deserts me. This man has strangely conquered me and it deeply affects my feelings to leave him. He has grappled me to his own soul with unseen hooks which are harder than steel, although he has sought only to restore a man to himself, to set him free and not to enslave him. He has taken me into the benign presence of my spiritual self and helped me, dull Westerner that I am, to translate a meaningless term into a living and blissful experience.

I linger over our parting, unable to express the profound emotions which move me. The indigo sky is strewn with stars, which cluster in countless thousands close over our heads. The rising moon is a thin crescent disc of silver light. On our left the evening fireflies are making the compound grove radiant, and above them the plumed heads of tall palms stand out in black silhouette against the sky.

My adventure in self-metamorphosis is over, but the turning axle of time will bring me back to this place, I know. I raise my palms and close them together in the customary salutation and then mutter a brief good-bye. The sage smiles and looks at me fixedly, but says not a word.

One last look towards the Maharishee, one last glimpse by dim lantern light of a tall copper-skinned figure with lustrous eyes, another farewell gesture on my part, a slight wave of his right hand in response, and we part.

I climb into the waiting bullock-cart, the driver swishes his whip, the obedient creatures turn out of the courtyard into the rough path and then trot briskly away into the jasmine-scented tropic night.

THE END